BUSINESS AND ENVIRONMENTAL POLITICS IN CANADA

BUSINESS AND ENVIRONMENTAL POLITICS IN CANADA

DOUGLAS MACDONALD

Dedicated, with all my love,
to my wife Lorraine Wai Chun Cheng

Originally published by Broadview Press 2007

Library and Archives Canada Cataloguing in Publication
Macdonald, Doug, 1947–
   Business and environmental politics in Canada / Douglas Macdonald.

Includes bibliographical references and index.
ISBN 978-1-44260-032-4
(Previous ISBN 978-1-55111-277-0)

   1. Industries—Environmental aspects—Canada. 2. Environmental policy—Canada. 3. Business and politics—Canada. 4. Environmental protection—Economic aspects—Canada. I. Title.

HC120.E5M233 2007   333.70971   C2007-900824-0

We welcome comments and suggestions regarding any aspect of our publications — please feel free to contact us at the addresses below or at news@utphighereducation.com

North America
5201 Dufferin Street, North York
Ontario, Canada, M3H 5T8
2250 Military Road
Tonawanda, New York, USA, 14150
Tel: (416) 978-2239; Fax: (416) 978-4738
email: customerservice@utphighereducation.com

UK, Ireland, and continental Europe
NBN International, Estover Road, Plymouth, UK PL6 7PY
Tel: 44 (0) 1752 202300; Fax: 44 (0) 1752 202330
email: enquiries@nbninternational.com

www.utphighereducation.com

This book is printed on paper containing 100% post-consumer fibre.

Higher Education University of Toronto Press acknowledges the financial support of the Government of Canada through the Book Publishing Industry Development Program (BPIDP) for our publishing activities.

Designed by Chris Rowat Design, Daiva Villa

PRINTED IN CANADA

Contents

LIST OF TABLES

Acknowledgements

I am grateful for financial assistance provided at the beginning of this project by the Social Sciences and Humanities Research Council, in the form of a postdoctoral research fellowship. I would also like to thank the University of Toronto which more recently provided the leave time that allowed me to complete the manuscript.

I have learned much through working with my students in a number of courses in which different aspects of this work were explored. Students who have helped me through research or co-authoring of articles include Andrew Bjorn, Tracey Brieger, Sao-Jan Chan, Elfreda Chang, Trevor Fleck, Christopher Gore, Kyle MacIntyre, Mary McGrath, Shawn Morton, Bryan Purcell, Leanne Wall and Joanne Wolfson.

I would like to express my appreciation to all of the professionals in government, business and the environmental movement who have helped me to develop my understanding, both those who participated in interviews and the many others with whom I have discussed this subject over the years. A number of academic colleagues have spent time participating in seminars, discussing the subject with me individually, or providing comment on conference papers. Of those, I would particularly like to thank Sonia Labatt and David Powell, with whom I co-taught a course on business and environment for several years. I would also like to thank Robert Boardman, Kathryn Harrison, Don Munton, Robert Paehlke, Liora Salter, Debora VanNijnatten and Mark Winfield. I am grateful for the hospitality extended to me by the Département de science politique, Université Laval, where I spent a six-month sabbatical stay and have twice presented seminar papers on this subject. In particular, I would like to thank two colleagues in that department, Jean Crête and Jean Mercier.

Anonymous comments by two peer reviewers were of direct assistance, as was the guidance given by my two editors at Broadview Press, Greg Yantz and Martin Boyne.

CHAPTER ONE

Introduction

During the summer and fall of 2002, Canadian business, in an effort to prevent the Chrétien government from ratifying the Kyoto Protocol to the United Nations Framework Convention on Climate Change (UNFCCC); carried out the single largest political campaign intended to influence environmental policy since the modern regulatory system was first put in place in the late 1960s. The business campaign, which saw millions of dollars spent on television and print advertising, was led and largely financed by the oil and gas industry, the sector most threatened by the Kyoto policy goal of stabilization of greenhouse gas emissions, some two-thirds of which result from the burning of fossil fuels. The oil and gas sector's lobbying arm, the Canadian Association of Petroleum Producers, was not alone, however. It was joined by other industrial sectors with an economic stake in the issue, represented by trade associations such as the Canadian Energy Pipeline Association, the Automotive Parts Manufacturers' Association, the Canadian Chemical Producers' Association, the Canadian Electricity Association, and the Canadian Steel Producers Association. Standing shoulder-to-shoulder with them were the broad-based associations that represent the interests of capital as a whole, most notably the Council of Chief Executives of Canada (formerly the Business Council on National Issues), the Canadian Chamber of Commerce, and the Canadian Manufacturers and Exporters Association. Altogether, 32 business associations came together to hire an Ottawa consulting company, National Public Relations, to carry out a co-ordinated lobbying effort under the name of the Canadian Coalition for Responsible Environmental Solutions (CCRES).

The Coalition campaign was carried out concurrently with similar lobbying by the provinces most vigorously opposed to Kyoto, most notably Alberta and British Columbia, and by the two then-existing political parties, the Alliance and Progressive Conservatives, who were also in the opposition camp. On the other side, but with nothing like the same financial resources for advertising or guaranteed elite-level access enjoyed by business, were the environmentalists, many labour unions, health practitioners, churches, and other progressive social movements. They were supported by two provinces,

Manitoba and Quebec, and, within the House of Commons, a clear majority of Liberal back bench MPs, the New Democratic Party (NDP), and the Bloc Québécois.

When they spoke in public, through advertisements, position papers, and open letters to the Prime Minister and members of his cabinet, members of the business coalition made two major arguments. Because the US had pulled out of the international Kyoto regime, they said, Canadian ratification would hurt this country's competitiveness, causing individual citizens to suffer through job losses and reduced economic growth. Second, it was argued that ratification was premature because the federal government had not yet developed a detailed plan for emission reduction (Macdonald, 2003). Full-page newspaper advertisements made both points, in large type. These arguments were accompanied by a threat of capital flight—newspaper articles appeared, quoting oil and gas executives who suggested the industry would pull billions of dollars out of Alberta oil-sands development if Kyoto were ratified (Chase, 2002; Nguyen, 2003). Instead of "rushing" to ratify (five years after the Protocol had been brokered at an international meeting in Kyoto, Japan), the government of Canada should eschew foreign ways and instead take the time necessary to develop a "made in Canada" policy. Despite the slogan, the policy advocated by business was continentalist. Business wanted Canada to pull out of the international regime and instead follow the same policy as that of the United States, announced by President George W. Bush in 2001, which was intended only to limit the ratio of greenhouse gas emissions to economic activity, without imposing any specific objective or imposing an overall limit on emissions.

At the end of the day, as we know, business was unable to achieve its political objective; ratification was approved by a decisive vote in the House of Commons on December 10, 2002. This does not mean, however, that lobbying by the oil and gas industry had no impact on federal government climate policy. At the same time that it was carrying out this very public campaign to block ratification, throughout the fall of 2002, oil and gas industry representatives were also meeting behind closed doors with officials from Natural Resources Canada in an attempt to fashion a policy compromise (Macdonald, 2003). Eight days after the ratification vote, the results of those negotiations became public when Herb Dhaliwal, then Minister of Natural Resources, sent a letter to the industry guaranteeing that its share of total Canadian reductions would not be more than 15 per cent (Natural Resources Canada, 2002). After that, as is the norm for the development and implementation of environmental policy, government and industry representatives engaged in extensive, detailed negotiation of the regulatory measures the federal government would take to achieve the Kyoto objective. It became apparent in 2005, when the Martin government released yet another plan for climate policy, that business had wielded considerable power in those closed-door negotiations: the total amount of greenhouse gas emission reductions the federal government was asking it to make had been cut by 29 per cent (Macdonald and VanNijnatten, 2005). Business may have lost the Kyoto battle, but as of 2005 it was still winning the climate-policy war.

Although they were writ larger than usual, the anti-Kyoto campaigns contained all of the elements found in business efforts to influence environmental policy: threats to move investment to other jurisdictions; arguments that action is premature due to uncertain science and insufficient study; very visible appeals for public support, based in projected job losses and economic impacts, combined with secret, closed-door lobbying. Prior to 2002, the most recent business campaign using this format was the successful effort exerted during the final stages of House of Commons passage of the amended *Canadian Environmental Protection Act* (CEPA). In that case as well, the industrial sector most directly threatened by new environmental regulation, the chemical industry, led the charge and worked by creating a coalition of industries. Although a number of issues were in play, a central one was the recommendation made by the House of Commons Standing Committee on Environment and Sustainable Development (chaired by Charles Caccia, a prominent environmentalist, and on which the governing Liberals, of course, held a majority of votes) that CEPA be applied not only to regulate more rigorously the release of chemicals into the environment, but also in some cases to ban chemicals used as manufacturing inputs. Like climate policy, which to be effective requires a reduction in the total quantity of the product sold by the oil and gas industry, chemical bans addressed a product rather than the by-product of pollution, and for that reason posed a fundamental economic threat to the industry and its trade association, the Canadian Chemical Producers' Association (CCPA).

The CEPA Review Industry Group, chaired by Claude-André Lachance, a former MP and at that time a public-affairs official for Dow Canada, was the body created to manage this campaign. Letters and meetings were used to make the industry group's arguments to virtually all MPs. A letter dated April 19, 1999, expressed the "sense of dismay and growing alarm" over the legislative recommendations being developed by the Caccia Committee (Lachance, 1999; Winsor, 1999). The letter was sent to Liberal MPs, over the signature of Lachance and on behalf of the CCPA, two firms — Dow and Imperial Oil — and another nine trade associations. It listed eleven "key problems" with the revisions made by the Standing Committee, one of which was the "Use of Toxic Substances." Under that heading, the basic argument was made:

> The federal government's focus has consistently been on managing releases of toxic substances, not their uses.... This approach has been altered by [Committee] amendments.... It is not the use of toxic substances that is cause for public concern and government attention, but their improper management and releases causing adverse effects. The government's clear policy to control releases should be maintained by returning to the original language in the Bill ... (Lachance, 1999)

During enactment of the bill in June 1999, the Chrétien government did exactly that. Instead of adopting the recommendations made by the House Committee, the Liberal government proposed legislation focussed only on releases. This led Caccia and two other Liberal members of the Committee to vote against their own government when the revised Act was finally adopted in the House. After the vote, the Committee Chair gave this assessment: "Caccia accused the government of being convinced by the chemical industry to water down the bill" (Eggerston, 1999).

The fact that two industrial sectors have spearheaded business coalitions engaged in political activity to influence pending environmental regulation is hardly surprising. What does give pause, however, is the *timing* of these policy interventions. Just a few years earlier, both sectors, and business as a whole, had very publicly claimed to have undergone a transformation of core values respecting environmental performance. This greening of business in Canada and other countries had its origins in the 1980s and was given global expression by the creation of the World Business Council on Sustainable Development, which in 1992 publicly stated its new-found creed through the title of its first publication, *Changing Course* (Schmidheiny, 1992). Throughout the 1990s, business in Canada and elsewhere stated that it was ready to go "beyond compliance" — bringing its environmental management performance to a more effective level than that required by law. In policy terms, this new attitude was expressed as a willingness to work with governments to establish rigorous new pollution-control standards, codified in memoranda of agreement and then met through voluntary action.

In 1995, seven years before wading into the Kyoto battle, the oil and gas sector had signed such a memorandum of agreement with the federal minister of natural resources, committing to extensive action, voluntarily undertaken, to reduce its own greenhouse gas emissions (Macdonald and Smith, 1999). In 1986, the chemical industry in Canada, followed by that in other countries, had without government prompting established the Responsible Care program, a series of measures intended to improve beyond current regulatory requirements the occupational health and environmental safety of chemical management (Moffet, Bregha and Middelkoop, 2004). During the following decade, the CCPA and member firms entered into a number of voluntary agreements with the federal and provincial governments for improved environmental performance. These two sectors, and others, had apparently moved away from their earlier policy stance of denial of responsibility and efforts to delay the imposition of new regulatory requirements. Instead, they were actively *embracing* such new requirements. Why, then, a few years later did they devote such significant time and money to efforts to *weaken* pending environmental regulation? Surely one would expect to have seen such large-scale political campaigns in the early days of environmental regulation, before corporate culture had changed, in tune with changing values in the larger society, and before firms and their trade associations had purportedly come to accept environmental protection as a basic objective of business.

In the decades following World War II, the emergence of modern environmentalism posed a new threat to the profitability of Canadian resource and manufacturing industries. In response to the growing political power of environmentalists, by the late 1960s both federal and provincial government regulators were enacting laws and regulations requiring that sectors such as pulp and paper, smelting, steel, chemicals, and manufacturing put in place new measures to reduce pollution emissions, steps that would require both initial capital investment and increased operating expenditures each year afterward. The initial response of the resource and manufacturing sectors in Canada and other countries was to negotiate with regulators for weaker standards and lengthy time delays before full compliance would be required —a process often referred to as "grudging compliance." Cairncross (1995: 178) gives this description: "For many years, most companies regarded environmentalists as enemies and environmental regulation as something to be fought off as long as possible and then complied with reluctantly." Both the Canadian pulp-and-paper and smelting sectors, for instance, engaged in successful defensive action over a period of fifteen to twenty years before making significant pollution-control expenditures (Macdonald, 1991).

Other sectors, however, moved beyond a defensive posture and actively intervened in the policy process. The most notable example is the Ontario soft-drink industry, which during the 1970s and 1980s was subject to regulatory demands that it revert to selling its product in refillable glass bottles rather than recyclable cans, in accordance with the established solid-waste management principle that reduction be the first priority, followed by re-use and then recycling. Initially, Coca-Cola and other companies followed the normal practice of lobbying for weaker standards, in this case the portion of total sales that had to be in refillable containers. By the mid-1980s, however, the industry had adopted a very different strategy: it was actively reaching into the policy process, working to convince governments that the policy objective of re-use, requiring glass bottles, should be replaced by that of recycling,

5

to be achieved by selling pop in aluminium cans. This was done by offering to subsidize municipal curb-side recycling programs (Macdonald, 1991).

As noted, the chemical industry in the mid-1980s also sallied forth from its defensive position and moved to voluntarily put in place new standards governing the handling and transportation of chemicals under the rubric of the Responsible Care program. As discussed below, sector representatives were candid in admitting that this was done both to forestall new regulatory demands and to win back lost public legitimacy. Throughout the 1990s, the CCPA pointed to its voluntary program to support its argument that new government regulation was unnecessary. Other sectors followed suit, entering into a variety of agreements with the federal and provincial governments for voluntary improvement of their environmental management. But then, in 1999, faced with the new regulatory threat of chemical bans being incorporated into CEPA, the chemical sector did not again use the tactic of pre-emptive voluntary action. Nor did the oil and gas sector, faced with the threat of Kyoto ratification in 2002.

When we look at the more than thirty years of environmental regulation in this country, we do not find the linear progression of response to societal and regulatory demands for improved environmental management that we would expect either from the claims of business itself or from a number of studies of business environmental management (Cairncross, 1995; Frankel, 1998; Schmidheiny, 1992). Generally speaking, these studies paint a picture of business going through three distinct phases in its response to the new values of environmentalism and resulting changes in regulation: initially, denial of the problem and resistance to regulation; then, by the mid-1980s, active participation with environmentalists and government regulators in multi-stakeholder development of new environmental policy; and finally, by the 1990s, voluntary implementation of improvements in environmental performance going well beyond the demands of government. These analysts claim that this evolution of responses has come about through two fundamental changes in corporate culture. The first is a slowly dawning recognition that money spent on environmental management is a good investment, since reduced waste-disposal costs, less regulatory liability, and new consumer demands for improved environmental performance all translate into increased profitability. The second is a steadily growing acceptance of the values of environmentalism by company executives: in other words, money is spent on improved environmental performance simply because it is the "right thing to do." In fact, however, as demonstrated by the short histories related above, the business response to environmental regulation has not been linear at all, leading one to suspect that other factors are at play beyond the greening of corporate culture.

As discussed below, corporate culture is clearly one factor that must be examined if we wish to understand political activity by the firms and sectors subjected to environmental regulation. Furthermore, the claim by Schmidheiny, Cairncross, and others that corporate culture has been progressing steadily toward accepting and concurring with the values of environmentalism seems reasonable. Values held by those working inside the firm, as is the case for all organizations, are not completely immune to changes in the values of those working and living in the world outside. But therein lies exactly the problem with this school of thought: if corporate culture were the major factor driving both the firm's environmental management and its attitude toward government regulation, we would expect to find a corresponding steady movement toward both improved environmental performance and increasingly cooperative relations with regulators. In the case of the latter, we do not find any such linear movement. Instead, we are faced with the difficulty of explaining the timing of the Kyoto and CEPA policy interventions. If corporate culture were the most significant explanatory variable, surely we would have seen such flexing of political muscle in the late 1960s, since it was then that the new values of environmentalism were most at odds with those held by managers. Instead, we see it thirty years later, when a new generation of managers, exposed to environmental values from birth, was directing the political activity of the firm. Corporate culture by itself, therefore, cannot fully explain the environmental political activity of firms.

PURPOSE OF THE BOOK
The purpose of this book is to explore the full range of factors that must be examined to answer questions such as the following:

Why do we see, within the same industrial sector, different political responses at different times, when presumably the corporate culture of firms within that sector has been becoming steadily greener?

Alternatively, when we compare sectors at a given time, why do we see a defensive adaptation response by one sector (e.g., in the 1980s, the smelting industry facing new acid-rain regulations) and an activist, interventionist policy response by another (e.g., the soft-drink industry being asked to sell its product in refillable bottles)?

If differences in corporate culture amongst firms and sectors cannot fully explain these differing policy interests and strategies, what other factors must we consider?

7

When regulated firms do engage in such activist political activity, to significantly change the environmental standards to which they are subject, why do they sometimes pursue a strategy limited to private, elite-level lobbying while at other times they also very publicly seek allies and work to stimulate public support?

Why do some firms offer to cooperate with environmentalists, while others seek to cripple them by means of court actions, while yet others (the majority, most of the time) effectively ignore them?

How do we explain the fact that in some instances firms or sectors *invite* regulation, thus departing from the norm of seeking only to weaken or delay it?

When the answer is clearly because environmental regulation contributes directly to the profitability of the sector, such as demand for the pollution-control services or equipment sold by the environmental industries sector, do such business actors then take on an active political role, allying themselves with environmentalists to lobby governments?

How do firms work to achieve legitimacy with respect to their environmental performance in the eyes of relevant audiences?

What decides the political strength of industry in the arena of environmental politics?

As we have seen, the chemical industry successfully lobbied the Chrétien government in 1999, but the oil and gas industry was unable to exert equally successful pressure on the same government three years later. What factors explain that difference?

Finally, has the power exerted by business been the decisive factor influencing the way in which Canadian environmental policy has been developed and implemented since the 1960s?

I pursue these questions by providing an historical account, accompanied by exploratory analysis, of the ways in which regulated industries and other business actors have participated in the Canadian environmental policy process since the present regulatory system was first established. To date, little research has been done on the topic in this country, which means this work is a venture into new territory. As such, it attempts to provide a comprehensive account of all aspects of the subject represented by questions such as those posed above.

By exploring such questions in the pages that follow I hope to accomplish two things. The first is to document political activity by Canadian business in the arena of environmental politics. I do this by gathering existing information in the secondary literature and by presenting the findings of the primary research conducted for this project. Second, I hope to begin to make sense of that political activity by taking steps to develop a theoretical, generalized understanding. I do this by exploring three main research questions, along with subsidiary questions for each.

These questions flow from the focus of this work upon three aspects of business engagement with Canadian environmental politics. The first is the interest pursued by the firm, sector or coalition of sectoral and broad-based associations as each undertakes political activity in this field — both the policy interest, defined as what the business actor wants the relevant government agencies to do, and the broader political interest, defined as what it wants other, non-government actors (including the general public) to do or to think. The second is the strategy used to achieve that policy or political interest. Third, the book focuses on the political power of business with respect to environmental policy — defined as the ability of the business actors in question to achieve their objectives by influencing government actions.

This focus upon business interest, strategy, and power in the arena of environmental politics is explored through the following three research questions:

(1) What have been the political objectives of business actors engaged with environmental politics in Canada since they first became subject to modern environmental regulation in the 1960s? This leads to two subsidiary questions. First, in terms of the narrowly defined policy interest, what has business wanted government to do with respect to environmental policy? Second, in terms of the broader political interest, to what extent has business worked not only to maximize profit but also sought other objectives, most notably legitimacy?

I divide the potential business policy interest into three categories: to invite regulation, to seek to delay or weaken regulation, to seek to completely block or fundamentally change a given regulatory policy initiative. As discussed below, instances of firms or sectors actively encouraging regulation, in the belief that it will impose greater costs on competitors than on themselves, have been rare. The bulk of the analysis, for that reason, addresses the second two categories.

Negotiating with environmental regulators in order to delay and usually also to water down regulatory standards has been by far the most common policy interest pursued by regulated firms. It is essentially an adaptive response to policy initiatives, based in acceptance of the need to make improvements in environmental management, albeit with an interest in keeping the cost of those improvements to a minimum. Although it has the effect of limiting the ability of governments to achieve their environmental policy objectives, it poses no fundamental challenge to those objectives. However, such fundamental challenges have occurred, as evidenced by the two stories briefly told in the first pages above. When successful, as was the case with the 1999 CEPA amendments, business brings about major changes in environmental policy. Because it potentially has such significant implications for policy effectiveness, it is essential that we understand the factors which induce firms to mount major policy challenges, instead of simply adapting while negotiating to reduce the imposed cost. The effort to understand why most firms adapt to proposed environmental policy while some intervene to stop or fundamentally change it lies at the heart of the first research question.

As noted above, the second aspect of the business interest addressed here is the extent to which legitimacy has come to be pursued as a political objective. In this case, we are looking at efforts by the firm to influence not only governments, but also a variety of societal actors. The history recounted here shows that little effort was made to achieve environmental legitimacy in the early period of the 1970s, but that by the 1990s it had become a major preoccupation of the large firms. Why was that? The *ways* in which firms have sought legitimacy are discussed in response to the second research question.

(2) What have been the political strategies and tactics used to influence the thinking and actions of environmental regulators and others, such as environmentalists or the general public? As discussed below, the inherent power of business in Canadian society means that it has ready access to government decision-makers in a way that its critics in the environmental movement do not. The normal practice is for environmentalists to work publicly to influence government policy, taking actions that will both highlight issues in the news media and generate and demonstrate public support. Business, on the other hand, normally makes its case to government ministers or officials in private. Occasionally, however, business too will engage in outside lobbying, seeking to influence public opinion in support of its policy interest. What prompts that second strategy? The second subsidiary question explored here has to do with business relations with the environmental movement. For the most part, the regulated firms have ignored their critics, providing some financial donations and responding to their critique in the news media, but doing little else. In some instances, however, they have actively cooperated

with environmentalists, while in others they have used litigation in an attempt to weaken them. What prompts these different strategies?

The third aspect of business political strategy explored here is the effort to achieve legitimacy in the eyes of relevant audiences, such as regulators, environmentalists or the general public. Legitimacy is an essential source of political power, and one of the premises of this work is that firms, like all other political actors, actively seek it for that reason. Furthermore, based on Suchman's analysis (1995), I assume that while environmental legitimacy can be achieved by improving the firm's environmental performance, it can also be achieved in two other ways. One is to change the *image* of that performance, largely through media relations and advertising, in the eyes of those audiences. The other is to change the environmental norms that those audiences are using to evaluate the environmental legitimacy of the firm. The major example of this, I suggest, has been the concept of sustainable development, which business has sought to define primarily in terms of increased efficiency, to reduce the consumption of raw materials and the generation of waste by-products. Like the first two questions in this second category, the question here is what prompts the firm to adopt one or more of these three strategies for achieving legitimacy?

(3) What are the sources and extent of business political power in this policy field, and how effective have those strategies been? This third research question is addressed by means of two subsidiary questions. First, why has the power of business to influence environmental policy fluctuated? Understanding why business power declined in the 1980s, relative to the preceding decade, and then rebounded in the 1990s will tell us something about the sources of such power. Second, to what extent has business succeeded in influencing the environmental policy to which it has been subjected? I do not suggest that political power can be precisely measured. Nor can this work give a definitive statement of the extent to which our environmental policy has been shaped by business wishes, since other important factors, such as the institutional and ideational context and the political power of the environmental movement, are not addressed in detail. This question is explored, however, in preliminary terms.

SCOPE OF INQUIRY

Having set out these three lines of inquiry that are used to structure the text, it is necessary to set the parameters of the field within which they are pursued, in terms of both public policy and the business actors examined. The policy field, of course, is "environmental protection" — which includes all aspects of government action pertaining to solid waste and toxic pollution generated during resource extraction, the design, manufacture, transport, sale, use, and eventual disposal of products, and all other individual or organizational activities that generate pollution of whatever kind. A current description of the mandate and activities of environmental regulation, in the regulator's own words, is this:

> The people of Ontario deserve clean, safe, livable communities. The Ministry of the Environment (MOE) safeguards our environment by working to ensure cleaner air, water and land, and healthier ecosystems for the people of Ontario. The ministry has built a strong foundation of clear laws, stringent regulations, tough standards and rigorous permits and approvals.
>
> The ministry monitors pollution and restoration trends in an effort to determine the effectiveness of its activities and to assess risks to human health and the environment. In turn, this information is used to develop and implement environmental legislation, regulations, standards, policies, guidelines and programs to enhance environmental protection. The ministry's inspection, investigation and enforcement activities are key components of achieving Ontario's environmental goals. (MOE, 2005)

In Canada, the lead regulatory agencies are provincial environment departments, but other provincial government departments also have mandates for pollution control. To continue with the Ontario example:

> MOE is not the only agency with responsibility for environmental issues. The Ministry of Natural Resources (water quantity), the Ministry of Agriculture and Food (nutrient management), the Ministry of Municipal Affairs (land-use planning; brownfields; water and sewer infrastructure), the Ministry of Health and Long-Term Care (water testing, West Nile Virus), and the Ministry of Northern Development and Mines play a role in protecting the environment through their respective regulatory and enforcement mandates. (MOE, 2005)

Looking beyond the boundaries of a given provincial jurisdiction we note that the federal department, Environment Canada, and other Government of Canada departments with mandates for pollution control, corresponding to the provincial departments listed above, also play significant roles, as do local governments and a variety of international bodies, such as the United Nations Environment Program, courts, administrative tribunals, and various governmental advisory and audit agencies such as the federal Commissioner for Environment and Sustainable Development.

While these government actors play lead roles, the nature of the pollution issue is such that other parts of government are integrally involved. Air pollution from transportation is strongly influenced by land-use planning decisions made by relevant provincial and municipal bodies; climate change is more an energy issue than anything else, which is why Environment Canada and Natural Resources Canada have squabbled from the outset over which has lead jurisdiction; and of course government departments charged with a mandate to promote industrial growth and export-trade competitiveness have a keen interest in the costs being imposed upon Canadian business by their brethren, the environmental regulators.

Further broadening the scope of government activity that is the subject of this research, the term "environment" today connotes far more than just pollution: resource and energy conservation, habitats for species biodiversity, and the virtually limitless array of economic and social activities represented by the ambiguous phrase "sustainable development" also fall within its ambit. Indeed, "sustainable development" is usually interpreted as calling for a wide-ranging transformation of virtually all governmental and societal activity in order to achieve full integration of environmental and economic decision-making. For these reasons, while the central policy subject examined here is pollution control, in particular with respect to highly visible and politically charged issues such as toxic chemical contamination, acid rain, smog and climate change, a number of other policy fields and relevant state and non-state actors are also examined as needed.

The core policy activity examined here, regulation of pollution emissions and wastes, has gone through four distinct phases. The regulatory system was established and implemented in the 1960s and 1970s; it became increasingly stringent and punitive during the 1980s; and then regulatory pressure was significantly relaxed during the deregulatory period of the 1990s, followed by a partial return to previous practices after the shock of deaths caused by water pollution in Walkerton, Ontario, in 2000. Each of these phases is presented chronologically in the pages that follow.

Having thus described the policy field examined here, I now turn to the central subject of the book: the business actors who have both responded to and influenced this historical unfolding of environmental policy. When the pollution issue first moved onto the policy agenda in the 1960s, it was taken, both by environmentalists and by the governments responding to their demands, to involve very few business activities beyond those of the resource and manufacturing sectors. As it has evolved, however, others have been drawn in. Critical attention is now being paid to what had previously been seen as relatively benign industries, such as tourism or electronics industries. Beyond that, it has been extended to those who do not themselves directly generate any pollution but who play a role, and who now worry about potential environment-related liabilities: the banks, insurance companies, and others that comprise the financial sector. Writing in 1994, Doern and Conway categorized into four groups the business sectors which had by that time been drawn into the world of environmental policy-making: "traditional polluting industries," "clean" industries such as telephone companies, environmental industries that sell goods and services to the market created by environmental regulation, and "other components of the corporate world from auditors to lenders, to securities regulators" (115).

While terms such as "business community" are often used to refer loosely to all such actors in a collective sense, we can only examine their political activities by more carefully distinguishing amongst groups of business actors, ranging from the individual CEO through to capitalists as a social class. Brooks and Stritch (1991: 11) state that "the political interests of business can be arranged along a spectrum from the most general, those shared by virtually all businesses, to the most specific." They divide their spectrum into four categories, and for each they state the political goal pursued and the means of political organization used to achieve it. The first category is "capital" — those who own the means of production and share a common interest in generalized goals such as the maintenance of social order, private property rights, and the acceptance of capitalism as the prevailing form of social organization. Their second category is composed of business interests that pursue broad, but more specific, policy goals in such fields as tax or trade policy and that are represented by broad-based associations such as the Canadian Chamber of Commerce or Canadian Council of Chief Executives. Third, they list specific industrial sectors, such as oil and gas or banking, which take political action by means of their trade associations, in those two cases the Canadian Association of Petroleum Producers and the Canadian Bankers Association. Fourth, they list individual firms, which pursue political goals such as government financing which may conflict with those of both other sectors and other individual firms within their own sector (Brooks and Stritch, 1991: 11-12).

The categories I use here are modelled on theirs, modified to fit the needs of my particular subject. Accordingly, I divide "business" into these categories: (1) the business community as a whole, speaking on environmental policy issues through broad-based associations such as the Chamber of Commerce; (2) the industrial sector, represented politically by its trade association (although firms may also undertake their own political activity); (3) the individual firm; and (4) the relevant sub-units and individuals within each firm, such as the environmental management or public affairs departments. The rationale for this categorization and reasons for paying far less attention to the two categories at either end of the spectrum — capital as a class and the heroic individual business person who has been bitten by the bug of environmentalism — are set out below.

Whatever system of categories they use, those studying business and politics usually focus more on one than the others, as dictated by the purposes of their research. Carroll (1986: xiii-xiv), for instance, defines his subject this way:

> In Canada and other developed market societies, economic resources exist as capital, and the dominant class makes up a bourgeoisie. The class power of capitalists is expressed, through the corporations they control, as corporate power.... capitalists in the control of corporations decide when, where, and how to invest.... This book is about Canada's bourgeoisie — particularly its most powerful fractions — and that class's relationship to Canadian capitalism.

His subject is the first of the four categories listed by Brooks and Stritch, that is, capitalists constituting a social class. Since they use the corporation as a vehicle for generating return on investment, Carroll necessarily considers the firm but focusses more on the owners of the firm — those who make investment decisions and thus decide in which jurisdiction the firm will be built and will operate — than on the firm itself, the organization operated by its board of directors and senior executives on behalf of its owners.

Because the subject and purpose differ, this study focuses primarily on a different category of business actor: the individual firm. It is true that environmental regulation is at least a minor factor influencing plant siting (Olewiler, 1994) and companies do, as seen above during the Kyoto ratification conflict, sometimes threaten to pull up stakes and invest elsewhere as one means of influencing policy (referred to as "job blackmail"). However, because the costs of complying with environmental regulation are minor in comparison with other costs, most notably the cost of labour, they have little influence on siting. As Olewiler notes, "the available evidence suggests that international investment flows have been relatively unresponsive to differences in environmental regulation across countries" (1994: 111). Accordingly, the subject considered here is almost exclusively the political performance of the corporation *after* the investment decision has been made, once the firm is up and running. This means that both investors as a class and shareholders in a given firm are less relevant for this study of the corporation's dealings with environmental regulators than they would be for a study of other aspects of business-government relations. That said, the basic interest of owners in seeing return on investment, and their power to change firm management if that interest is not being met, is necessarily part of this subject matter.

In the same way, the political power that accrues to capital because governments compete to attract investment and thus, as Carroll notes, put themselves in a position of dependency has to be considered here. The dominant political power held by business does not flow only from government dependency; current ideas respecting legitimacy of state and market are at least as important. A theme running through this work is the fact that environmental regulation was only one aspect of the overall expansion of the state in the 1960s and its subsequent shrinking in the 1990s. I argue below that the relaxation of regulatory pressure in the latter decade had less to do with business lobbying in the specific policy field of environment than with the more general business attack on the credibility of government that had been carried out at least since Ronald Reagan and Margaret Thatcher held power in the 1980s. Relations between state and market, and the broader social power of capital, necessarily form the context for this study, but the nature of the subject matter is such that they are not a central subject.

Finally, capitalists as a class are not directly relevant to this study for the simple reason that the social movement of environmentalism has never gained sufficient political power to threaten their dominant social position. The values originally espoused by environmentalism — a steady-state economy instead of economic growth, full recognition of the inherent moral worth of non-human species, and government treatment of the environment as a public rather than a private good — are threats rivalling anything penned by Marx or Engels. But as the movement grew and moved closer to the centre of policy-making, environmentalists focussed instead on more immediately achievable goals, thus allowing the rich to recycle as assiduously, and feel themselves to be as green, as the rest of us.

Just as the political power of capital cannot be completely ignored in a work such as this, the personality of individual executives, particularly the CEO, must also be considered. This is because he or she is a major source of corporate culture, one of the explanatory variables considered here. Individual personality, however, is constrained by the duties of the office held. Any given officer of the firm must meet the dictates of the job description, and while some may do so in more aggressive, conciliatory or capable ways than others, the role is more important than the personality traits of the person playing it at any given time. This fact limits the importance of the variable of individual human foible. More importantly, the purpose here is to understand political action by business across all the resource and manufacturing sectors, to say nothing of a variety of others sectors, over a period of roughly half a century. From that perspective, individual business leadership is less significant than it might be for explaining the day-to-day tactical manoeuvrings in a particular regulatory conflict.

More attention, accordingly, is paid to the two categories, the industrial sector and individual firm, placed between the business community at one end of the spectrum and the firm sub-unit or individual business person at the other. That said, the political activities of "business as a whole" respecting environmental politics are noted whenever organizations such as the Canadian Chamber of Commerce have moved to play a role in a current environmental issue. The major question explored is what prompts such actions and the extent to which such a coalescing of forces works to increase the political power of business.

The succession of environmental issues that have moved onto the policy agenda over the years, as the result of lobbying by environmentalists, have for the most part been defined in terms of the relevant industrial sector. Pollution from the pulp-and-paper industry, for instance, was the subject of environmental policy-making early on, while that from agriculture was largely ignored until some twenty years later. While different standards may be applied to different firms within the sector, pollution-control policy is largely developed on a sectoral basis. For that reason, considerable attention is paid here to the next category of analysis, the industrial sector. It is not suggested, however, that a sector can be considered to be a unitary policy actor. While networks of common interest unite firms, suppliers, customers, and associated service industries faced with pending regulatory action that will force internalization of cost, they are not bound by sufficiently strong institutional mechanisms to ensure coordinated action. Firms in a given sector compete with one another in the marketplace and often do so in the political arena as well, seeking government action such as subsidies or the imposition of new regulations that will benefit them and disadvantage their competitors. When all share one policy interest, a given firm may work with those competitors to lobby government by means of the trade association or hired public-affairs company, but it will lobby individually when its interest varies from that of others in the sector (Brooks and Stritch, 1991: 12).

Since it largely exists to play a policy role, both as lobbyist and as partner with government in implementing some forms of industrial policy (Coleman, 1988), the sectoral trade association is very much part of the subject explored in these pages. Just as firms within each sector are engaged in market competition, so do they compete to decide the policy interests pursued by the trade association as it lobbies governments (Trent Environmental Policy Institute, 1999: 5). While that phenomenon is recognized here, it is not explored in depth. Instead, it is assumed that the trade associations discussed are by and large working in pursuit of the policy preferences of the larger firms in the sector. The internal politics that decides the policy interest of the trade association is a subject requiring further research (Kelley, 1991).

While business as a whole and the industrial sector are important parts of the subject treated here, greatest attention is paid to the individual business corporation. During the past century the corporation has become the primary organizational form used by investors to carry out market activity. Unlike the previous two categories, the corporation has sufficient internal organization and discipline that it can function something like a unitary actor in both the world of the market and that of politics. It has a culture that is to at least some extent distinct from that outside its boundaries, and it has a tangible identity to which, for the larger firms at least, its managers devote considerable care. For all of these reasons, it is the primary unit of analysis. The theoretical perspective used here to understand business participation in environmental politics is anchored neither in sociological class nor in the psychology of the individual, but instead in a view of the firm as an organizational entity.

I discuss below the question of whether the firm can be seen as a completely unitary actor and thus treated as a black box for analytical purposes, with no need to consider its inner workings. I start from the assumption, like many analysts, that it cannot (Clancy, 2004). Those internal processes—both the basic conflict between labour and management over division of the wealth created by the firm and the conflicting goals and demand for shares of the firm's resources of the different sub-units—have at least some influence on the way in which the firm sets and works to achieve its objectives. Furthermore, as noted, I address here the argument made by some analysts that corporate culture is the most important factor influencing the firm's environmental performance. For those reasons, the internal machinery of the firm is also included in the subject of this work.

Finally, in terms of the business actors examined, the subject is limited to the large, visible firms such as Inco, Dow or Shell which have been at the centre of environmental controversy. This is in part because it is the large firms that wield the most political power, but also for the more mundane reason that they have been studied by environmental policy analysts in a way that small business has not. I do not suggest the analysis here can be applied directly to the small firm, flying for the most part below the radar of societal and regulatory concern and without the resources needed to actively seek to influence regulators. Like many other aspects of this subject, the environmental politics of small and medium-sized business requires further study.

RATIONALE

Why is this study needed? The simple answer is because no comparable book-length treatment of the subject exists in Canada, despite the fact that business influence is one of the major forces shaping environmental policy. This book makes a contribution in the first instance simply by pulling together existing factual accounts, and thus for the first time providing a comprehensive documentation of political activity by business in this policy field.

Beyond such documentation, this study provides a preliminary analysis of *why* business political activity takes the form it does. As discussed below, there are now extensive bodies of literature on both environmental policy-making and environmental management by business. These provide only peripheral analysis, however, of the firm as an environmental policy actor. It is hoped this study will help fill this gap in our understanding of environmental policy-making.

Beyond simply providing detailed study where little existed before, this study contributes to scholarship by challenging two of the dominant themes found in the environmental policy and environmental management literatures. The first is the assumption that the policy role played by business is determined solely by the way in which environmental regulation influences the firm's primary goal of profit maximization. This study advances a different view: that in addition to profit, the firm has a dominant interest in legitimacy, since, among other reasons discussed below, both are essential for the over-riding organizational goal of survival. It is argued that this legitimacy interest significantly influences the firm's policy role. In part, of course, it contributes to the firm's willingness to compromise the profit goal and cooperate with regulatory demands. But the legitimacy interest can also be achieved by *influencing* those demands. Beyond that, it can be achieved by influencing the way in which the firm's environmental performance is viewed. I argue that environmental policy analysts cannot fully understand how and why firms, sectors, and business as a whole engage in environmental politics so long as they start from the assumption that the only goal pursued by those actors is profitability.

Second, as discussed above, the findings of this study challenge the view that corporate culture is the primary determinant of the firm's political response to environmental regulation. The argument is made that the external variable of the degree of threat posed by environmental regulation, both coerciveness of the instrument used and the subject of regulation — the firm's product or its pollution — is a more important factor in deciding the way in which business engages with government on the issue than are any of the internal factors associated with the greening of the boardroom or plant floor.

Better understanding of the policy role played by the regulated industry is also important to environmental professionals. The objective of environmental regulation is behaviour change by regulated firms to bring their environmental management into compliance. Ideally, this should be achieved in the most cost-effective manner possible, in terms of costs borne by both the firm and the regulatory department. We can be confident that in the majority of cases firms do comply, albeit after bargaining with regulators over both standards and compliance timelines in order to minimize their costs. However, we also know that in many cases firms and sectors do not follow that norm; instead, either they ignore the law and deal with the attendant problems of prosecution or, as in the case of Kyoto and CEPA, they use their political strength in an attempt to bring about fundamental changes in the law. The more they know about the factors that elicit the desired response of compliance, the better able government professionals will be to do their job.

RESEARCH METHODOLOGY

Two primary research methods have been used for this study. The first is a review of secondary literature, for the most part Canadian and American, on the subjects of the political power of business, the nature of the firm, Canadian environmental policy, and business participation in environmental policy processes in Canada, the United States, European states, and at the international level. To the extent it exists, that literature has been used to provide the chronological account of business environmental policy activity in this country which makes up the bulk of this work. That literature is limited, however, and for that reason has been supplemented by primary research, in the form of a review of documents generated by the relevant actors themselves. To a very limited extent this reliance on documents has been supplemented by personal interviews.

Taken as a whole, the methodology used here is decidedly qualitative. The focus upon variables such as the firm's choice between adaptive or interventionist responses to the external regulatory threat with which it must cope carries with it a hint of reductionism, but throughout there is recognition that many variables are at play, not all of which can be identified or ranked in order of priority for analytical purposes. More than anything else, this work tells a story. Such reliance on narrative and chronological organization of the data presented clearly stamps the methodology as being qualitative.

THEORETICAL PERSPECTIVE

To help the reader evaluate the argument developed in this work, I provide here a statement of the basic assumptions and theoretical focus upon which it is based. This is done for each of the three subjects that lie at the heart of the overall subject of business engagement with environmental politics. Those are the firm as a political actor, the policy process in which it participates, and, more specifically, the environmental policy process.

The Firm as a Political Actor

As stated, I start from the assumption that we can most usefully understand the firm as it engages with governments and other political actors by viewing it as a unitary, rational actor. As discussed in the next chapter, the organizational theory perspective that sees corporate bodies as systems, made up of interactions amongst their internal units, which in turn are interacting with other systems in the external environment, is an excellent starting point. Clancy (2004) does a good job of using that perspective to explain why analysts must look inside the firm, seeking to understand the motivations and actions of its internal units. Nevertheless, we must remember that the firm, unlike actors such as social movements, has sufficient internal discipline to act in a coordinated manner in pursuit of whatever political goal has been decided by senior management. Furthermore, I assume that despite all the difficulties of inadequate information and unconscious, unexamined biases and assumptions, the firm is to at least some degree able to pursue its political self-interest in a logical, rational manner.

Second, I think it helps to bear in mind that the firm was not created in order to achieve political ends. Unlike social movements, political parties or government departments, politics is not its primary focus. Instead, it engages in politics to the extent necessary to achieve its primary purpose of successful market activity. This is the basis for the common assumption in the literature, discussed below, that the political objectives of the firm are decided by its market strategy. Although in some instances, such as the search for government contracts or cartel-type regulation, the firm is the first mover when it engages government, in areas such as the environment this is rarely the case. Instead, the firm is on the defensive, reacting to changes in social values and government policy, rather than initiating political action. Business firms first engaged in environmental politics because they had to, as they encountered regulatory demands for behaviour change, not because they themselves had decided upon a particular environmental policy objective. This essentially defensive posture helps explain, I suggest, the arc of business engagement with environmental policy from the 1960s to the present as firms have adopted the various goals of ignoring, complying with or intervening to influence environmental policy.

Finally, I start from the assumption that profit, while the dominant goal, is not the only objective pursued by the firm. I share the view presented by Mitchell (1989), discussed below, that during the course of the twentieth century business executives came to view their functions and responsibilities as extending beyond the market, into society. I assume that the large firms studied here accept the fact that they have social responsibilities and work to meet them. This leads to one of the central premises that provide the foundation for this analysis: the large firms seek legitimacy in the eyes of society and governments with respect to the aspect of social responsibility studied here, namely their environmental performance. That desire for legitimacy is one of the factors that must be recognized if we wish to fully understand the political objectives pursued by business with respect to environment. As discussed, however, we must also recognize that this desire does not simply lead to accommodation with regulatory demands for improved performance. It also leads to efforts to project an image of legitimacy, regardless of performance, and to efforts to redefine the norms of environmentalism by which it is being judged.

The Policy Process

In terms of policy-making in general, I start from the perspective of pluralist policy analysis, which rests on the assumption that government policy action results from interaction, in the form of conflict, bargaining, and compromise, amongst a variety of state and non-state actors. The term "pluralist" refers only to the fact that policy in this view is seen to be made by a number of actors; it does not imply equivalency of power amongst them. I share the common view, discussed in the next chapter, that business is the dominant non-state actor.

Unlike Marxist or rational-actor approaches, which look to the variables of class or the self-interested individual, it is assumed here that the most important policy actors in regulatory policy are organizational entities, in particular the government department and the regulated firm. This assumption brings with it the need to disaggregate the state (Coleman and Skogstad, 1990). From this perspective, government departments are seen as state policy actors with at least some marginal autonomy who pursue the policy interest of their mandate, such as increased environmental protection. This interest often is in conflict with that of other departments, particularly those that exist to further the well-being of particular industrial sectors. Those departments, again because of their mandate, pursue a contradictory interest, such as continued externalization of cost by the industries they seek to foster (Pross, 1992). To accomplish those ends, each department works in alliance with the non-state actors that are politically active and pursuing a policy interest similar to theirs.

Although no attempt is made here to apply formal policy network analysis, in terms of seeking correlations between network structure and policy outcome, the basics of that approach—recognition that technical specifics of policy emerge from interaction amongst a limited number of state and non-state actors that possess the expertise necessary to participate—inform the analysis of environmental policy provided here (Atkinson and Coleman, 1996; Montpetit, 2003). One aspect of the functioning of the environmental policy network—the question of whether or not environmentalists are relegated to the status of members of the "attentive public" watching closely but excluded from the private, closed-door negotiations between firm officials and regulators that is almost always found at the core of environmental policy-making (Cotton and McKinnon, 1993) — is assumed to be of particular relevance to the political power of the regulated firm.

It is assumed here that public policy-making, despite the fact that it is almost always a somewhat messy and incoherent process, can usefully be understood by focussing separately on different stages of the process (Howlett and Ramesh, 1995). These begin with the social construction of the policy problem. That definition, or framing, of the problem largely decides the spectrum of options that will be considered for its solution. This is followed by the adoption of policy objectives, even if only vaguely stated. Inaction or purely symbolic action may well be objectives. This in turn is followed by the selection of the policy instrument and its implementation. All of this takes place within the institutional framework of jurisdiction and established decision-making procedures and within the context of currently dominant ideas.

Generally speaking, policy analysis seeks to understand by looking to those three primary variables: the interests of the actors involved and the context of institutions and ideas that stimulate, constrain, and shape their actions as they pursue those interests. Michael Atkinson gives us this picture of the way in which the three are used in current policy analysis:

> ...there are three typical avenues of interpretation. First, it is possible to explain ...policy...by focusing on political ideas. In this view, contentious concepts such as equality, freedom, rights, and authority lie at the heart of our political disagreements and our policy disputes.... For many policy analysts...what is required is attention to a second source of policy, namely political interests.... [This approach] asks the simple question: who benefits? ...The third approach is, in some respects, the most traditional. It involves an assessment of political institutions such as federalism, Parliament, cabinet and the bureaucracy. (Atkinson, 1993: 101)

I assume that to fully understand any given process of environmental policy-making, we must look to all three variables: ideas, such as the dominant values governing our relationship with nature or the scientific understanding of the relevant pollutants and their effects; interests, in terms of the goals of environmentalists, industries, government agencies, and others involved; and, finally, the institutional framework that sets the rules within which governments and others negotiate environmental policy, such as Canadian federalism, environmental assessment, standard-setting or compliance processes. Heclo (1994) discusses the inherent connections amongst the three. The focus of this study, however, is the variable of interest. Yet discussion necessarily includes the other two variables, since they clearly are significant for the business role; from the outset, business has been actively engaged in producing and discussing the science that forms the basis of environmental regulation, and, as discussed above, it is the institutional framework that decides who is or is not given a voice in the policy process. My purpose, however, is not to contribute to understanding variables such as those.

There are two reasons for focussing instead upon the policy interest of the regulated industry and the related subject of its ability to achieve that end. The first is that it is a subject largely ignored in the literature to date. Hessing, Howlett and Summerville (2005: 294) make an important point when they note that the term "interest" is often used interchangeably with "actor," which precludes any possibility that a given policy actor might conceivably pursue more than one political objective:

> For the most part, "interests" are defined in subjective terms: that is, in terms of the definition of the policy "actors" themselves.... As a result, political interests are made synonymous with political actors in a somewhat tautological manner, and the difficult question of the relationship between interest and actor is explained away.

As discussed, little has yet been written on business and environmental policy at all, and no works that I am aware of focus upon the political objective of the regulated firm. In addition, the subject of the firm's environmental policy interest is more complex than currently available analysis would lead one to believe. Most current research rests on the questionable assumption that when business negotiates with environmental regulators it seeks only one objective, weaker regulation, in order to minimize the impact on profit. Usually that is the case, but sometimes it is not. Furthermore, there is a need to examine the *degree* of that interest, since this is an essential factor in deciding what resources the firm will commit to the conflict with regulators and, accordingly, its political power. Finally, we must recognize that, almost always, interest in minimizing the economic impact of regulation is compromised by pursuit of other objectives, most notably regaining the legitimacy lost when environmentalism first began to attract public support. By focussing upon these two related variables of firm policy interest and power I can only give a partial picture. I hope, however, that providing a more complete and fully nuanced understanding of that one aspect of the business role than is available to date will give other researchers firmer purchase for exploring the other essential aspects of the ways in which firms influence industrial pollution regulation.

Environmental Policy

The basic understanding of environmental policy-making used here starts with a model of the regulatory department using policy instruments of sticks or carrots as it attempts to improve the environmental performance of the firm. The majority of the time, only those two actors are found in the policy network, as regulators operate in a routine manner to apply, through discussion and negotiation, their general guidelines and policies to the particular environmental permit that sets out the operating conditions applying to the individual firm. In the case of new policy development, the arena is often enlarged. There, in very general terms, environmental policy-making is done through negotiation between two groups, the first consisting of the environment department, working in alliance with ENGOs and others, and the second of the regulated firm, which in turn works with the relevant industrial development departments and other business actors, such as buyers and sellers, whose shared economic interest leads them to the same policy interest.

Pollution is regulated within Canada by governments at the local, provincial, and federal levels, and national, federal-provincial environmental policy now takes place within a complex web of international agreements (Boyd, 2003; Porter, Brown and Chasek, 2000). By far the most important, direct regulatory role, however, defined as putting in place and enforcing legally binding pollution standards, is played by the provincial governments. It is now clear from court decisions that the federal government has the constitutional authority itself to directly regulate, using federal law (Harrison, 1996a). Yet it has only rarely done so, most notably in the early 1970s and again in the early 1990s. It is engaged with international environmental policy and coordination of provincial policy, but it is seldom the direct regulator. Local governments play important roles respecting solid waste management, treatment of human wastes, and provision of safe drinking water but beyond that have no environmental policy mandate. When firm officials sit across the table and negotiate with environmental regulators, they are almost always looking into the eyes of officials from provincial environment departments.

The basic instrument used for environmental regulation of industry has from the beginning been administrative law, implemented through a licensing system that sets out allowable quantities or toxicity levels of pollution emitted and controls the methods used for its disposal (Benedickson, 2002; Boyd, 2003). The history of environmental policy is largely one of successive changes in environmental policy instruments and the degree of coerciveness with which they were used by regulators (Macdonald, 2001). Environmental law was first implemented by means of an "abatement" approach in which regulators, almost always engineers, engaged in technical discussion with their counterparts in the firm, with only rare recourse to court prosecution. Such enforcement practices became more common in the 1980s. By that time a very different form of regulatory pressure, positive or negative financial incentive, was coming into vogue. Very few economic instruments were actually put in place, however, and by the mid-1990s regulatory fashion had turned to voluntary programs. Administrative law is still the basic regulatory tool in current use.

A variety of other instruments are also potentially available, although for the most part they have been more discussed than actually used. These include provision of environmental services by governments, such as technical engineering assistance provided to industries asked to change product design or manufacturing process; economic instruments such as tax reductions for pollution-control equipment, and pricing of energy or waste disposal; systems for trading pollution-emission credits, intended to allow the market to decide which firms abate by how much, within the umbrella of an overall regulatory cap; labelling programs to influence consumer choice; purchasing decisions made by governments themselves, which by ensuring markets can stimulate green product design; and various measures used to induce industries to "voluntarily" improve environmental management. Any of these instruments, but in particular the way in which law is enforced, can be used in a more or less coercive fashion. The central theme of the history that follows is steadily increasing coerciveness, measured by number of prosecutions and convictions and level of associated fines, from the early 1970s to early 1990s, followed by a distinct relaxation of regulatory pressure in the deregulatory era of the 1990s.

The simple model of the regulatory system described in the preceding pages is officials from a provincial environment department agreeing with firm officials on steps the latter will take to reduce the toxicity or quantity of pollution from their factory and then issuing an environment permit which gives legal force to those standards. This simple model may have represented the bulk of regulatory activity in the 1970s, when the system was established, but since then a whole series of concentric rings of policy activity has been added. Environmental policy has expanded spatially, from a primary focus on control of local emissions to recognition of the impact of long-range, often transboundary emissions to global atmospheric issues such as the stratospheric ozone layer and concentration of greenhouse gases. It has also expanded in terms of the type of activity considered, not only product design and bans, but also the implications of such things as intensity of urban development and implications for transportation-related smog or the quasi-regulatory role played by banks and insurance companies as they have come to concern themselves with the environmental performance of their industrial clients. The focus of this study is upon the way in which resource and manufacturing industries engage with environmental regulators, but inevitably that process is influenced by these other policy fields, and they are for that reason discussed when necessary.

In the same way, firm-regulator engagement takes place within the larger ambit of business-government negotiation over a host of issues such as plant siting, employment practices, and fiscal and monetary policy. Because the balance of power between the firm and its environmental regulators, which is the central subject of this work, is directly influenced by this larger field of state-market relations, the latter is also discussed as needed.

As mentioned, one of the central arguments made here is that we must recognize that the regulated firm pursues two independent and sometimes contradictory objectives: profitability *and* legitimacy. Equally central to this analysis is another aspect of firm interest: *how much* it is motivated to pursue either. I assume the degree of interest in legitimacy is directly related to social acceptance of the environmental critique, that is, the extent to which its behaviour has come to be generally seen as illegitimate. The degree of interest with respect to profitability flows from the extent to which environmental regulation poses an economic threat. Simply put, regulation of pollution is less threatening to profitability than is regulation of products.

Both waste and pollution represent that portion of manufacturing input materials that have been purchased by the firm but are not included in the finished product, thereby precluding the ability to recoup that purchase cost. Waste and pollution management and disposal also impose costs which, as regulatory controls have become more stringent and disposal sites less numerous during the past half-century, have increased sharply. The higher the cost of raw materials and waste disposal, the greater the incentive for the firm to spend on efficiency improvements to reduce waste quantities. Such improvements are usually associated with plant modernization, which for sectors such as pulp and paper and smelting have been key to pollution reduction.

Since pollution is a by-product, an unwanted and wasteful use of one portion of the total resources fed into the resource and manufacturing processes, the firm has an inherent economic interest in seeing it reduced. The Inco plant at Sudbury, for instance, significantly decreased the annual quantities of sulphur dioxide emitted to the air, in order to increase efficiency and profitability, throughout the first half of the twentieth century, long before those emissions were the subject of any government policy. The firm prefers, of course, to get rid of its wastes at the lowest possible costs, while regulators want them to spend more money on the process, to reduce environmental impacts. But since pollution control is a relatively minor portion of total business spending, usually less than five per cent even in the pollution-intensive sectors like steel, chemicals or pulp and paper, and in many instances improved efficiency saves money spent on raw materials, this is not a major conflict. This congruence of interest between the firm and regulators increases to the extent that waste disposal costs increase, as noted above. Not surprisingly, regulation of pollution by-products has been the most successful aspect of environmental policy to date and the area in which business has been most willing to voluntarily go beyond regulatory requirements.

This same congruence of interest is not found with respect to products. An inherent objective of environmental policy is to influence the design of products such as motor vehicles, buildings or beverage containers so they will generate less pollution while used, require less energy and, when disposed of, lend themselves more readily to re-use or recycling. As discussed below, regulation of the motor vehicle and soft drink industries has since the 1970s consisted largely of efforts to bring about changes in product design, so as to reduce smog emissions, increase fuel efficiency and, in the latter case, allow the beverage container to be re-used. Here, and more recently in the case of chemical and fossil-fuel products, industry resistance has been much greater. This is because the firm's strategic search for profit is centred on decisions made concerning the nature of the product it will sell. As consumers become increasingly environmentally conscious, the firm may well wish to move to a strategy of selling green products, but there is no inherent reason it would wish to include regulators in that decision-making process.

An even greater challenge for regulators than influencing product design is to completely ban a product. In the early 1970s, DDT and PCBs were banned in Canada and other countries, as were CFCs some fifteen years later. The 2001 Stockholm Convention on Persistent Organic Pollutants is intended to place a global ban on a handful of particularly dangerous chemicals, which for the most part have already been banned by domestic legislation. Such examples of successful regulatory bans, however, are rare.

The goal of the 1992 UNFCCC is to bring about, if not a complete ban, a substantial reduction in the use of fossil fuels, in the hope that their economic function will be performed by energy sources that do not generate greenhouse gases. Ontario in the late 1980s adopted a policy goal of cutting pesticide use in that province by half. At that same time, Greenpeace in Canada and the US began demanding a complete ban on the manufacture and use of chlorine. None of those policy efforts has succeeded. With respect to product bans, the clash between business and government is fundamental. The companies that make their living by selling the products or substances slated for complete elimination are faced with a much greater economic threat than is the case for improved pollution management, which makes compromise with regulatory demands very difficult indeed. Those firms are strongly motivated to use whatever political power they can muster to prevent governments from adopting such a policy.

The challenge is compounded by the fact that those who buy the product, as well as those who make and sell it, will resist bans. Total prohibition of alcohol was a policy failure because of resistance not so much by the manufacturers, but instead by the users of the product — as has been the case for recreational drugs such as marijuana or cocaine. Cigarette regulation has attempted to reduce demand by education, price, and placing controls on advertising, but has never attempted a complete ban. There is no serious discussion of banning the manufacture of handguns, despite the harm they cause. In the same way, to give just one example from our policy field, environmental policy seeking to reduce automobile use is hampered as much or more by the political power of drivers as it is by the automobile industry.

ORGANIZATION OF THE TEXT

The book is organized, in the first instance, by means of narrative. I provide a chronological account of the various ways in which business, and most particularly the firms and sectors engaged in resource extraction and manufacturing activities, have undertaken political action in response to the new demands and opportunities presented by environmentalism. A separate chapter is devoted to each of the three major phases in the evolution of environmental policy from the 1950s to the present: establishing the regulatory system (although initial regulatory action was taken in 1956, a comprehensive system only began to appear in the following decade), significantly increasing regulatory pressure in the 1980s, and then relaxing it in the decade following. Events since 2000, primarily the battle over Kyoto ratification in 2002 and the evolution of climate policy since, are not treated in a separate chapter, partially due to the lack of published analysis, but also because it is not yet clear whether we are currently witnessing a change in policy comparable to that of 1980 and 1993, or simply a prolongation of the relaxed regulatory pressure of the 1990s. For that reason, no attempt is made to comprehensively treat events since 2000, but climate policy is presented as a coda to the third of the three history chapters.

While the flow of time from the creation of the Ontario Water Resources Commission in 1956 to the Chrétien government's ratification of the Kyoto Protocol in 2002 is the organizing principle, this historical account does not emulate the straight-cut lines of a barge canal but is more akin to the meandering path of a northern river. When the narrative bumps up against political activity by firms at the centre of the most salient issue of the day, such as acid-rain emissions by Inco in the 1980s, or oil-and-gas industry action on climate change a decade later, those sandbanks or islands are explored in detail. Nor is our speed constant as we move through this half-century; we slide through some time periods quickly, noticing few details on the way while in others we move at a more measured pace, one that provides opportunities for observation. Finally, it should be noted that to give the reader the necessary context, each of those chapters begins with a short description of the activities of environmental regulators spanning the entire time period of the chapter, before reverting to chronology to structure a description of the activities of the regulated industries and other business actors.

Beyond chronology, the other organizing principle is examination of the subjects addressed by the three principal research questions set out above, namely the objective sought by the firm as it engages in environmental politics, the strategies it uses, and its power to achieve its purpose. Chapter Two provides a review of the current state of research knowledge of those subjects, both in Canada and in other jurisdictions. At the conclusion of that chapter, I provide a short statement of the things upon which analysts agree, other issues that are the subject of academic debate, and yet other aspects that are still largely unresearched and thus represent gaps in our knowledge. Since this work aims to contribute to those debates and to fill those gaps, such an understanding is essential to the reader before embarking on the historical voyage that follows. The voyage is punctuated at the end of each of the three history chapters by a brief discussion of business interest, strategy, and power during the period examined.

The concluding chapter is also organized by means of those aspects of business political activity. My purpose there is to draw upon the findings presented in the historical account in order to use them as evidence to support the analysis and argument made in that chapter. That argument is presented in summary form here, developed in stages in the concluding sections of each of the historical chapters, and then presented fully in the final chapter. The book then concludes with a discussion of two things: the first is possible avenues for future academic research, while the second is the implications of my argument for the future evolution of applied environmental policy, as governments, business firms, and environmentalists continue to contest the purpose and methods of environmental policy.

SUMMARY OF THE ARGUMENT

To help the reader wrestle with the argument developed in the following chapters, I present it here in abbreviated form, structured by means of the three research questions.

Political Objectives

The firm subject to environmental regulation takes political action primarily in order to minimize the impact that regulation has upon its fundamental interest of profitability. In some instances, it may invite regulation as a means of contributing to profitability, but instances of that objective are rare. For the most part, the policy goal sought by regulated firms is to negotiate weaker standards and to delay their implementation. In some instances, firms have pursued more ambitious goals, attempting to completely block new policy initiatives or fundamentally change them. It would seem that the most important factor causing firms to adopt this more radical goal is the relative severity of the regulatory threat. The greater the economic consequences to the firm of proposed regulation, the more likely it is to take more ambitious political action with the intent of nullifying or significantly reducing that threat.

Contribution to its economic goals, however, is not the only political objective sought by such a firm. It also seeks legitimacy, in the eyes of both regulators and the larger public. It does so because legitimacy is a principal source of both economic and political power, and thus a longer-term strategy for achieving profit. More than that, however, legitimacy is necessary for basic survival. Because it is seen by the firm in such life-or-death terms, the need for legitimacy is not just a secondary interest, contributing to the primary political goal of profit. It is instead a distinct and separate interest, for the achievement of which the firm is willing to sacrifice some considerable degree of the profit interest.

Despite their dominant political power, managers of large firms have felt their firm's survival to be imperilled during several periods in the last hundred years. In the US, these included "trust-busting" threats in the early years of the twentieth century and attacks by labour after 1945. In both countries, the critiques of the new social movements in the 1960s caused another loss of legitimacy and political power. The external threat represented by the political power of environmentalism, which reached its peak in the late 1980s, was another such period. In all of those cases, business has taken active steps to restore legitimacy, and thus political power.

Strategies for Achieving those Objectives

The usual strategy for influencing environmental policy has been private negotiation with regulators, taking advantage of elite-level contacts. The firm engaged in such negotiations usually seeks to strengthen its hand by bringing allies into that closed-door process, either other firms with comparable policy interests or state actors. The latter may be other departments in the same government as the regulatory department — most usually the firm's client department, such as industry, natural resources or agriculture — or actors in central agencies such as the prime minister's or premier's office, or yet others located in another level of government. While seeking to bring such allies in, the firm also hopes to keep environmentalists out. With the advent of multi-stakeholder consultation, business has had to accept the presence of environmentalists in at least that one bargaining forum. In rare instances, business has broken out of those private negotiations to make its case in public, seeking political support.

To achieve or regain legitimacy in the eyes of relevant audiences, business firms, like all individuals and organizations, have three available means: change their own behaviour, change the image of their behaviour in those eyes, or change the norms by which those audiences are judging them. Business in Canada has used all three means to regain environmental legitimacy. They have changed their own behaviour, in terms of environmental management, to bring it more closely into line with the values of environmentalism. They have been far more willing to do this with respect to pollution control, which often results in cost savings, than product design or bans, which usually entail greater costs. They have pursued the second strategy by going to great lengths to publicize that improved performance and by advertising and public-relations efforts to give their products and the corporation itself a new green image. The third strategy, an attempt to change the environmental values by which it is judged, has been pursued by embracing the concept of "sustainable development" and thereby working to redefine the environmental problem as nothing more than a lack of efficiency, within the dominant paradigm of economic growth.

Success in Achieving those Objectives — Political Power

During the 1960s, an era of steadily increasing government revenues and belief in the value of activist government, the political power of new social movements and associated loss of business legitimacy in the eyes of the public resulted in the imposition of a number of new regulatory regimes, including that of environment, upon resource and manufacturing industries. Business still held sufficient political power, however, to fend off meaningful implementation of environmental regulation during the 1970s. Business political power relative to that of environmental regulators was then eclipsed during the late 1980s and early 1990s. That balance of power was then again reversed in the 1990s, as business regained environmental legitimacy, the role of the state was called into question, and federal and provincial environment departments were stripped of financial and human resources. The events of Walkerton and September 11, 2001, have restored some power to both regulators and the state in general, but business still exerts significant power in the environmental policy arena.

The sources of the political power of the firm, relative to that of environmental regulators, are many and vary according to individual circumstance. I do not pretend to be able to give a definitive picture here. I suggest, however, that the political power of business with respect to environmental politics depends less upon its own actions than upon factors external to the firm. Choice of lobbying strategy, organization of business coalitions, efforts to garner public support, and the total magnitude of the resources committed to the political battle are important factors. More important, however, are three external factors. The first is the institutional context, which decides if the environmental policy decision is made by regulators solely through private negotiation with the firm or with the addition of some form of public debate and countervailing lobbying by environmentalists. The second factor is the extent to which government is motivated, primarily by perceived electoral advantage, to impose behaviour change on the firm. This decides whether the environment department must act in isolation or with the active support of central agencies, such as the prime minister's or premier's office. The third factor is the prevailing context of ideas respecting both the relative legitimacy of state and market and, within that context, the framing of the environmental problem. The former has played itself out in debates over government regulation and deficit financing, from the expansionist period of the 1950s and 1960s through to the shrinking of the state in the 1990s. The latter has seen a fundamental redefinition of the environmental problem and its solution from the original "limits to growth" and "bioequity" to the now dominant paradigm of "sustainable development" that incorporates economic growth into the environmental solution and extends ethical regard only to future generations of humans, granting virtually no moral worth to other beings, alive today or tomorrow, who do not happen to be of our species.

CHAPTER TWO

The Current State of Understanding

This chapter provides a review of the current state of knowledge and debate concerning political activity by the environmentally regulated firm. The first section, after documenting the emergence of the firm as an organizational entity, the political issues associated with its current legal structure, and the role of corporate culture, reviews literature dealing with the larger context of "business-government relations" within which environmental regulation takes place. The second section of the chapter reviews the current state of research on the more specific topic of environmental policy-making, with the focus primarily on research done to date in Canada.

EMERGENCE OF THE CORPORATION

Without going into detail, we can quickly trace the evolution of the firm as a legal entity. The modern legal status of the corporation as an entity, in some ways analogous to an individual human being, having similar rights to sue and be sued, to due process, to freedom of speech, and so on—that is, as a body with agency of its own, distinct from that of the individuals managing its affairs at any given time—has its origins in church law:

> Indeed, it must have early become evident to the church that it was essential to find some way of differentiating the individual acts of a priest, bishop or abbot from those carried out in his official capacity. Once the notion of a separate corporate person had evolved to even an elementary level within the ecclesiastical sphere, it was highly likely that it would be exported into the secular realm, given the extent to which the clergy controlled the early administrative regime of the English Crown. (McGuinness, 1999: 9)

This extension beyond church governance occurred first in the realm of government, through the establishment of incorporated municipalities (McGuinness, 1999: 12). In the realm of business, the companies created in the seventeenth century by special acts of the Crown, such as the Hudson's Bay Company, created in 1609, were composed of individuals who shared the benefits of the royal grant of lands and trading monopolies. During the years that followed, the company then emerged as an agent distinct from those individuals:

> Over time, in addition to sanctioning individual trading activities, companies began to operate as independent commercial ventures. Members would subscribe for capital to fund the venture. This capital was jointly held with all other capital for the benefit of the company. Members became known as "joint stock-holders." ... Eventually, private trading by each member was eliminated and the joint stock company emerged with a separate legal personality. (Johnson, 1999: lxxiii)

Initially, individual investors fully shared both benefits and liabilities incurred by the joint-stock company. In common with the partnership, which during the eighteenth and early nineteenth centuries was the most common legal structure for business operations, this potential liability was a challenge to attracting investment (Bakan, 2004). That changed in 1855, when the British government passed the Limited Liability Act, which meant that losses of an individual investor could not be larger than the size of the investment, thus making it easier for the corporation to raise capital. It was around that time that the corporate form of business organization had become more common than the partnership. Under limited liability, the larger society is potentially at risk for costs of bankruptcy, beyond those absorbed by investors up to the limit of their liability, which acts as a form of insurance for risk-taking by investors. Since encouragement of financial risk is essential for capitalist wealth creation, the limited liability of the corporation is an important legal doctrine that is unlikely to be changed. The other major trend in the evolution of the legal status of the firm in the closing years of the nineteenth century was a loosening of state control over the initial fact of incorporation. Governments began to grant incorporation upon request, thus transforming corporate status from a privilege to a right.

Today in Canada, corporations are established under either federal or provincial law. In addition to limited liability, Canadian law gives them the attribute of separate personality, essentially agency distinct from that of the individual human personalities who own and manage them. In terms of the political functions of the firm, this has two ramifications. The first is the claim that corporate advertising for harmful products such as cigarettes is protected by the same rights of freedom of speech given to human individuals. The second is the question of whether the legal system, as it seeks to deter illegal behaviour by corporations, should impose sanctions upon the firm, usually in the form of fines, or upon individual directors and managers. As discussed below, one of the most significant indications that regulatory pressure was increasing occurred in the 1980s, when individual business people were first prosecuted for environmental-law infractions committed by the company for which they worked.

The other political implication of the system of law governing the creation and management of corporations (as opposed to bodies of law such as environment, occupational health, and others regulating particular actions of the firm) concerns the fiduciary duty of directors. For very understandable reasons, they are subjected to legal obligations to act in ways that further the financial well-being of the corporation rather than, for instance, themselves. Both Glasbeek (2002) and Bakan (2004) discuss the problem this poses for efforts to convince firm owners and directors to act in a more socially responsible manner. In Bakan's words,

> The people who run corporations are, for the most part, good people, moral people.... Despite their personal qualities and ambitions, however, their duty as corporate executives is clear: they must always put the corporation's best interests first.... The money they manage and invest is not theirs. They can no sooner use it to heal the sick, save the environment, or feed the poor than they can to buy themselves villas in Tuscany. (Bakan, 2004: 50)

The ongoing debate over corporate social responsibility (Brummer, 1991) in which one side argues that firms should both do more to reduce the social impacts of their market activities and take a more active role in positively addressing social problems, while others argue they should not exercise such unaccountable social power and instead simply obey the law, is not directly part of the subject explored here. It has important implications for it, however, most notably in terms of the implicit argument made by business in the 1990s that it was by then ready and willing to act in a socially responsible manner respecting the environmental impacts of its activities and, therefore, law was no longer needed. We will return to this subject. Suffice it to say here that the legal form of the corporation has these political ramifications: the contested right of the corporation to freedom of speech, through advertising; the fact that legal financial liability for actions of the firm on the part of those who own it, investors, is limited to the amount of their investment; the contested question of the extent to which regulatory systems such as environmental law should pierce the corporate veil and hold directors and officers personally responsible; and, finally, the extent to which fiduciary duty places limits on managers' ability to ensure that the firm acts in a socially responsible manner.

We now turn from the legal structure of the corporation to the less sharply defined world of values and assumptions internal to the firm.

CORPORATE CULTURE

No matter how intangible or difficult to define or dissect, there is no doubting the fact that some aspect of the shared values found within organizations influences the ways in which they view and interact with the world outside their boundaries. An illustration is provided by Robert Graves, comparing two virtually identical organizations, regiments in the British Army, located in exactly the same environment, the World War I trenches. Graves originally joined the Royal Welch Fusiliers (which prided itself on the "c" spelling and regimental history going back to the American Revolution), but when he first went to the trenches he was posted to the Welsh Regiment. He served there, and then returned to the Royal Welch:

> The first night I was in the trenches [with the Royal Welch] my company commander asked me to go out on patrol; it was the regimental custom to test new officers in this way. All the time I had been with the Welsh I had never once been out in No Man's Land, even to inspect the barbed wire.... But with battalions of the Royal Welch Fusiliers it was a point of honour to be masters of No Man's Land from dusk to dawn.... The Second Royal Welch, unlike the Second Welsh, believed themselves better trench fighters than the Germans. With the Second Welsh it was not cowardice but modesty. With the Second Royal Welch it was not vainglory but courage; as soon as they arrived in a new sector they insisted on getting fire ascendancy.... The Welsh [on the other hand] seldom answered a machine-gun. (Graves, 1995: 122-26)

Johns (1996) defines the element that produced the different behaviours described by Graves in this way: "organizational culture consists of the shared beliefs, values and assumptions that exist in an organization. In turn, these shared beliefs, values and assumptions determine the norms that develop and the patterns of behaviour that emerge" (288-89). Schoenberge (1997) provides a similar picture of the ideas held internally within the organization—which she presents as three layers: assumptions, values, and, arising from those, norms—which determine the behaviour of individuals as they interact within the organization and which have at least some influence on the way the organization as a whole behaves as it interacts with its external environment. To that picture, she adds the concept of "identity," making the key point that the identity of the organization is distinct from that of the individuals of which it is composed: "The corporation is both a collection of individuals and a self-reproducing institution whose identity is linked with, but not the same as, those of the people who work in it" (113). Other analysts point to "rites, rituals and symbols of the company" (Kono and Clegg, 1998: 5). Those who write on corporate culture agree that it emanates largely from top management. Deal and Kennedy (1982) go so far as to add "leadership" as a part of the definition of corporate culture.

To what extent do analysts see corporate culture as a factor determining objectives and strategies as firms interact with governments? The authors referred to above, who have taken corporate culture as their subject of study, quite understandably and correctly believe it is a factor that cannot be ignored. Those writing more generally on organizational behaviour or business-government relations, however, take as their subject the firm situated within its external environment. For them, the nature of the economic or political risks and opportunities which the firm sees in that environment tend to be more significant factors as they work to understand firm behaviour.

In the world of environmental policy, culture has been most often examined in terms of the apparent split that developed in the late 1990s amongst transnational oil companies with respect to climate change (Rowlands, 2000). Hard-liners such as Exxon, who continued to dispute the physical reality of the phenomenon, are contrasted with firms such as BP which have acknowledged it is a problem that must be addressed. A comparative study of the two firms done in 2003, however, found more similarities than differences:

> Even though BP is renowned for its "proactive" stance on climate change, it is clear that the company cannot afford to neglect to demonstrate [to shareholders] that increased oil production remains a priority; just as ExxonMobil, despite the company's continuous attempt to delegitimize the issue of climate change, can no longer afford not to take action to reduce emissions. The case study of BP and ExxonMobil shows that even though these two companies have often taken opposing stands on climate change, their current strategies are actually not that different. Both companies experience a similar exposure to risks associated with carbon-intensity, and both companies are taking limited action to reduce this risk while remaining heavily committed to the expansion of their fossil fuel resources. (Malmqvist, 2003: 26)

The difference between the two firms lies not in their environmental management behaviour, but in the different *images of that behaviour* which each tries to project. Given the similarities between the two and the fact that they operate in the same external environment, we can only conclude, as was the case for Graves's two regiments, that this difference in image-making must be attributed to differing corporate cultures. The greening of the corporate image is an important aspect of business political activity on environment, as discussed in Chapter Five. However, it is only one strategy, part of the overall bid to regain legitimacy. Far more important for the subject examined here are the basics of that political behaviour — the difference between firms which actively work to block or shape environmental policy and those which, through negotiation with regulators, adapt to it. The evidence presented in the pages that follow leads to the conclusion that it is the nature of the external threat, not internal culture, which decides those differing responses. To give just one example here, the split between hard-line and accomodationist Canadian oil firms disappeared in the fall of 2002, in the face of the external threat of federal government ratification of Kyoto. A western Canadian writer put it this way: "At this point [mid-October, 2002], industry insiders agree that the oil patch is 100% united against Kyoto, with even liberal laggards like Shell Canada determined to resist" (Byfield, 2002: 13).

BUSINESS-GOVERNMENT LITERATURE

Interest: what does business want from government?

As mentioned, Brooks and Stritch (1991) begin their discussion of this question by noting that at the first level of organization, that of capital as a class, business actors share only very general political goals, such as preservation of private property rights. For more specific policy goals, unanimity is not found. Given this fragmentation of business interests, perhaps it is more useful to put the question this way: what does the individual firm want government to do? Brooks and Stritch tell us that the firm pursues "narrow corporate interests, e.g. government contracts; grants; loans; subsidies; licences" (1991: 11). In other words, the policy interests pursued by the firm are those that will contribute directly to its basic goal of profitability. Mitchell (1997: 11) states that this is the view commonly held by political scientists:

> How to account for corporate political activity? The principal goal of business is economic success, not to participate in politics. While political scientists have no general political theory of the firm, we have come some way in testing a set of propositions to explain this activity derived from the general assumption of the firm as profit maximizing.

Assumptions concerning the basic political goals of the firm arise, accordingly, from the view one holds of the basic nature and organizational goal of the firm. The firm, from this perspective, is an organizational form that has largely come to replace other forms, such as individual proprietorship or partnerships, because is has proven to be more effective in achieving the goal of investors, providing return on capital. Because state and market are fundamentally interdependent, business has always engaged closely with government, but it does so not for ideological reasons, to fashion what it sees as the perfect society, as do some actors, but instead for self-interested reasons. It temporarily leaves its home-ground of the market and enters that of the state. Once there, it seeks government policy which will help it generate profit in that original venue.

Another political scientist, Graham Wilson, has done empirical research on the question raised by Mitchell as to why firms engage in political activity (which is another way of asking what interest they pursue when they do so). He surveyed 250 of the largest US firms, hoping to obtain "a deeper understanding of why corporations are, or are not, politically active" (Wilson, 1990: 282). His expectation was that regulatory pressure, one factor influencing economic self-interest, would be the greatest motivator of political activity. His findings, however, led him to another variable, one more directly tied to profitability, namely "the size of a corporation's federal contracts," which in turn led him to conclude that "the scale of the contracts obtained from the federal government is the best predictor of the scale of a corporation's political activities" (Wilson, 1990: 287). According to this study, what business most wants from government is money.

Other disciplines also share this perspective. Economists use the term "rent-seeking" to refer to political activity intended to confer economic benefit (Stigler, 1971). The most common examples are transportation or communications industries that have actively sought to be regulated in order to make it more difficult for potential competitors to enter their field of activity (Strick, 1990).

A similar approach is found in the field of management studies, the domain of schools of business. Mahon and McGowan (1996) unabashedly state the purpose of their research to be that of helping business find ways to use its political activities, which they define as including not just engagement with governments, but also relevant societal actors, to contribute to the search for competitive advantage in the market. Their book is intended to fill a gap in the management literature: "The teaching of political strategy is not as well developed as the more conventional business strategy; indeed, it is often downplayed or even totally omitted in most strategic management textbooks" (Mahon and McGowan, 1996: 5). Firms must learn to exercise strategic management in their political environment, just as they attempt to do in their market environment: "If ... the operating assumption is that political and social issues are environmental factors to be considered in shaping an organization's strategy, and that they are part of an overall pattern of situations that can be managed or influenced, then organizational strategies for anticipating, shaping and responding to such issues and problems makes sense" (20). Mahon and McGowan define this process as the exercising of political power by the firm: "corporate political strategy is defined as those activities taken by organizations to acquire, develop and use power to obtain

an advantage (a particular allocation of resources or no change in the allocation) in a situation of conflict" (29).

The view from these different disciplines—that the firm exists primarily
to maximize profit and that it pursues that same goal when it temporarily
leaves the arena of the market and enters that of politics—is clearly valid.
Some analysts, however, while accepting that initial assumption, have
explored other basic interests of the firm, which in turn have implications for
its policy interest. During the course of the twentieth century, business managers have largely come to see the basic goal of the firm as more than simply
profit maximization. They see the firm as fully engaged with the surrounding
society and therefore having social responsibilities it must meet, even at the
expense of some foregone profit (Post et al., 1996). In step with these changing views in the professional world, a number of university-based analysts
are now investigating goals of the firm not directly related to short-term
profitability. An example, again from the field of management studies, is
given by Marcus, Kaufman and Beam (1987). They fully agree that financial
benefit is the first goal of the politically active firm, but then point to an
important secondary goal—legitimacy: "Although corporate advantage is
the primary objective of the public affairs function, social legitimacy is an
equally compelling consideration, which typically acts as a constraint on
unbridled self-interest" (7).

Marchand has written a history of the first search for legitimacy, undertaken by the newly emerged large-scale corporations in the United States,
which had obtained both size and economic powers that dwarfed other institutions such as the family, church or community: "The crisis of legitimacy
that major American corporations began to face in the 1890s had everything
to do with their size, with the startling disparities of scale" (1998: 3). For
whatever reason, corporate leaders began to take a series of actions, both
concrete, e.g., related to the health and welfare of their employees, and imag-
istic, e.g., advertising campaigns intended to put a human face on the giant
firm, to demonstrate that it was possessed of a "corporate soul."

The first company to initiate what Marchand refers to as an "institutional
advertising campaign" (1998: 48)—advertising intended less to sell a particular product than to influence the recipient's attitude toward the firm itself—
was undertaken by the telephone company AT&T in 1908. The company's
patent-conferred monopoly had expired in 1894, and since then it had strug-
gled to hold on to market share through a number of cut-throat tactics used
to weaken competitors. The result was that by the early 1900s it was largely
detested. AT&T feared that the example of publicly owned telephone
monopolies being put in place in Europe and Canada would be followed in

the United States. In response, the newly appointed president, Theodore Vail, initiated a coordinated campaign combining action and advertising:

> Thus began the first, most persistent, and most celebrated of the large-scale institutional advertising campaigns of the early twentieth century. Its primary purpose was political — to protect a corporation with an odious public reputation against threats of public ownership or hostile regulation. Among the methods deployed to publicize Vail's new emphasis on quality and service were measured argument, emotional appeal and transformed corporate behaviour. (Marchand, 1998: 48)

There are striking parallels between the methods used by AT&T to regain lost legitimacy in 1908 and the combined behaviour change and image greening carried out by large corporations in the 1990s.

Mitchell (1989) has documented the ways in which, during the 1920s, the large US firms took actions such as increasing wages and providing pension plans which were neither required by law nor in the direct, immediate service of profitability. He explores and rejects two possible explanations. The first is the separation of ownership and management, first noted by Berle and Means (1932). According to this theory, the fact that by this time many large firms were managed by executives who no longer themselves owned the company, but rather acted on behalf of the shareholders who did, meant that those same executives were more willing to divert potential profit into such expenditures. Mitchell did not, however, find significant differences in socially responsible actions between public and private companies. The difference he did find was between large and small firms, with such actions being limited to the former. He also found differences over time. As earnings plunged in the 1930s, such spending was reduced apace. The other possible explanation is that such action was taken to pre-empt the power of labour unions within the firm. Again, however, Mitchell finds no correlation between union strength in different firms and these benefits provided to employees (1989: 43-51).

Instead, Mitchell explains these actions as responses to the growing social criticism of large corporations from the 1890s onward. President Theodore Roosevelt's anti-trust policies, and in particular the breaking up of J.P. Morgan's Northern Securities Company in 1904, were a threat that business could not ignore (Mitchell, 1989: 92-93). In response, Mitchell argues, big business developed a new ideology. No longer, as they had in the nineteenth century, did business leaders argue they had no responsibility to act in the face of social ills. Instead, they accepted the new norm which stated that they held at least some responsibility for the well-being of their employees and

43

also for others outside the firm. At the heart of business motivation, according to Mitchell, was exactly the same search for legitimacy documented by Marchand, above:

> If it is accepted that corporations have power, then they, like the state, face the problem of legitimizing their power. That power requires legitimacy is one of the classical axioms of politics.... Corporate social policies originated as an expression of a new ideology of business power. They represented an attempt to legitimize that power in the eyes of government and other groups. (6-7)

By the middle years of the century, American business again found its legitimacy under attack, this time from organized labour, which in 1946 had launched a round of strikes intended to give it not only a greater share of profit but also a greater say in the management of the firm (Fones-Wolf, 1994). By the 1950s, the capital-labour compromise, whereby wage settlements ensured that a share of the increased wealth generated by increased productivity was passed on to labour and, in exchange, management was assured unfettered control of the corporation, was firmly in place. In the years before that, however, corporate leaders saw themselves as operating in a largely hostile and risky world in which nationalization of the enterprise was a distinct possibility.

Again, the response was a combination of action and advertising. The large firms and broad-based associations such as the United States Chamber of Commerce used the methods of "lobbying, campaign finance and litigation" to influence federal government policy in Washington (Fones-Wolf, 1994: 5). Locally, programs were initiated to undercut the power of labour unions, both on the plant floor and in the community. At the same time, paid advertising and public relations efforts to influence news media coverage were used to change the image of business:

> To achieve these goals, employers tried to construct a favorable image of business as a good neighbor by demonstrating both their social consciousness and the importance of the company to the community. Efforts ranged from publicizing company contributions to the local economy to beautifying plants and opening them to the public. Equally important were local public relations campaigns selling business's political agenda. (Fones-Wolf, 1994: 6)

The authors who have researched the business search for legitimacy throughout the twentieth century make it very clear that the motive for such campaigns was not purely altruistic. Instead, they paint a picture in which fear for the very survival of the firm as a privately owned entity combined with the normal profit interest to motivate such campaigns. It might be argued, then, that this does not constitute a distinct thread in the literature, since self-interest is basic to their analysis. Such an argument, however, fails to take into account the behaviour change that legitimacy-seeking firms mixed in with their lobbying, advertising, and public-relations efforts. Because it usually involves genuine actions above and beyond simply image change, be they employee pension plans in the 1920s or improved pollution management in the latter part of the century, I argue that legitimacy is a firm goal distinct from, and perhaps equally important as, profitability. Certainly, self-interest in terms of profit is one basic source of the search for legitimacy. But internalization of changing societal norms is also a factor.

Miles and Cameron (1982) have studied the way in which the US cigarette industry coped in the 1950s and 1960s with both the new scientific understanding that the product they sold was deadly to the user and the ensuing regulatory pressures (in that case, a drive to modify or completely ban cigarette advertising). That case study directly parallels the way in which resource and manufacturing industries coped with similar pressures relating to science, risk, and regulation a few years later (Macdonald, 2002a). Their theoretical perspective was based in an attempt to understand how organizations adapt to external change, but then added to that recognition was the fact that organizations also seek to *influence* their external environments: "Virtually no attention is paid by these theorists to the possibility that organizations, individually or collectively, may influence the environments upon which they depend for their effectiveness and persistence" (Miles and Cameron, 1982: 11).

An important component of Miles and Cameron's analysis was the organization's need for social legitimacy. They argued that organizations search for legitimacy in the face of changing external norms in three ways: by changing their own behaviour to adapt, by changing the external norms, or by seeking to have their behaviour identified with other, more legitimate norms. Their case study of the cigarette industry examined all three industry responses to new views of the product that had been successfully marketed throughout the century: changing product design, to introduce "safer" filter-tip cigarettes; lobbying governments in order to change regulatory behaviour governing cigarette advertising; and marketing their product to associate it with traditional, prized values of individual freedom and responsibility on the part of those who smoke, through such symbolism as the Marlboro man, dressed in cowboy gear, proudly independent astride his horse in the American West.

Since Miles and Cameron wrote their book in 1982, the tobacco industry has lost more legitimacy than perhaps any other. At least one American cigarette company, however, continues to seek it. Writing in *The New York Times Magazine*, Nocera (2006) has described the new strategy adopted by

Philip Morris (but not by others in the industry) of inviting regulation of the industry by the US Food and Drug Administration:

> Although Altria's [the company that owns the cigarette firm Philip Morris USA] stock price has performed well in recent years, it should be much higher based purely on its financial performance. But it's not, in part because it owns a tobacco company with a tarnished reputation, under constant attack.... There is no question, then, that Parrish [Steve Parrish, Philip Morris Senior Vice-President for Corporate Affairs] and Philip Morris USA are hoping that regulation could help the company to reclaim some legitimacy. From a business perspective, that could result in a higher stock price.... He [Parrish] also wants to see the company accepted as having a legitimate seat at the table when tobacco policy is being debated.

In this case, the firm seeks legitimacy both for reasons related to market performance and as a source of political power.

Suchman, also writing from an organizational theory perspective, holds that recognition of the search for legitimacy as a motivator of all organizations is transforming his discipline: "Drawing from the foundational work of Weber and Parsons, researchers have made legitimacy into an anchor-point of a vastly expanded theoretical apparatus addressing the normative and cognitive forces that constrain, construct, and empower organizational actors" (Suchman, 1995: 571). He too argues that legitimacy is gained by changing behaviour to better match new external norms, associating one's behaviour with symbols of desired values and, key to the analysis presented here, reaching into the external environment to change norms: "Even though most organizations gain legitimacy primarily through conformity and environment selection, for some, these strategies will not suffice.... In this case, managers must go beyond simply selecting among existing cultural beliefs; they must actively promulgate new explanations of social reality" (585-86).

Strategies to Achieve those Objectives

There is agreement in the literature that the primary method used by business firms to influence government policy is to take full advantage of its privileged elite-level access in order to privately make its case. On occasion, however, business will speak publicly, hoping to attract political support.

Kollman (1998: 4) defines "outside lobbying" as "attempts by interest group leaders to mobilize citizens outside the policymaking community to contact or pressure public officials inside the policymaking community." He suggests those seeking to influence policy will sometimes use the tactic of outside lobbying for two reasons: first, to demonstrate to government officials that the policy objective they seek has popular support, and second, to increase the amount of that popular support. The advertising campaign to prevent Kyoto ratification is an example of outside lobbying by business. As discussed below, research findings from Smith (2000) suggest that outside lobbying may be counter-productive for business, since such public political conflicts mobilize those working against business. Again, the Canadian example of the 2002 failure to block Kyoto ratification lends support to his argument.

The distinction between inside and outside lobbying is useful for this study because it relates directly to the two very different means by which business actors and their opponents in the environmental movement seek to influence government action. As discussed, a major source of the political power of business is the fact that it has elite-level access to government decision-makers. Environmentalists, with some exceptions, have no such guaranteed access. The *only* tactic they can use is outside lobbying, done largely through the news media, to move issues onto the policy agenda and to demonstrate popular support for their resolution. Business, on the other hand, has a choice. This raises the question of what factors induce firms or other business actors to sometimes supplement their normal method of closed-door lobbying with outside, public lobbying. A second question concerns the effectiveness of such campaigns.

Power: The Privileged Position of Business as a Political Actor

In the closing years of the nineteenth century, the emerging discipline of political science shared with legal studies a focus upon the institutional structure of constitutions and laws. With the publication of *The Process of Government* by Arthur Bentley in 1908, however, American political scientists recognized that government drafting and implementation of law was subject to external lobbying and thus began the century-long study of "interest groups." Prominent among those groups, of course, were business firms and trade associations, lobbying for economic benefit. Interest groups were the subject of Truman's 1951 study, *The Governmental Process: Political Interests and Public Opinion*. In the years following this conceptualization of interaction, lobbying and bargaining amongst state and non-actors, referred to as a pluralist perspective, scholars writing from that viewpoint did not single out the political power of business for particular attention.

During the 1960s, that started to change. In 1969, the American political scientist Edwin Epstein published a study focussed specifically upon the firm as a policy actor, entitled *The Corporation in American Politics*. Epstein laid out the basic themes that have been explored in the business-government literature since then: a focus upon the individual corporation, with the attendant question of why competing firms will at times collectively lobby by

47

means of a trade association and at other times act independently; an examination of the ways in which corporations influence government decisions; and the normative question of whether corporate political power represents a threat to democracy. Political scientists today, however, looking back over the evolution of their discipline's treatment of business political power, usually point not to his work but instead to Charles Lindblom's 1977 book *Politics and Markets* as an indicator of this change. The book is considered significant because Lindblom—whom Luger (2000) has called "one of the deans of postwar pluralism" (24)—originally saw pluralism as connoting some parity of power, but in this work portrayed business as having political power not available to labour or other societal actors, a view at variance with his earlier writings on power and the role of business. Brooks and Stritch (1991) give this view of the way in which mainstream political scientists came to view the subject: "While there is no doubt that business does not have matters all its own way in the political system (the diversity of material interests within the business community alone ensures that there will be both winners *and* losers among business interests), there also is no doubt that business occupies a privileged position in the politics of capitalist societies" (16).

Other schools, such as those writing from a Marxist perspective (Panitch, 1977) or sociologists exploring the influence of elites (Mills, 1956; Clement, 1975) had always assumed that business exerted disproportionate political influence. What is significant about the evolution of the understanding of business power is that analysts like Mills, who wrote from an explicitly critical perspective, had by the closing years of the twentieth century been joined by their mainstream, pluralist colleagues.

There is less agreement on the sources of business political power, the ways in which it is exercised, or even the definition and ways of understanding the term "political power" itself. Before turning to those debates, however, it is necessary to set out the ways in which most researchers today qualify the picture of business as the dominant political actor. With respect to both the power of business *relative to that of government* and, what is a very different but directly related subject, the power of business to influence government *relative to that of other non-state actors*, there is general agreement in the literature on three things. First, business power is far from absolute—there are occasions when government can force a business actor to do things it would prefer not to do or prevent it from doing things it would like to (such as the Canadian government's prohibition of bank mergers or more recently income trusts). Second, the political power of business has varied over time, most significantly during the late 1960s when it was unable to resist regulatory encroachment upon a number of its activities. Finally, the power of a business actor relative to that of the government of a jurisdiction in which it plans to begin operations is greater prior to making the investment decision than it is once it has incurred the sunk costs of building the mine, mill or factory. I will now briefly discuss each point.

Brooks and Stritch (1991) point out that business political power is limited by internal conflicts, as different sectors or firms pursue competing political goals. However, even when business closes ranks, as it did in 2002 during the Kyoto ratification battle, business may lose a political conflict with other actors, such as labour or environmentalists. Mitchell (1997) uses examination of the rare instances in which business does not prevail as a window through which to study the more usual case of business dominance. More specifically, Smith (2000) has studied the question of whether closing ranks automatically generates political power and finds, counter-intuitively, that it does not.

Since social power flows from organization, one would assume that in those instances where the different levels of business, including firms, sectors, and capital as a whole, unite around a given political objective and then devote their considerable financial and elite-access resources to the task of lobbying governments, policy success is assured. Smith has studied a number of political issues in the US that have seen such a closing of ranks, as indicated by the US Chamber of Commerce moving in to play a direct political role, and found that this is not the case. More often than not, such a united business front has lost the political battle, because the issue has energized and united those on the other side, such as labour, social movements, and churches. Smith argues convincingly that business wields greater political power at the sectoral level, when the Chamber is not involved, and business is not united, but where the battles are less public and opposition, accordingly, less stiff. This suggestion that business influence is greater when it engages in closed-door negotiation with environmental regulators than in open conflict with environmentalists, aired in the news media, is central to the analysis presented here.

The third factor working to ensure that business political power relative to that of governments is not absolute is the mutual interdependence of market and state. A major source of business political power is the fact that in a society dedicated to economic growth, governments depend upon business to invest and thus generate wealth and jobs in their jurisdiction. Dependence flows two ways, however. In the first instance, business is equally reliant upon government to provide those collective-action goods, such as infrastructure, internal security, and defence from external threat, which it cannot provide itself. Beyond that, the embeddedness of state and society that increased as government grew throughout the post-war years and began to operate in a wide number of societal domains that had hitherto been private,

49

doing so through a diversity of partnerships, co-funding arrangements, and quasi-governmental organizational forms (Cairns, 1986), means that state-market-society interdependence is reciprocal and pervasive.

We therefore find in the literature three factors that work to limit, at least marginally, the dominant political power of business: fragmentation of business interests, at least some instances in which other societal actors are sufficiently mobilized to exert counter-vailing political power, and the reciprocity of dependence between business and government. I argue below that to that list we must add one other factor, namely the business need for legitimacy in the eyes of external audiences, which leads it, admittedly, to devote considerable resources to manipulating the image appearing in those eyes, but which also induces cooperation and compliance with societal norms.

The second aspect of business political power on which there is general consensus in the literature is summed up in the title of David Vogel's 1989 book, *Fluctuating Fortunes: The Political Power of Business in America*. Vogel paints this picture: "The political position of business was relatively secure during the first half of the 1960s, declined significantly between the mid-1960s and mid-1970s, increased between the mid-1970s and early 1980s and has since slightly eroded" (6). Vogel argues that the political power of business, in terms of its ability to withstand pressures from government regulators, flows ultimately from public support, which in turn is decided by the state of the economy. In good times, when citizens feel secure in their jobs, public support for government regulation is high, but during economic downturns, the public is more receptive to arguments that regulation will lead to reduced profit and job losses. Although some analysts quarrel with this analysis of the sources of business power as incomplete because it ignores the basic issue of government dependence in a capitalist society (Luger, 2000: 22-23), there is agreement that business political power is not in fact constant. Certainly it declined during the expansion of government regulation in the late 1960s and was in the ascendant in the "shrinking the state" days of the 1990s.

James Q. Wilson, like Vogel, points to the significant loss of business political power in the 1960s. His explanation, however, goes beyond the complacency associated with the economic growth in that decade and includes as well the emergence of the new social movements, such as consumer advocacy, symbolized by Ralph Nader, feminism, and environmentalism. Wilson (1996: 413) describes the process this way:

In the quarter century between the early 1950s and the mid-1970s, the American corporation changed dramatically the manner in which it engaged the political process. Most of these changes were born of necessity: declining success in

Congress with respect to matters of fundamental importance to corporate management, a profound alteration in the ways in which money and information could be converted into political resources, the resurgence of intellectual opinion favourable to markets with respect to some transactions and unfavourable to them with respect to others, and a steady erosion in the prestige of business executives and the legitimacy of the large corporation.

As we will see below, Canadian business writers painted a similar picture of events in this country (Finlay, 1994).

The third aspect of business power noted by analysts which is relevant here is its decline after the investment decision is made. Richards and Pratt (1979), citing Moran (1974), give us a graphic picture of the way in which business power declines relative to that of government once the investment decision has been made:

> The large international firm [negotiating with a government such as Alberta over terms governing its potential resource extraction activities] begins from a position of monopoly control over information, expertise, and skills—a monopoly control that only a few alternative competitors can supply at a similar price. It has the experience, access to markets, and capital which the government needs to exploit its resource base, and it is initially in a powerful position to dictate terms for development. Government, on the other hand, typically starts with a very incomplete knowledge of its resource base or of the complex inner workings of the industry itself. (72-73)

Once the firm has sited its operations, however, government expertise, and therefore relative power, increases as it regulates and thereby learns more about the industry: "The power of resource companies to exact rent is greatest at the point before they have transferred their capital into fixed assets in place, and while they enjoy a temporary monopoly over skills and information; thereafter, this power tends to be whittled away until another round of major investment is pending" (73). As previously noted, the great majority of Canadian business political activity on environment to date has been associated with regulation of *in situ* plants. Therefore, in the area of environmental policy, business is operating from the basis of diminished political power identified by Richards and Pratt.

As we have seen through the constant allusions made to it above, it is impossible to discuss the political power of business without having some idea of what it is and where it comes from. For neither subject do we find consensus in the business-government literature. Although central to many areas of social-science research and analysis, political power is difficult to define, identify or measure. When exercised overtly it can, at least, be readily recognized, if not precisely measured. We can say with confidence that the failure by business to prevent Kyoto ratification in 2002 was a rare instance in which business lacked sufficient political power. However, it is often exercised in other, less easily recognizable, forms. Political actors may exert political power unconsciously, as when others mould their behaviour solely around the *expectation* of how that actor might behave, with no direct communication between them. In other cases it is even more invisible, when those actors do not themselves realize that their behaviour is being influenced by the power of others. For many women in the nineteenth century, denial of legal and political rights was part of the natural order of things, in no way related, in their eyes, to political or social power held by men.

Because of the inherent difficulties of definition and measurement, some analysts simply refuse to discuss the subject, even though it is a central part of their subject matter. DeSombre states that the power of actors influences global environmental politics, but she takes the position that "discussion of a definition of power can become unwieldy and is not worth addressing in this context" (2002: 184). Luger describes that unwieldiness in this way:

> the concept of power remains contested. Debates have raged decade after decade, generating a voluminous literature, with little hope for any resolution. For years battle lines have been drawn over questions concerning what is actually meant by power, where power is located, how to study power and how to evaluate the results of such studies. Sometimes the conclusions of a study tell us more about the perspective and assumptions of the researcher than about the material presented. (2000: 16)

It is not my intention here to wade into those troubled waters by attempting to use this study of power exercised by one set of actors in one policy field, in one country, to contribute to theoretical understanding of political power in general. Instead, I simply want to lay out the definitions and conceptualizations used in this study.

We begin with the ways in which analysts define power, be it exercised in society, the family, the state or elsewhere. Boulding (1989: 15), referring to power exercised by individual humans, defines it as "the ability to get what one wants." Lukes (1974) suggests it is the "capacity to produce, or contribute to, outcomes — to make a difference in the world" (504). Russett and Starr, for their part, define power as the "ability to prevail in conflict and overcome obstacles" (1992: 126-27). And Galbraith defines it by quoting Weber's definition of power as "the possibility of imposing one's will upon the behaviour of other persons" (cited in Galbraith, 1983: 2).

These authors agree that power must be seen as a form of social relationship. Directly flowing from that conceptualization is the view that power can most usefully be understood in terms of the relative portions held by actors bound together in a power relationship. Baldwin (1989: 3), summarizing the areas of consensus amongst students of power, takes that as his starting point and then adds two more: "Examples of fundamental areas of agreement by large numbers of power analysts include the following: (1) agreement that power should be treated as a relationship between two or more people rather than as a property of any one of them; (2) agreement that the bases of power are many and varied; and (3) agreement that power is a multidimensional phenomenon that varies in scope, weight, domain, and cost."

It is precisely because power is multidimensional, taking many different forms, that any one definition is likely to be seen as incomplete and only partially adequate. In an oft-cited work, Lukes (1974) defines three types of power pertinent to government and politics: (1) the ability to influence behaviour of others in situations of overt conflict; (2) the ability to keep issues off the policy agenda, outside the realm of overt conflict, thus leading to inaction by government; and, (3) the ability to induce "false consciousness" — influencing the interests and desires of those who might otherwise take political action contrary to one's own interests. All three forms of political power are germane to this study of environmental politics. In that field, firms most commonly exercise power to influence the behaviour of environmental regulators. Lukes's second type, however, is also at play, although for the most part in an implicit manner. To give one example, by persistent insistence that economic growth be our dominant goal, the call for a steady-state economy has effectively been kept off the environmental policy agenda. Finally, I argue below that the whole-hearted endorsement of sustainable development as the central paradigm for environmental protection is an effort to induce false consciousness — an effort to convince citizens sympathetic to the goals of environmentalism that in fact those goals are defined as economic growth, with blue-box recycling on the side.

The definition of political power that I use here is this: "the ability to influence government environmental policy decisions and the ways in which they are implemented." As noted, most of this work deals with that ability on the part of business in situations of overt conflict, but it also includes other forms of political power that exert indirect influence on government decisions and actions, by influencing prevailing societal images of business impact on environment and norms related to environment. While the focus here is upon the political power of the non-state actor in question, namely business (and to a lesser extent environmentalists and others), this definition also encompasses the political power of state actors, such as the provincial environment departments that exercise regulatory powers. What is being examined is the *relative* power of the firm and regulator. When in December 1985 the CEO of Inco, pressed to cut acid-rain emissions more than he was willing to do, went over the head of the Environment Minister and directly lobbied the Ontario Premier, he was successful in changing the relative power of Inco and the MOE. The political conflict between his firm and the ministry was resolved a few weeks later by a decision of the Ontario Cabinet, through a compromise. As defined here, political power is exercised by *both* state and non-state actors. To understand the political power of a business firm engaged in overt conflict with regulators, we must also seek to understand the political power of the regulators.

As stated above, the pluralist approach to policy analysis used here means that government is disaggregated. Environment departments are seen as pursuing policy objectives that often are in conflict with those of other departments. This means that when governments, with the final decision being made by cabinet, are developing new environmental policy, as in the acid rain example given above, we must attempt to understand the relative power of the firm and environment department to influence that cabinet decision. The fact that the firm is lobbying from outside government while the department, as part of government, is in effect lobbying from the inside, is irrelevant. From this perspective, the governmental policy decision is determined by the relative political power of those two actors, along with whichever others, state and non-state, may be involved.

What does the literature say about the "many and varied" sources of business political power? Lindblom (1977) points to three: (1) ideological power, defined as the ability to influence public opinion; (2) the fact that business decisions that influence the economy are essential to government success in re-election, leading to the governing political party's dependence on business; and (3) the fact of having greater resources to participate in the political process than other actors. Brooks and Stritch list four: the cultural dominance of business (similar to the first, above, but less focussed on agency power such as public-relations efforts and more upon currently prevailing ideas respecting the role of business in society); the structural dependence of government upon business (similar to Lindblom's second source); elite linkages between the two; and lobbying power (1991: 16-24).

The first source discussed by Brooks and Stritch refers to the dominant materialist and consumer values of capitalist societies, and more specifically to the fact that while business investment decisions have deep, widespread ramifications for the entire society, they are, nevertheless, considered "private" and therefore not automatically open to influence by the state. The second flows from the mobility of capital, which means governments are continually engaged in a competition with one another to convince business to invest, build plants, and provide jobs within their borders rather than within another jurisdiction. Business, thus wooed, gains power from the interest and dependence of government. Elite linkage refers to the fact that business and government leaders have traditionally come from the same class and thus hold common values and world views, to say nothing of continually bumping into one another at the same church or club. Lobbying power depends upon both elite access and availability of resources.

In discussing the sources of political power of business to influence policymaking, there is value not only in looking to such categories but also in making a basic distinction between two sources: that which inherently accrues to an actor, with no conscious effort made to obtain the power, and that which *is* the result of conscious effort. The term "structural power" is used by some analysts to refer to the former category (Mitchell, 1997; Luger, 2000). Structural power flows, first and foremost, from the basic fact of government dependence in a capitalist society upon those who make the investment decisions. This form of power is held here also to derive from the context of currently dominant ideas (cultural dominance) and in particular those concerning the relative legitimacy of the state and the market. Such power can be thought of as "latent power," defined as the starting point from which the actor can begin to consciously make the effort to exercise political power. The power flowing from that conscious effort is referred to as "agency power." In the environmental policy arena, in instances in which we see Lukes's first category of power on display, agency power flows from the ability to deploy resources such as money, people or expertise and to coordinate them so that their application is focussed upon a particular policy objective. Inevitably, however, the latent power of business, government, and environmental actors is also coursing through that arena.

Agency power is in part determined by the resources the actor possesses. In general terms, business can devote more money to lobbying governments than can environmentalists. The simple availability of resources, however, is only part of the story. Just as important is the question of what portion of total available resources will be committed to a given political battle. That in turn depends upon the motivation of the actor. Agency power is thus linked directly to the variable of interest. To understand the political power of a firm engaged in environmental politics we must not only determine its interest, i.e., the policy objective it hopes to achieve (which, as discussed, is not always self-evident), but also the *degree* of interest. How important is the policy objective in the eyes of the firm, and therefore what resources is it willing to gamble to achieve it? The inherent links between interest and power are a major theme of this work, expressed in terms of firms' different motivations associated with product regulation and pollution regulation.

Another theme, relevant to both structural and agency power, is the importance of legitimacy as a source of both. Legitimacy is of central importance because it allows power to be exercised *with the consent and willing participation of those whose behaviour is being influenced.* It is the most important source of Lukes's third category of power. Carroll makes the point this way:

> Hegemony is about the brute dominance of capitalists over other interests in society. Indeed, naked dominance is, as Gramsci (1971) insisted, the opposite of hegemony. The class hegemony in which the corporate elite participates is an ongoing accomplishment of *business leadership,* which includes the absorption of leaders and ideas from other spheres into the world of corporate business and which relies not on coercion but on persuasion. Hegemony is rule with the consent of the governed—but consent does not necessarily mean democracy. (2004: 8)

Another analyst makes this observation: "Machiavelli's argument is that pure power is impotent; its stability therefore depends on voluntary acceptance, and voluntary acceptance depends on its legitimacy" (Zelditch, 2001: 36).

Thus, the political power of business relative to government rests on the perceived legitimacy of each. As we have seen, political scientists associate the decline in public confidence in business, as measured in opinion polls, with the expansion of the regulatory state in the 1960s. But while business legitimacy is an ongoing sub-theme in Canadian politics—symbolized by such things as the resonance of the NDP phrase "corporate welfare bums" in the 1970s—the issue is more usually framed in terms of legitimacy of the state. It was that concern, not a renewed confidence in business, which drove the triumph of neo-liberalism and the shrinking of the state in the late 1980s and 1990s.

During that period, business continued to tout its own value to society, but not in any way markedly different from the way it had throughout the previous century. It gained traction not by pointing to its own virtue, but instead by tearing down that of the state. Two arguments, the first that steadily increasing public debt was not sustainable and the second that taxes could be cut without causing harm to the middle class, led to a shifting of political power from government to business. In the analysis that follows, the legitimacy of the regulated industries is a key variable, in terms of both this larger context of state and market-relative legitimacy and the efforts made by business to gain its own environmental legitimacy. Power is seen as a relationship, not an absolute, and as the sum of agency and structural factors.

BUSINESS AND ENVIRONMENT

Within this context of business-government relations in general, we now turn to two interrelated bodies of literature: scholarship dealing with business as an actor in environmental policy-making and works addressing the non-technical aspects of the firm's environmental management practices. The connection between the two comes from the fact that the whole purpose of environmental policy is to improve the firm's environmental behaviour — those practices are the stakes being bargained over during policy-making, and the firm regularly offers up *some* behaviour change, but not as much as is desired by regulators or environmentalists, as a bargaining tactic. This means that the question that comes automatically to mind is whether the firm's motivations in one area carry over to inform its actions in the other. Are firms with good environmental management practices also more constructive and cooperative participants in the policy process than their renegade counterparts? Beyond that specific question, I review the ways in which these two literatures address the firm's environmental policy interest, strategies, and political power.

Environmental Policy Literature

In recent years there has been, as VanNijnatten and Boardman (2002: xiv) point out, "a significant expansion of the environmental policy literature in Canada, which uses the tools and perspectives of political science, the policy sciences, public administration, economics and the environmental sciences (among others)." That literature has not as yet, however, focussed extensively upon the role played by the regulated industry. To date, Canadian environmental policy analysts have paid more attention to other policy actors, most notably environmentalists (Wilson, 1992; Hanigan, 1995; Paehlke, 1997; Mercier, 1997; McKenzie, 2002; Wilson, 2002) and governments (Paehlke, 1989; Macdonald, 1991; Boardman, 1992; Doern and Conway, 1994; Winfield, 1994; Harrison, 1996a; Paehlke and Torgerson, 2005), labour (Adkin, 1998), or to the policy process in general (Harrison and Hoberg, 1994; McKenzie, 2002; Dwivedi et al, 2001; VanNijnatten and Boardman, 2002; Montpetit, 2003; Hessing, Howlett and Summerville, 2005). Writing specifically addressing business and Canadian environmental policy includes Schrecker (1984; 1985), Harrison (1996b), Labatt (1997), and Macdonald (2002). The list of English-language works on the same subject in other countries, or on business as an actor in global environmental politics, is not a great deal longer (Chatterjee and Finger, 1994; Vogel, 1995; Welford and Starkey, 1996; Welford, 1997; Beder, 1997; Gunningham, 1998; Newell, 2000; Rowlands, 2000; Gunningham, Kagan and Thornton, 2003; Levy and Newell, 2005).

Like this study, a considerable portion of the literature on Canadian environmental policy-making comes from a pluralist perspective, looking to the variables of interests, ideas, and institutions for explanation. A current, explicit statement of that approach is given by Amos, Harrison and Hoberg, whose study of the politics of the attempts by the federal government to enact endangered species legislation is based upon "a policy regime framework that seeks to explain policy outcomes as a function of three regime components: actors, institutions and ideas" (2001: 138). They provide their definitions of each, saying this about the first one:

> The first regime component, *actors*, is defined as the individuals and organizations, both public and private, that play an important role in the formulation and implementation of public policies. The pursuit of interests within a competitive political arena is structured both by the resources that each actor can draw upon to influence policy outcomes and by the strategies employed to maximize the impact of those resources. (138, emphasis in original)

Their definition suggests that what is most important about a policy actor is interest—the government policy action most beneficial to the policy actor and for which, accordingly, it is pressing. With their focus upon resources, strategies, and impacts, they also present the related subject of the power of interests to influence policy. They go on to note that pluralist analysis no longer assumes that all actors have a roughly equal ability to influence policy. For these authors, *degree* of interest is also a significant variable, noting as they do that those asked to bear a concentrated cost will devote more effort to influencing a given policy decision than will those who will share a diffused benefit (147-48).

However, for these scholars, and for others working from such a pluralist perspective, the *way* in which actors pursue their interests and their *abilities to do so* are considered to be significant variables, but the interest *itself* is not. The implicit assumption is that the interests of actors are self-evident. As we have already seen, the concepts of "actor" and "interest" are conflated.

In terms of business, the assumption is made that firms seek only policy ends that contribute to increased profit. Carter (2001: 302-03, emphasis in original) provides a good example of this view, in which the term "interest" refers only to profitability:

> In practice, the typical response of business is to resist *any* form of imposition on their activities, whether tax or regulation. If change is seen as inevitable, an industry, provided it is sufficiently organized, may offer a voluntary agreement as a means of preventing or delaying a regulation or MBI [market-based instrument], in the hope that the government will regard it as quicker and less costly than legis-

lation or taxation. If the path to self-regulation is closed, then industry will lobby for the instrument — whether regulation or MBI — that better suits its interest.

Carter, like other analysts, recognizes that economic self-interest may lead firms to different policy objectives, including actively seeking out environmental regulation, but his perspective does not include any interests beyond profitability which might influence the firm's political goal. Hessing, Howlett and Summerville (2005: 179) also note that the conflicting economic goals of resource industries mean that for a given issue we often find "a wide range of [business] policy proposals being developed for government rather than a monolithic one." An example of this phenomenon is the conflict that emerged in the 1990s between the gasoline and automotive industries with respect to additives in gasoline, which impaired the functioning of pollution-control devices. This led the latter industry to ally itself with regulators, in opposition to the gasoline industry (Curtis, 1999).

During such conflicts, one business camp may seek alliances with environmentalists. Greve and Smith (1992: 60) have used the term "bootlegger and Baptist coalition" to describe such conflicts when one business actor works closely with environmentalists to press for policy that serves its economic interests. Like those who profit from selling illegal alcohol and those who want to see it illegal, differing motivations lead to common political objectives. The Ontario beer industry, which sells its product in refillable containers, has reached out to environmentalists lobbying for re-use in preference to recycling (Macdonald, 1996). In other instances, what would seem to be natural bootlegger-Baptist alliances, such as the insurance industry beset by soaring severe-weather damage claims and environmentalists pressing for action on climate change, have failed to materialize.

For these writers, the policy interest is determined completely by the market interest. Levy and Newell, however, argue that business interest with respect to environmental policy is not so automatic or self-evident as Carter and others might suggest: "We need a better understanding of the connections between corporate strategies in the market and political spheres, and of the underlying processes by which corporate perceptions of interests develop" (2005: 47). They start from the writings of Gramsci and go on to incorporate insights from organization theorists and others writing on corporate political strategy. Their arguments are that firms' interests in the two spheres of market and state can never be completely disentangled, and that the objective of legitimacy and the power flowing from it are always found in both:

> Gramsci's conception of hegemony thus provides a basis for a more critical approach to corporate political strategy that emphasizes the interaction of material

and discursive practices, structures, and strategems in sustaining corporate dominance in the face of environmental challenges. Corporations practice strategy to
improve their market and technological positioning, sustain social legitimacy, discipline labor and influence government policy. (58)

Turning to the subject of strategy, we find consensus in the environmental
policy literature that private lobbying is the norm, but there have been studies of business outside lobbying, in the form of public relations (Beder, 1997;
Fagin and Lavelle, 1999). Other business strategies have also been researched.
The move to "private governance," such as the ISO 14000 system for granting labels to firms that have put in place environmental management systems, has been examined (Clapp, 2005), as has the subject of voluntary
action in general (Wood, 2003; Webb, 2004). Cashore (2002) has studied
the efforts by the forestry industry to counter the environmentalists' tactic of
establishing the Forestry Steward Certification program, a non-state system
for labelling lumber taken from old-growth forests and thus applying direct
economic pressure on the industry. In response, the industry established its
own private labelling system, with less onerous standards. Cashore's study is
one of the few in the environmental policy literature to discuss the role of
legitimacy in environmental politics.

With respect to the subject of political power, we find consensus in the
environmental policy literature on the fact of business dominance. To give
just one example: "Among interest groups, business is generally the most
powerful, with an unmatched capacity to affect public policy" (Hessing,
Howlett and Summerville, 2005: 124). Most analysts explain this dominant
power by pointing to the structural power flowing from government dependence, the agency power associated with elite access, and the ability to bring
significant financial resources to bear. As Carter notes, "Structuralist and
neo-pluralist theories of the state help explain how business interests have
retained a privileged position within the policy process despite the increasingly large, vocal and professional environmental lobby" (2001: 173).

Only two Canadian works have attempted to address more specifically
the sources of business political power in the environmental policy process:
Schrecker (1984) and Harrison (1996b). Within the context of the structural
power flowing from government dependence, Schrecker looks to the greater
financial resources that business, in comparison with its critics, could bring
to bear. These allow it to fund scientific research, engage fully in the regulatory policy process, carry out litigation, "absorb" court-imposed sanctions,
and fund advocacy advertising (Schrecker, 1984: 67). In an effort to determine if there was a "race to the bottom" as Canadian provinces set new
pulp-and-paper mill standards in the late 1980s, Harrison developed a listing

of factors that determine the political power of that industry as it negotiates standards with the government of the province in which it is located. Rather than resources available to the firm, she deems most important the number of jobs provided by a regulated industry relative to the number of members of environmental organizations in that province. To that she adds other factors: "A firm's ability to oppose environmental regulations is strengthened to the extent that it sustains a large number of jobs, that the costs of regulation are high, that the plant in question is in a precarious economic position and that there are limited alternatives available to displaced workers, as in a province with a high rate of unemployment or a community heavily reliant on a single industry" (Harrison, 1996b: 479).

While both analyses seem reasonable, neither can be considered complete. To date, Canadian environmental policy analysts have taken no further steps to build on these foundations, either on the level of theory or on that of empirical research, to build a more complete picture of business power with respect to environmental policy.

Environmental Management Literature

The other body of literature to be surveyed here is that which deals primarily with environmental performance of business and treats environmental policy as the context for that subject. These academic and professional writings can be divided into three categories. The first is made up of those works written exclusively for a professional audience, primarily environmental managers, which provide either technical information on pollution control systems (Hirschorn, Jackson and Bass, 1993) or information on the regulatory system with which they must comply (Thompson, McConnell and Heustis, 1993; Ibbotson and Phyper, 1996; Phyper and Ibbotson, 2003). The former tend to be written by engineers and the latter by lawyers. Since this literature does not address the question of what motivates the environmental management of the firm, or how that motivation influences the firm's environmental policy objectives and strategies, it is not considered here.

The second category develops the normative argument that business *should* improve its environmental performance. Environmentalists, of course, have been saying that for many years, at least since Rachel Carson published *Silent Spring* in 1962, and have generated a vast body of eloquent, forceful works to that effect. This category of the environmental management literature differs, however, in that it has the tone of being written by one hardheaded, practical businessperson, to be read by another. The major argument, accordingly, is that spending on waste and pollution management will contribute to achieving the firm's financial goals. Although some of this literature (e.g., Reinhardt, 2000) treats only this subject and is completely silent on the moral implications of business environmental performance, most presents such ethical aspects as a subtext to the business case. This leads to the celebrated "win-win" picture, in which business is both on the side of the angels and generating even more profit than before (Hawken, 1993).

When business first became the subject of environmental regulation, in the 1950s and 1960s, managers and analysts alike assumed that increased spending on pollution control was simply a drag on profitability. The intellectual basis for that view came from the economist's theory of externalities, which formed the basis for the "polluter pays principle," adopted in 1972 by the OECD. Although it carries overtones of moral obligation, in fact the principle enunciated by the OECD in those early years of environmentalism had no such intent. Rather, it was meant to ensure that market prices included environmental costs, and therefore could fulfil their function of maximizing allocative efficiency. The evolution of the view that environmental management expenses were only cost internalization, to a recognition of the potential for such spending to *contribute* to profitability, is the major theme in the environmental management literature.

One of the first such works along those lines, in this case generated by an ENGO, was a report published by Pollution Probe in 1982, *Profit from Pollution Prevention* (Campbell, 1982), which drew upon the experience of the 3M company in setting forth the argument that reductions will generate savings, in terms of both raw materials needed and waste-disposal costs. Some years later, the profitability derived from marketing green products was the subject of an extensive literature (Smith, 1998).

Frances Cairncross, an *Economist* editor writing from the pro-business perspective found in that newspaper, argued in her 1991 book *Costing the Earth* that many firms were in fact recognizing these new profit opportunities and that this recognition, combined with changes in corporate culture, were driving the greening process. A few years later Piasecki (1995) offered a similar analysis, but placed greater emphasis upon the external shock of the Bhopal accident, documenting the way in which that accident, at a Union Carbide plant in India, led all firms in the chemical industry to review and upgrade their environmental management. He noted that the basic objective of the firm respecting its environmental practices should be "strategic environmental management," consisting of three fundamental aims: "regulatory compliance," "liability containment," and "money making" (4).

Far more influential, both because of the source, a wealthy Swiss industrialist, and because the views expressed were institutionalized by the creation of a global business lobbying organization, was Stephen Schmidheiny's 1992 book, which was discussed in the first chapter. This was essentially the founding manifesto of what has become the World Business Council on

Sustainable Development (WBCSD). Schmidheiny's central argument was that business should reduce the environmental degradation it causes for two reasons: first, the traditional view, that doing so provides opportunities for improved profitability; and second, at the time a novelty coming from the pen of a business representative, because it was the right thing to do. The story of the eagerness with which business adopted the mantra of sustainable development in the late 1980s is told below.

Some have questioned the notion that environmental management spending does in fact pay for itself and, beyond that, contribute to profitability. The argument that greening automatically leads to financial rewards came under critical scrutiny during the 1990s, in particular in the oft-cited article "It's Not Easy Being Green" (Walley and Whitehead, 1994). They took issue with the "win-win" picture presented by Al Gore and others, in which business could effortlessly green its operations and thereby increase profit and stock value, while saving the planet in the process:

> Questioning today's win-win rhetoric is akin to arguing against motherhood and apple pie. After all, the idea that environmental initiatives will systematically increase profitability has tremendous appeal. Unfortunately, this popular idea is also unrealistic. Responding to environmental challenges has always been a costly and complicated proposition for managers. In fact, environmental costs at most companies are skyrocketing, with little economic payback in sight. (Walley and Whitehead, 1994: 46)

They go on to argue that this does not mean firms should pay no attention to possible environmental management improvements or "obstruct environmental regulatory efforts" (50). Instead, they say, business should move carefully in the area of environmental management, with shareholder value always used as the guiding criterion. Six years later, Hoffman (2000) provided a similar analysis, rejecting both the notion that environmental spending always made economic sense and the reverse argument that it never did. Like Walley and Whitehead, he explored ways in which firms could selectively choose those improvements that would benefit the environment while minimizing the trade-off cost to profit.

Reinhardt (2000) has provided a comparable analysis, which concludes that in some cases improvements in environmental management will be profitable and that in others they will not. He argues that instead of improving environmental management either from a blind belief that doing so will increase profits or, conversely, that the firm must do so from a sense of social responsibility even if it decreases profit margins, business managers should approach the environment in the same way they handle all other aspects of firm management. They should undertake a rational calculation of opportunities and costs and then, if the results are promising, improve environmental management as one more way to contribute to overall profit. He explores five opportunity areas: (1) differentiating products from those sold by competitors on the basis of environmental performance; (2) imposing costs upon competitors either by inducing government regulation (he gives the example of DuPont, which in 1987 lobbied in favour of the Montreal Protocol, an international agreement to restrict CFC production and thus protect the ozone layer, to ensure that its European competitors were subjected to regulation comparable to that in the United States) or by developing systems of private regulation (for instance, the chemical industry's Responsible Care program); (3) reducing costs through increased efficiency, less waste, and less money spent on manufacturing inputs; (4) redefining markets and the firm's role in them, such as Monsanto's development of genetically modified, herbicide-resistant crops; and (5) improved environmental risk management, including more cooperative work with environmentalists, local communities, and others to expedite the process of gaining regulatory approvals.

Although it is central to their subject, these writers do not focus upon environmental policy. The argument that improved environmental management will contribute to profitability, either through reduced material and waste-management costs, or due to other factors examined by Reinhardt and others, ultimately depends upon the regulatory context within which the firm finds itself. Profit from waste reduction, for instance, was unheard of, for the very good reason that it was not available, in the first half of the century when waste disposal was essentially free. Only in the 1970s and 1980s, when waste-disposal costs began to rise due to regulatory restrictions on disposal options, did the argument become viable. For the most part, however, the link between policy and improved environmental management as a source of profit is not explored. Writers like Reinhardt simply take the policy context as a given and then explore the opportunities available within that context. Factors leading to changes in the regulatory context, and therefore changes in the financial incentives facing managers, are not explored.

The third category of works dealing with environmental management consists of those which do not so much present and analyze the argument that firms *should* go green, but instead explore the factors deciding *why* firms select a given level of environmental performance. These works explore a variety of internal and external factors, of which government regulation is only one. Various forms of societal pressure are also at work, inducing business to improve its environmental management (Hoffman, 1997, 2000; Frankel, 1998; Buchholz, 1998; Macdonald, 1998, 2002). These include economic pressure brought to bear by environmentalists urging consumers to boycott products such as lumber made from old-growth timber, and more recently setting up non-state regulatory systems such as the Forest Steward- ship Council (Cashore, 2002); other business firms, in the form of suppliers or customers requiring ISO or EMAS certification; customers looking for green labels such as Eco Choice on products (Harrison, 2004); and insurance firms and banks, worried about their liability and therefore insisting upon environmental audits (Macdonald, 2002). The study by Prakash (2000) sup- plements this examination of external factors by returning to the subject of corporate culture, in this case arguing that the self-interest of individuals within the firm who stand to benefit from greening, in the form of expanded powers, budgets, and salaries, constitutes another important variable.

A review of this environmental management literature in 2003 led Gunningham and his co-authors to conclude that social scientists had not yet determined exactly which factors most heavily influence the environmental performance of the firm, particularly when it is exceeding regulatory require- ments, but that the answer was to be found in an interactive mix of internal factors — "attitudes and commitments of the managers" — and external pres- sures, which they put in three groups: economic, legal, and social (Gunning- ham, Kagan and Thornton, 2003: 35-38). Economic pressure is applied by buyers, whether individual consumers or other firms, investors, and lenders. Legal pressure, of course, refers to regulation, while social pressure is exerted by the local community, environmentalists, and the voting public. With respect to the latter, they note that "a company's failure to meet social expec- tations concerning environmental performance can impair the firm's reputa- tion, adversely affect recruiting, and trigger demands for more stringent and intrusive legal controls" (37). They make the valid point that the three forms of pressure are interactive (i.e., social pressure triggers regulatory pressure) and for that reason bundle them into the one concept of "social license to operate." Their analysis is limited, however, to the ways in which firms change their behaviour to fit the demands of the social license, without exploring actions by firms to manipulate the "social expectations" to which they are subjected.

These researchers have to date paid little attention to the links, or lack thereof, between the firm's environmental management strategy and its politi- cal strategy for dealing with regulators. It has been suggested that researchers in the field see the two as being directly connected:

> Most of the business environmental management literature operates with a rough
> distinction between reactive/defensive, proactive/offensive, indifferent and inno-
> vative strategies (see e.g. Steger, 1993). Given a certain environmental risk inher-
> ent in a company's activities, a proactive company motivated by profits and

survival will exploit market opportunities and support environmental regulation. (Skjaerseth and Skodvin, 2003: 13)

This assumption that a firm willing to improve its environmental manage- ment for profit reasons will not intervene in the policy process to weaken or delay regulation has not been subjected to extensive research.

Frankel, on the other hand, has pointed to the fact that business in the US, well after it began its self-proclaimed greening process, did little to object to the deregulatory initiative launched by the Newt Gingrich Republicans in Congress in 1994 and in a number of cases participated in the drive to relax regulatory standards (Frankel, 1998: 107-09). He continues: "All of which is to suggest that companies can be green inside their factories and in their environmental-management policies, and brown inside the Beltway" (109). In the same way, business in Ontario made no objection to the deregulatory agenda of the Harris government, elected in 1995, and in a number of instances actively sought to benefit from the new willingness of that govern- ment to weaken its environmental law by lobbying for specific relaxations of standards governing their behaviour. And, as noted at the outset of this work, both the chemical and oil-and-gas sectors mounted major policy inter- ventions intended to water down regulatory standards a number of years after they had voluntarily agreed to improve their own environmental per- formance.

Frankel explains the lack of connection between environmental perform- ance and policy behaviour by pointing out that the firms are composed of internal sub-units and systems whose activities are not fully coordinated:

> Far from being integrated entities, corporations contain what amount to multiple, parallel, and often unaligned universes, with each responding to different — and often contradictory — rules of engagement. As a result, it is the rule, not the excep- tion, for environmental management and lobbying to occupy entirely separate tracks within a corporation — for the two have nothing whatsoever to do with each other. (1998: 109)

It is difficult to accept his claim that the two spheres of firm activity are com- pletely unrelated, given the fact that it is precisely the details of environmental management that the firm lobbyists are negotiating with regulators. I sug- gested at the outset that while the firm can be considered a unitary actor we must also look at the internal units. Haveman and Dorfman (1999) have writ- ten on the "green wall" that separates the environmental management unit from the rest of the firm. I would argue, however, that while lack of internal coordination may be one factor, we need to search for a more comprehensive explanation for the fact that a firm may, on occasion, be simultaneously greening its operations and lobbying to weaken regulations. It is entirely plausible to imagine a firm, functioning as a unitary, rational actor, consciously pursuing both strategies as a means of achieving its political and market goals.

DEVELOPING THAT UNDERSTANDING

This concluding section of the chapter is intended to summarize very briefly the current state of research reviewed above and to show the way in which those bodies of literature provide a launching pad for the historical review and analysis to follow. It is organized by means of the three research questions and subsidiary questions for each, set out above. Each question is discussed first in terms of the literature on business-government relations in general and then in terms of the specific policy field of environmental protection.

Political Objective

Those writing on business-government relations in general share the picture presented by Brooks and Stritch of a commonality of business interest only at the most general level of political objective, such as maintaining the sanctity of private property rights. Specific sectors and firms within the business community seeking policy favourable to their economic interests almost always find themselves in conflict with other business actors seeking conflicting policy goals. The environmental policy literature also assumes that differing economic interests will generate political conflict amongst firms and sectors engaged with a given environmental issue. There is also agreement in both literatures that all such policy goals, from the general to the specific, are determined primarily by the way in which the relevant business actors see them as contributing to their economic goals. The other motivation explored here, the search for legitimacy, is considered more fully in the business-government literature than in that devoted to environmental policy.

Neither literature has explored in depth the question of what prompts either an adaptive or interventionist response to proposed government policy. My hope is that discussion of that question in terms of environment, which focuses upon the degree of regulatory threat, might contribute to our understanding not only of environmental policy but also of business-government relations in general.

Legitimacy as a political objective is explored by at least one political scientist, Mitchell (1989), and is a dominant theme in the management studies and organization theory literatures (Marcus, Kaufman and Beam 1987; Miles and Cameron, 1982). Legitimacy as a motivating interest has for the most part been ignored, however, by business and environment writers, with the exception of Howlett and Raglon (1992), Cashore (2002), and Levy and

Newell (2005). This, to my mind, has resulted in an incomplete understanding of business participation in environmental policy-making. Accordingly, in the history that follows I document the efforts by business to gain environmental legitimacy, using all three of the methods set out above, and then to use that to influence policy.

Strategies

Both bodies of literature address the means by which business works to influence government, and there are no great discrepancies in approach. For both, the secret world of private business-government negotiation is, understandably, largely *terra incognita*. Sawatsky's *The Insiders* (1987) is one work which peers into that process. Harrison (1996a; 1996b), through the use of confidential interviews, has provided a similar service for environmental policy and, unlike Sawatsky, used the data thus gained for academic analysis. In the pages that follow, I attempt to add to our store of knowledge with respect to environmental lobbying, both inside and outside, but I describe only the broad contours of private lobbying, as revealed by primary documents. More interview research is needed to gain anything like a full understanding of that process. I also touch upon the question of why firms will sometimes supplement private lobbying with outside, public campaigns intended to generate political support.

Neither of the two bodies of literature reviewed above addresses the two other aspects of strategy explored here, namely relations with NGOs and different means of achieving legitimacy. I discuss both in a preliminary fashion, but do not provide definitive answers.

Political Power

This subject, in all its complexity, is treated fully in the business-government literature, although this has not led to consensus. In this area, as with political objectives, the two bodies of literature diverge. Environmental policy analysis, to the extent it treats the subject at all, shares the view of business dominance and the distinction between inherent and agency sources. Very little research has been done, however, on the factors that have led to changes in the power exercised by firms in the environmental policy arena. Perhaps Levy and his colleagues have done the most, but much more is needed. I hope the historical account that follows is a step in that direction.

Although the subject is addressed by a number of those writing in the environmental policy literature, an overall assessment of the extent to which Canadian policy has been shaped by business has not yet been done. Again, I do not pretend to provide a final answer here, but do provide an initial examination.

CHAPTER THREE

Establishing the Regulatory System, 1956-1980

During this time period, the first of the three historical phases examined in this and the next two chapters, business seems to have paid little attention to the fact that it was becoming subject to new federal and provincial environmental regulations. This is probably because, at the time, environment was only one small part of the overall expansion of the governmental regulatory sphere. That larger phenomenon certainly was noticed by business, which during the 1970s began to arm itself for political battle and by the end of that decade was pressing for a roll-back of the regulatory state. As is the case for the deregulatory period of the 1990s, political action by business on environment during this period can only be understood by seeing environmental politics as one part of the larger subject of business-government relations.

The story told in this chapter begins with a short overview of the major environmental policy actions taken by governments during the entire period. It then provides a detailed examination of the way in which one industrial sector, the pulp-and-paper industry, reacted to the initial regulation of its waste-discharge processes. The story of that early regulatory initiative is told here primarily because it is the one that has been most extensively studied by scholars. Although other historical research would be needed to verify the claim, I assume we can treat it as broadly representative of the ways in which other sectors engaged with regulators in the late 1960s and early 1970s. The remainder of the chapter is then devoted not to one particular sector but to the ways in which firms, trade associations, lobbyists, and business as a whole began to take political action during the 1970s to regain the ground lost in the previous decade.

POLICY EVOLUTION, 1956-1980

Prior to World War II, industrial pollution was not subject to any form of regulatory control. Environmental policy had originated in the nineteenth century, but the focus then was upon infectious disease found in human and animal waste and carried by drinking water, or transmitted in food or by various forms of contact amongst humans. Local boards of health, operating under provincial jurisdiction, had made significant progress by the early years of the century,' but neither industrial wastes nor products were considered by society or governments to be a cause for concern. Health effects associated with toxic substances first became the subject of government policy in terms of indoor pollution in the workplace (Proctor, 1995). Provincial and federal labour departments were established in the first half of the century, and occupational-health regulatory standards governing pollution that could harm workers were then developed and implemented.

Outdoor pollution did not move onto the policy agenda of governments until the 1950s. Both steadily increasing scientific knowledge and major events, such as the London smog of 1952 which caused thousands of deaths and the above-ground nuclear tests carried out by the United States and other nuclear powers, drew public attention to the issue. Pollution from pesticides started to become a subject of concern after the publication of Rachel Carson's famous 1962 book, *Silent Spring*, while other pollution issues such as oil spills at sea, the eutrophication of Lake Erie, and litter on sidewalks and highways followed on the pages of daily newspapers. These concerns, coupled with the social activism of the 1960s, gave rise to the modern environmental movement, which demanded government action on the issue (Paehlke, 1989; Macdonald, 1991).

In response, provincial governments began to act. In 1956, Ontario created the Ontario Water Resources Commission (OWRC), primarily to provide capital funding for municipal sewage treatment and drinking-water purification plants, but also with a mandate to provide assistance to industries wishing to reduce their pollution impacts and to impose upon them legally binding controls. Similar action was taken, in 1967, to move air-pollution regulation from the municipal to the provincial level, with a division of the Ontario Department of Health acting as the regulatory body (Macdonald, 1991). In July 1971, Ontario enacted the *Environmental Protection Act*, to be administered by what is now the Ontario Ministry of Environment (which assumed the regulatory powers that had been vested in the OWRC and Department of Health during the previous decade), and in that same year Alberta also both enacted pollution-control legislation and established the environment department that would administer it (Winfield, 1994). Other provinces followed suit during the early 1970s.

During the latter part of the 1960s, the federal government had taken the position that it need not act, since primary constitutional authority rested with the provinces. That position changed, however, as the issue became more politically salient. The newly elected Trudeau government announced in the Throne Speech of 1969 that it would take action. This was followed by the enactment of five environmental statutes — most of which were later combined into the 1988 *Canadian Environmental Protection Act* (CEPA) — and the creation of the regulatory department, Environment Canada, in 1971 (Doern and Conway, 1994; Harrison, 1996a). Despite this legislative action, during the course of the 1970s it was the provinces, not the federal government, that took the lead in regulating pollution emissions.

In 1972, the countries of the world gathered for the first time to discuss global environmental problems and to seek cooperative solutions. Canada, true to its multilateralist tradition, played an active role. Maurice Strong was secretary-general of the Stockholm Conference, and the Canadian delegation, assembled after extensive consultative discussions throughout the country, was led by Jack Davis, the first federal minister of environment, and accompanied by his counterparts from Alberta and Quebec (Macdonald, 1991: 101). Thus was started the process, which has continued ever since, whereby Canada is an active participant in international environmental policy development; as a result, much Canadian national (defined as loosely coordinated federal and provincial action) environmental policy is developed in order to meet international commitments. Both Canadian business and environmentalists are often active participants at the international level, as are provincial governments.

Domestically, although laws had been passed and departments established to administer them, this new regulatory threat did not become more serious for the industries involved during the remainder of the 1970s. During that decade, as the social activism of the 1960s waned, the environmental movement remained politically weak and the newly established federal and provincial environment departments operated with small budgets and little support around the cabinet table for aggressive regulatory action.

Two new policy initiatives were taken, however, in the mid-1970s which potentially had significant implications for resource and manufacturing industries. The first was the introduction of procedures, based on the model of the US *National Environmental Policy Act* of 1969, for assessing the potential environmental impacts associated with new undertakings such as a mine, road or waste site. The Ontario government, under lobbying pressure by environmentalists and about to fight an election, enacted the *Environmental Assessment Act* in July 1975 (Winfield, 1994). Although not all followed this model of stand-alone legislation, all other provinces and the federal government introduced some form of environmental assessment procedure during the years that followed (Macdonald, 1991).

The basic method of regulating potential environmental impacts was not new. All the federal and provincial environmental laws enacted a few years before had licensing approvals as one of their core regulatory procedures. Any new or modified industrial operation that would cause pollution had to receive a permit from the relevant environment department (usually provincial), a licence that was issued only after consideration of the potential environmental impacts. (Existing processes, if regulated at all, were done so by means of administrative orders.) That permit, however, was granted after closed-door discussion between regulators and the regulated firm. The significance of overlaying environmental assessment on that process was that it could open the door for local citizens and environmentalists to participate in the regulatory decision-making process, in the extreme version through a litigated process before an administrative tribunal, with citizens' costs paid by the proponent seeking the regulatory approval. As such, environmental assessment represented, in theory at least, a significant threat to one of the major sources of business power in the environmental policy process: its ability to engage in private negotiation with regulators. In fact, however, few private-sector undertakings have been subjected to environmental assessment requirements since that time.

The second policy departure was the introduction of federal legislation intended not to regulate pollution as it came out the end of the pipe, but instead to regulate a given toxic substance as a *product*, one of the inputs to the manufacturing process. In 1975, the federal government enacted the *Environmental Contaminants Act* (also later rolled into CEPA), giving itself the authority to regulate, through licensing new substances before they could be used in manufacturing, and ultimately to ban chemical substances. Given the very large number of chemical substances in use and introduced each year, this enormous regulatory challenge has not yet been successfully met.

As such, the regulation of chemicals as products initiated by the 1975 law followed a general line of jurisdictional division of responsibility between the federal government and the provinces. While the former has given itself legislative authority to regulate pollution emissions, and had that constitutional authority confirmed by the courts, in fact regulation of emissions has almost always been done by the provinces. Regulation of products that cause environmental harm, on the other hand, such as pesticides, gasoline, and motor vehicles, is done by the federal government, using laws such as the *Motor Vehicle Safety Act* and *Pest Control Products Act* (Doern and Conway, 1994: 22). As discussed above, a major theme of the analysis presented here flows from the fact that environmental regulation directed at products, those things which are bought and sold in the market, poses a much greater threat to a firm's profitability than does regulation of unwanted pollution emissions. Potentially, then, federal regulation of products might have become a much greater threat to industry than provincial regulation of pollution emissions alone. Had that happened, industry-provincial alliances likely would have emerged to jointly resist such federal regulation. In fact, the federal government has not moved vigorously on product regulation, and such alliances have not become a major part of the policy dynamic. Like environmental assessment, federal product regulation was initiated in the 1970s but did not later emerge as a major threat to business interests.

During this decade, the newly established federal and provincial environment departments began to develop a coordinated system for administering Canada's two-tiered environmental laws. Since both levels of government had assumed responsibility for pollution regulation, it was necessary to reach agreement on ways in which these duties would be shared and coordinated. This was formalized by a series of bilateral federal-provincial agreements signed in the 1970s (Harrison 1996b), and on-going coordination services were provided by what is now named the Canadian Council of Ministers of the Environment (CCME), a federal-provincial secretariat with a small permanent staff and supported by a network of federal-provincial committees staffed by environment department officials. The federal government used its own law to directly regulate some pollution emissions from four sectors (metal-mining, lead-smelting, petroleum-refining and vinyl-chloride), as well as those from pulp-and-paper plants located on the ocean coasts, but for the most part its activities were concentrated upon scientific monitoring of conditions and the development of recommended standards for use by the provinces, participation in the international policy process, and overall coordination of national pollution-control programs (Doern and Conway, 1994).

The larger provinces, which had their own scientific and regulatory capacity, began to increasingly resist what they saw as federal intrusion in their jurisdictional field. Sensing an absence of political benefit at the polling station, the federal government acquiesced, and by the end of the decade had largely vacated the regulatory field to the provinces (Harrison, 1996a). They, in turn, regulated with a gentle hand. Standards were set in close consultation with industry, firms were given ample time to come into compliance, and prosecutions were rare. By the end of the decade, clouds were beginning to gather on the horizon (the new issue of acid rain had gained sufficient momentum that it resulted in the forced resignation of the Ontario environment minister in 1978), but the sun still shone on what was for the most part an amicable, benign business-government working relationship in the newly established field of environmental policy.

Table 3.1 presents a summary picture of the policy developments described above.

Table 3.1 Policy Evolution, 1956-1980

pre-1945	occupational health regulation of indoor workplace toxins outdoor industrial emissions regulated, if at all, by local boards of health
1956	Ontario Water Resources Commission
1962	Rachel Carson, *Silent Spring*
early 1960s	US legislation provinces begin to regulate
early 1970s	all provinces and federal government enact environmental law, create environment departments
1972	Stockholm Conference
1975	Ontario Environmental Assessment Act federal Environmental Contaminants Act
1978	Love Canal hazardous waste contamination Ontario Environment Minister resigns over acid-rain issue
1980	Canada-US Memorandum of Intent to negotiate acid-rain air treaty

During the period from the mid-1950s to early 1970s, Canadian governments developed and implemented the environmental regulatory system that exists today. By and large, the new system was focussed on pollution by-product emissions, but in two instances — motor-vehicle emissions and fuel efficiency and the question of whether soft drinks would be sold in refillable glass bottles or throw-away metal cans — regulators set out almost immediately to try to influence product design.

Before I present the industry response to this new web of regulatory controls that had been draped over its shoulders, two points must be made. The first is that in designing their administrative system, Canadian governments were consciously and explicitly following the pattern of the American system that had been put in place a few years earlier. The US government had passed the *Clean Air Act* in 1963, first regulated motor-vehicle emissions in 1965, and created the Environmental Protection Agency in 1970. Although the systems of government are different and the courts play different roles in the two countries (US court decisions have had a far more significant impact on government policy), movement of pollution issues onto the policy agenda and the ensuing standards tend to follow parallel tracks (Hoberg, 1991; Boyd, 2003; Howlett, 1994).

Given the increasing integration of the two economies, codified by the 1993 North American Free Trade Agreement (NAFTA), this is hardly surprising. It has the result, however, that industries that sell the same product in both countries, such as the motor-vehicle industry, have an automatic desire for harmonization of the two sets of standards. Others, like the Ontario beer industry trying to keep American competitors out of their domestic market, have had a contrary incentive, hoping to see environmental regulations favouring their containers, refillable bottles, over the metal cans used by the US industry. The business role in Canadian environmental policy has always been influenced by the close connections between Canadian and American policy.

The second point to be made is that environmental regulation was only one part of the larger process of "social regulation" of business taking place during the post-war years. Prior to the war, government regulation of business had been restricted to historic measures to ensure fairness in trade by regulating weights and scales, "economic regulation" of pricing and market entry to prevent problems associated with monopoly control in some industries, and a series of laws governing corporate relations with labour, including working hours, workplace safety, and collective-agreement bargaining. During the 1950s and 1960s, a series of new social issues associated with business activity, above and beyond environmental protection, gained sufficient prominence in the United States, Canada, and other industrialized jurisdictions that eventually resulted in the passage of new laws regulating business activity. Prominent among these was product safety. Harm caused by cigarettes became an issue in the 1950s, followed by legislative bans on most forms of advertising and restrictions on sales to young people (Miles and Cameron, 1982). Deaths from traffic accidents, in part attributable to motor-vehicle design, were made a political issue by Ralph Nader in the 1960s. The safety of drugs prescribed by doctors became an issue after the thalidomide tragedy of the 1960s, leading to a tightening of food and drug regulation. As had been done with pollution control, these issues and others led to the enactment of new consumer-protection legislation, with new departments to administer it, by both the federal and provincial governments. At the same time, other practices of the firm, such as hiring and promoting minorities and women, were coming under critical scrutiny.

This expansion of industry regulation in a variety of policy fields was in part a response to the social-equity concerns of the new social movements that came onto the political stage in the 1960s. Civil-rights workers, students, peace activists, women, and environmentalists began to crowd out the demands of the old left, centred in labour, as they demanded new forms of social justice (Gitlin, 1987). It was also, however, the first stirrings of the "risk society," an abandonment of the nineteenth-century belief that accidental death and illness were acts of God, to be accepted with stoic fatalism, in favour of the view that the expertise of administrative rationalism, both in corporate head offices, but more importantly in regulatory departments of government, could make risk something amenable to human control (Paehlke and Torgerson, 2005).

Governments, flush with the annually increasing tax revenues flowing from the post-war economic boom, were more than happy to accept this mandate. In the previous decade, the triumph of Keynsianism had led them to believe that the expertise of economics allowed them to manage the economy so as to avoid recession (and indeed there was none until the stagflation of the mid-1970s), and the 1950s advent of the welfare state meant that social engineering was now within their powers. Working to curb industry externalities in a variety of fields, using law administered by government departments, was a logical extension of this new trajectory of expanding powers of the state. US President Lyndon Johnson confidently set out to fight a war on two fronts, simultaneously beating back communism in Vietnam and poverty in American cities. Prime Minister Pierre Trudeau proclaimed a vision of expansionist government used to create a "just society." The failure of such initiatives to achieve anything akin to their visionary goals presaged the eventual triumph of neoliberalism and the shrinking of the state, but at the time, when the environmental regulatory system was being established, government power relative to that of business was at its maximum.

PULP-AND-PAPER INDUSTRY RESPONSE TO INITIAL REGULATION

The response of Canadian business to the imposition of environmental regulation was surprisingly muted. By the late 1970s, business was beginning to arm itself with the information on government activity and lobbying resources needed to play a more overtly political role. A decade earlier, however, the regulated industries simply entered into quiet negotiations with officials in the new environment departments.

Those new departments had limited staff resources and lacked procedural and technological expertise respecting the sectors they were regulating. They saw their role as one of patiently working with their fellow engineers in the firms to abate the worst problems, with court prosecution to be used only as an instrument of last resort. More important, the governments of which they were a part may have taken on a commitment to rub some of the rough edges off industry behaviour, with respect to environment and the other issues that had moved on to the policy agenda in the 1960s, but had never wavered from their goal of business-led economic expansion and job creation. The inherent power of business, based in the dominant ideas of capitalism, may have waned slightly during its loss of legitimacy in the 1960s, but this power was still sufficient to leave business in a powerful position when confronting environmental regulators. Regulated industries had a significant voice in deciding the environmental standards imposed upon them and, once regulations were in place, were then able to negotiate lengthy periods of time during which they would be free from prosecution while they worked to upgrade their environmental management to bring it into legal compliance. An example of this political power is seen in the development and implementation of regulatory controls for discharges of wood waste and toxic liquids to lakes and streams by the pulp-and-paper industry. That sector demonstrated both its ability to stave off regulators for years after standards ostensibly came into force, and a single-minded focus on profitability as the only factor influencing the policy interest sought.

The manufacture of newsprint, cardboard, paper for printing and photocopying, tissue paper, and other paper and paperboard products requires both the raw material, wood, and considerable quantities of water that is used in the process of pulping the wood and for the discharge of waste materials. The pulp-and-paper industry, which originated in the mid-nineteenth century when the method of making paper from wood was first developed, exists in countries like Canada that have bountiful supplies of both wood and running water, which provides energy and a flushing system for wastes. As Shaw notes,

> Throughout the industry's commercial history the economics of transportation have dictated that the manufacture of paper be located in relative proximity to the sources of its principal raw materials, rather than the marketplace. The availability of wood, water and energy also heavily influences the industry's choices between the adoption of various production processes, the different paper products to produce, and the rate of research and development of new products and production technologies, including their diffusion. (1989: 7)

For this reason, the global paper market has been supplied primarily by firms located in forested regions of Canada, Scandinavia, and the US. More recently, the industry has begun to expand into Indonesia and South-East Asia, seeking the benefits of faster grower times for softwood trees such as eucalyptus (Lohmann, 1996). Within Canada, these geographic constraints have meant that while pulp-and-paper mills are located in all provinces except Prince Edward Island, by far the largest production capacity is located in Quebec, followed by Ontario and British Columbia.

Within those provinces, and for Canada as whole, the industry is a dominant economic actor. In 1966, as the current regulatory system for pulp-and-paper mill pollution was being developed, it was the largest industrial sector, accounting for approximately 5 per cent of total Canadian gross national product (Jones, 1966: 5). By 1986, that portion had declined to 2.9 per cent, but the industry was still the "top ranked manufacturing industry in terms of value added, employment, and production and related wages" (Shaw, 1989: 24). In 2002, the industry contributed 3 per cent of Canadian GDP (FPAC, 2003: n.p.). The roughly 150 Canadian mills, owned by perhaps half that many firms, directly employ 70,000 people, and indirectly, including logging, government, and other related employment, provide jobs for somewhere between 350,000 and 921,000 Canadians (Price Waterhouse, 1994: 7; FPAC, 2003: n.p.). As we have seen, Harrison (1996b) looks to the portion of total employment in a given province provided by the pulp-and-paper industry as one source of its political strength. This may explain why, during the second wave of industry water-pollution regulation, discussed below, New Brunswick was less eager to impose new standards than were provinces such as British Columbia or Ontario.

Writing in 1981, Parlour provided an excellent depiction of the industry role during the development of the first federal regulations. He set out the basic economic interests of the industry, with respect to its environmental management. The first was a desire to reduce the quantity of wood waste as part of the ongoing search for efficiency, which had significantly reduced total suspended solids before imposition of any regulatory controls. The second was an interest in ensuring that any further spending on pollution controls be devoted to in-plant changes, which would yield further efficiency gains, rather than external treatment, which would produce environmental benefits alone:

> In-plant treatment cuts costs and provides useful by-products which can be profitably exploited, whereas external treatment is, from a firm's point of view, a complete waste of money since it has no effect on plant efficiency and provides no utilizable waste materials.... It is most unlikely that anything like the increases in expenditures in external treatment that occurred between 1969 and 1971 would have come about in the absence of government regulation (or at least the threat of such regulation). (Parlour, 1981: 137)

Prior to the advent of the modern regulatory system, the industry was subject to at least some form of governmental control. Using the constitutionally secure powers of the *Fisheries Act* as a threat, the federal government prior to the 1960s had negotiated some form of pollution abatement with mills on both the east and west coasts (Sinclair, 1990: 88-89). In Quebec and Ontario, the Canadian Pulp and Paper Association (CPPA), through a committee established in 1961, maintained close contact with the then-existing regulatory authorities, the Ontario Water Resources Commission (OWRC) and la Régie des eaux du Québec (Jones, 1966: 10). Although, by the 1960s, both levels of government had in place legislation allowing them to coerce mills through legally binding orders and the sanction of court prosecutions, such powers were rarely used. Sinclair says federal authorities "negotiated" abatement with individual mills and makes no reference to prosecutions (1990: 89). In Ontario between 1965 and 1971, the OWRC imposed twelve legally binding controls on the mills in that province, but prosecutions for non-compliance were rare, as they were to remain for many years (Macdonald, 1991: 138). The pollution reduction that occurred, not surprisingly, was in the area most aligned with industry profit motives: wood-waste pollution.

In 1922, before any regulatory controls existed, the CPPA had created a committee "charged with investigating techniques to reduce the losses of raw materials during production. This initiative was taken in response to increasing raw material prices..." (Parlour, 1981: 135). By 1966, total suspended solid pollution had declined from an estimated ten to fifteen per cent of total production to something like four per cent (Jones, 1966: 12). By then, however, the industry's renewed focus on its environmental performance was driven by pending regulatory action, as well as market forces. In that year, following a decade of increasing public attention to air and water pollution, the federal and provincial resource ministers met for a major conference on pollution. As the sector using and polluting more water than any other, the pulp-and-paper industry was of course a primary subject of discussion, which led to regulatory action:

> The first regulations under the [1971] amended [Fisheries] act were directed at limiting the discharge of BOD and TSS from pulp and paper mills. The major reason for starting with this industry was simply that it accounted for a very high—and frequently highly visible—proportion of total Canadian water pollution. In many cases, BOD and TSS emissions from mills had seriously degraded the quality of receiving waters and severely reduced or even eliminated fish populations. (Bonsor, 1990: 168-69)

A picture of the industry's initial response to this new external regulatory threat is given by a speech made to that ministers' conference on pollution by Douglas Jones, then president of the CPPA, in which he publicly staked out the industry position. Jones did not spend any time denying that water-pollution problems existed or that his industry was primarily responsible. Instead, he simply stated, "The pulp and paper industry, by the nature of its processes, is a large user of water, and is therefore deeply involved in the problem of keeping Canada's water resources clean" (Jones, 1966: 5). He outlined the successes achieved to date in reducing wood-waste pollution and then made these proposals for policy development: (1) establishment of a national system for monitoring and data management; (2) development of national policy, through increased federal, provincial, and industry consultation and co-ordination; (3) sharing of pollution control costs between the public and private sectors, by means of various financial aids to the industry, including tax write-offs, interest-free loans, and funding for research; and (4) "enlightened and flexible" regulatory requirements, based on consultation with the industry (Parlour, 1981: 137; Jones, 1966).

Parlour holds that the industry would not have acted without government prompting but does describe this initial 1966 position in these terms: "Jones's paper seemed to demonstrate a genuine concern for pollution control and is remarkable for its positive and conciliatory tone" (Parlour, 1981: 137). The industry was engaged in negotiated adaptation and did not mount any major policy intervention or outside lobbying campaign. Although using different terms, Clancy (2004: 77) gives a similar view:

> Few Canadian industries have found themselves so intensely affected by the rise of contemporary environmental movements, an experience for which most firms were poorly prepared and slow to respond. Bolstered by traditional clientelistic relations to state agencies, as well as a complacency linked perhaps to its strategic prominence in the nation's economic life, pulp and paper behaved in a reactive as distinct from a pro-active way until very recently.

In the years immediately following this speech, Jones and his industry colleagues did not witness the development of a national monitoring system, nor any great degree of national coordination. They did, however, receive considerable financial assistance as they worked to jointly develop with governments and then comply with a regulatory system that can best be described as "flexible." Harrison (1996b: 169) has found that during this period the industry stated a preference for provincial regulation. No major research has yet been done on negotiations of standards between mills and regulators in provinces such as Quebec, Ontario, and BC, but we do know they were developed individually for each mill. Writing some years after they were put in place, Bonsor describes provincial standards in this way:

> In a *de facto* sense, then, the major responsibility for controlling water pollution, especially in the case of the pulp and paper industry, rests with the provincial governments. The tool they use most often is the negotiated control order, whereby the regulatory authorities negotiate with an individual firm a control order that defines permissible effluent loadings and compliance schedules.... One of the results of this approach is that effluent-quality standards vary dramatically from mill to mill. (1990: 170)

Parlour tells us that the federal standards (implementation of which was then coordinated with the provincial environment departments) were based not on the quality of the receiving waters, since there were not sufficient scientific data available, but instead on the availability and cost of technology to reduce impacts, with those data coming solely from the industry representatives (Parlour, 1981: 142). During negotiations, the industry expressed concern about conflicting federal and provincial standards and took "every opportunity to weaken" the federal standards (Parlour, 1981: 141). They successfully insisted that only in-plant treatment would be required, and that the regulations would apply only to new or expanded mills. They also, in a letter sent to the new federal Environment Minister in June 1971, repeated the earlier request for financial assistance. As a result of the dynamic of government-industry negotiations, Parlour says, that request was granted by way of amendments to the Tax Act: "During the summer of 1971 the previous strong stand the government had taken against any form of financial assistance to the industry had weakened in the face of indications that the government would face stiff opposition from the industry in implementing the proposed regulations and the realization that some form of compromise was required if this opposition was not to completely undermine the force of these regulations" (Parlour, 1981: 143). At the end of the day, however, the federal standards, which came into effect in November 1971, were largely irrelevant. Because they applied only to new and expanded mills, by 1990 only 10 per cent of total Canadian pulp-and-paper water pollution was subject to federal regulation (Bonsor, 1990). As was the case with other sectors, the provinces were the primary regulators.

During the 1970s, the industry continued to press for government subsidy of pollution-control spending, within the context of the need for government assistance in modernizing the industry in order to regain its competitive international position. By 1985, it had received over half a billion dollars of subsidy from the federal and provincial governments, at least some of which was spent on pollution abatement (de Silva, 1988). It is likely that regulators used the industry desire for financial assistance to gain negotiating strength as they pressed for increased pollution control. A similar dynamic is found in the case of acid rain. The smelter modernization subsidy program of the 1980s was a comparable policy tool explicitly used by governments as part of their efforts to induce acid-rain reductions. In the case of pulp and paper, financial assistance as a policy measure complementing regulation did not produce policy success. Throughout the 1980s, the vast majority of firms were not yet in compliance with provincial or federal standards (Sinclair, 1990).

Clancy (2004: 119) provides this summary of the industry role: "The industry lobby exerted relentless pressure for moderate to minimal standards."

He attributes the industry success, both in weakening standards and using compliance agreements to delay the need to meet them, to the lack of interest and power on the part of governments, characterizing their role as a "permissive, or weak, state regulatory structure" (2004: 120). In the next chapter we examine the industry response when faced twenty years later with new regulatory demands made by much stronger and more vigorous environmental regulators. The industry response was similar — negotiated adaptation through private negotiation — but its political power was much less and it showed a concern for legitimacy completely absent in the 1970s.

Regulation of pulp-and-paper mill discharges to water in the late 1960s and early 1970s has been studied far more extensively than that of any other sector. There is no reason to suppose, however, that the response of any of those sectors was markedly different from the negotiated adaptation of the pulp-and-paper industry. What the regulated firms did *not* do during this initial period, then, is just as significant as that response. They did not offer to put in place voluntary, self-regulated programs as an alternative to government regulation. Nor did they undertake major political activities, going over the heads of the new, junior environment ministers to lobby premiers and prime ministers, accompanied by full-page advertising campaigns to engender public support. Instead, they relied upon private, technical negotiation of standards and compliance deadlines on a sector-by-sector and firm-by-firm basis.

In one sector, in a different country, we do observe a different response. In the United States at the time, the motor-vehicle industry mounted a significant lobbying effort in Congress against the first federal-government regulatory efforts, initiated in 1970, to impose emission controls (Luger, 2000). A few years earlier, the industry had fought a losing battle against the vehicle-safety regulations prompted by Ralph Nader's crusade. This time, recognizing that new tactics were needed, the US industry moved from exclusive reliance on inside lobbying to a more public campaign: "Industry officials decided to abandon their traditional low-profile stance.... Government regulation of car design forced the automakers to fight more openly for their interests" (Luger, 2000: 89). In doing so, they appealed for public support by painting environmental regulation as a threat to jobs and economic growth. No such public battle was fought by the industry in Canada, presumably since it was not needed, given the likelihood that Canadian law would adopt similar standards. The federal government imposed regulatory standards governing nitrogen oxide emissions from motor vehicles in 1974, apparently without any major political opposition from the Canadian industry (Mellon et al., 1986: 114).

Luger makes it clear that the US auto industry was taking more vigorous political activity in the 1970s than other industrial sectors subjected to American environmental regulation. He does not explore the point, but that may be because regulation of product design was a greater economic threat than was regulation of emissions from the factories manufacturing automobiles or other products. It may be that this same factor stimulated the Canadian chemical industry to lobby to weaken the 1975 federal *Environmental Contaminants Act*: "This 1975 legislation was essentially weakened through the intense lobbying of the Canadian chemical industry. The legislation required the pre-testing of new chemicals, but the law had virtually no teeth and was given little administrative support within the DOE" (Doern and Conway, 1994: 109). Whether the subject was product design or pollution emissions, however, business still saw environmental regulation as only one part of the larger problem of growing government encroachment on market activity. Accordingly, we now turn to the political response by business to this generalized threat.

BUSINESS BECOMES POLITICALLY ENGAGED

While the threat to resource and manufacturing industries during the 1970s posed by environmental regulation was relatively benign, firms in those sectors, and all others, were reacting to the unprecedented expansion of the regulatory state during the 1960s and in consequence felt themselves to be in a state of siege. Public writings from the time show clearly the extent to which business felt threatened by the rapidly expanding welfare state that was moving to regulate corporate activities on a number of fronts, of which environmental management was only one. This grouping of environment with other external threats to the firm was expressed by Richard Finlay, a Canadian public-affairs consultant, writing in 1978 about the new external threats facing the manufacturing industries. He pointed first to the activism of Ralph Nader in the United States on the issue of automobile safety and then went on to list the threats that followed:

> Growing brigades of consumers began to question the durability and reliability of products. Health and safety issues soon joined the list of criticisms and concerns about the manufacturing sector. The result was the consumer revolution of the 1970s. All of this was, of course, paralleled by the growth of an equally vocal environmental lobby that virtually transformed the manufacturing process and its relationships with government. (Finlay, 1994: 107)

Like all other analysts, Finlay traced a connection between loss of legitimacy in public eyes and loss of political power: "The costs of lost public confidence in business, consumer disaffection and the momentum of government intervention in business created during this period have also been substantial" (Finlay, 1994: 107-08).

At least some business representatives at the time saw this loss of legitimacy and political power as far more than simply a marginal problem, but rather as a fundamental threat to their continued existence. An example is provided by the following, written in 1982 by Robert Anderson, CEO of the American company Atlantic Richfield:

> ...today's business enterprise is critically affected by such matters as consumer and environmental protection, occupational health and safety, full financial disclosure, the political process at all levels, and the quality of life in the communities in which we are located and do business. (Anderson, 1982: xiii)

Anderson went on to express, in life-or-death terms, the need for this attention to the non-market demands being made of business:

> And so, after 20 years of debate, discussion, and confrontation, it's the rare chief executive officer who is not concerned with his company's public affairs program, who does not understand that the attitudes of employees, consumers, shareholders, government, the press, and the public in general have infinitely important consequences for business.... In fact, it's not stretching fact at all to say that business today has a new 'bottom line'—public acceptance.... The threat that the free market system could be more or less voted out of existence by a dissatisfied electorate in favor of alternative answers to its social expectations is the negative side of corporate public affairs. I do not think any such drastic occurrence is likely to happen. In fact, there is every reason to believe it is less likely than, say, 10 years ago when public hostility toward business was at its peak. (Anderson, 1982: xiv)

Some of these external threats, such as the political power of the consumer protection movement or of labour, waned during the following decade. The environmental movement, on the other hand, grew significantly stronger as the 1980s progressed. It is not surprising, then, that this same kind of apocalyptic tone, equating legitimacy and survival, was heard a few years later from what had by then come to be seen as the major business threat to ecological health: the chemical industry.

Business in Canada and other countries responded to this new climate of the 1970s by adapting to at least some extent to the new demands made upon it. Steps were taken to improve product and occupational safety, hire more women and minorities, and reduce environmental impacts. Business also responded, however, by becoming more politically active. The following pages briefly describe the evolution during the 1970s of four instruments used by business to influence provincial or federal government policy, including the newly established policy field of environmental regulation: the internal public-affairs department, whose focus on government meant that its mandate was coming to be distinguished from the traditional "public relations" function of the firm; the sectoral trade association, which provides both economic and political services to the firms in a given industry that establish and control it; the public-affairs consulting firms that came into being during this period; and, fourthly, the broad-based business associations which speak for capital as a whole.

The Growth of PA Departments

Prior to the expansion of regulatory activity in the 1960s, most firms did not have a stand-alone unit responsible for providing government relations analysis and advice to senior management. To the extent it existed, that function was located in public-relations or legal departments (as well as being performed, as discussed below, outside the firm, in trade associations). That changed as what came to be termed the "public affairs" function was distinguished from public relations, just as that in turn had earlier been separated from the paid advertising function. Although there is considerable overlap in the terminology, the primary demarcation between public affairs and public relations is the fact that the latter includes all aspects of the firm's external environment in its mandate, while the primary focus of the former is upon government alone. Writing in 1982, Anderson made exactly that distinction and then went on to explain the origins of corporate public-affairs units: "The public affairs movement was launched some 25 years ago when many in the corporate community became keenly concerned about big government and its impact — its massive impact — on business" (Anderson, 1982: 4).

Writing in 1983, Post and his colleagues reported on a survey of 400 large- and medium-sized US business firms, which revealed that public-affairs units for the most part came into being during the 1970s:

> Our survey reveals that more than one-half of all public affairs units were created during the 1970s and fully one-third since 1975. Corporate public affairs budgets and staff show comparable growth during that period.... In addition to their rapid growth in terms of personnel and budget, 60 per cent of the public affairs departments surveyed report directly to the company chairman, president, and/or chief executive officer, thus providing them with access to top management on a regular and continuing basis.... The implication of these facts and trends is that top-level general managers are becoming increasingly involved in public affairs activities. (Post et al., 1983: 136-37)

Similar change was taking place inside larger Canadian companies. Litvak reported in 1981 that, at that time, CEOs were spending anywhere up to half their time on public-affairs issues, that a number of boards of directors were creating new public-affairs committees, and that outside directors were being recruited who, because of their past experience and specialized knowledge, could assist in "identifying external threats and in ensuring that sound strategies are developed to deal with the emerging issues" (Litvak, 1994: 131). He provided this description of the public-affairs function:

> The key responsibility of the government relations executive is monitoring, analyz- ing and communicating government-related activity. Lobbying, including telling the company's story to legislators, bureaucrats and regulatory officials, has become a secondary although still important function. (134)

Litvak also provided a direct quotation from an internal document generated by a "Canadian resource-based firm," which set out its "government affairs objective" as follows:

> With specific reference to the Government of Province X and Canada, it shall be the objective of the department to:
> - Identify and assess relevant attitudes and actions at the political and public service levels;
> - Advise and counsel line management to ensure that the information thus gathered is taken into account in the company's decision-making process;
> - Provide information to politicians and public servants and facilitate their contact with company management that will contribute to the development of a governmental climate in which the company can continue to operate profitably. This is to be achieved in such a way as to be acceptable both legally and morally. (134)

He went on to note that "highly-regulated industries" were often opening an office in Ottawa to house their public-affairs department. Only a few of the larger companies, he reported, had more than three full-time public-affairs staff (134). He gave the example of "one of Canada's largest multinational resource-based firms" which began by hiring two public-affairs officials with primary responsibility to focus on the government of the province in which it was located, followed by another located in Ottawa "who had held the posi- tion of assistant deputy or deputy minister in a federal government depart- ment." Hiring a former federal high-level civil servant would, he said, provide "immediate respectability" (135).

Peter Bartha, who had served as Manager of Strategic Studies at Imperial

Oil, published an article in 1982 describing the model he had developed while with that company, to be used for generating analysis of the public policy process and to assist Imperial planners, managers, and communicators (Bartha, 1994: 138). The model, based on a "standard pluralistic view of the political system" (139) was intended to provide executives using it with an understanding of "how societal issues emerge, which of the issues are likely to result in government action, who the key movers and shakers are and what roles different segments of the public play in the policy development process" (138). As well as the roles of politicians and the public service, the focus was upon the general public, news media and interest groups.

Bartha gave a remarkably candid picture of the privileged, elite-level access to government enjoyed by business, in comparison with its critics. After noting that public policy invariably results in benefits for some and increased costs for the larger majority, he said that those lobbying for such benefits have two options: inside or outside lobbying (although he did not use that terminology). He described the first option as efforts to "keep the matter out of the domain of public discussion" (142). That method, he said, "is preferred by business groups" (142). The second option — "going public" — he said was "favored by groups that band together for some special purpose and are usually loosely structured and poorly financed" (142). Their only method of influencing policy was to generate and demonstrate to governments public support for their policy objective, largely through gaining news media reporting.

Trade Associations
Coleman (1988: 19) describes the factors that originally pushed industries to establish trade associations in the nineteenth century:

> After Confederation, a number of developments pushed business people to look to the formation of permanent associations that organized whole industries over a broad territorial expanse: the pressure of domestic competition, the need for protection against external competition, the growing fear of the labour movement both in politics and in the workplace, and the perception that other classes, particularly agrarians and liberal professions, were achieving political gains at the expense of business.

Such pressures led to the establishment of the Canadian Bankers Association in 1891, the Canadian Forestry Association in 1900, and the Mining Association of Canada in 1935.

Sectoral trade associations therefore exist to provide their member firms with services that meet two different sets of collective needs: those related to their market activities and those having to do with governments. As Kelley notes, "A trade association acts politically by representing an industry in political forums. They act economically by disseminating accounting, statistical, and technological information to their members" (1991: 95). While "acting politically" primarily involves lobbying governments, in some instances it also includes acting in a quasi-governance role, assisting governments in program delivery (Coleman, 1988). Beginning in the 1980s, trade associations in a number of sectors began to attempt to act in a quasi-regulatory role, trying to improve the environmental performance of firms in their sector. That role then became institutionalized in the 1990s, with the advent of voluntarism as a policy instrument, often with objectives explicitly stated in memoranda of understanding signed by governments, trade associations, and firms.

As we will see, the ability of trade associations to play such a role by influencing the behaviour of their member firms is hampered by not having the moral authority or legal powers of the state. They do not have the kind of delegated licensing authority that governments have given to the self-regulating professions such as law or medicine. Bodies such as the Ontario Medical Association which have the right to take away a physician's right to practice have an extremely effective instrument for regulating member behaviour. The closest that trade associations have come to that kind of authority have been efforts to negotiate agreements with governments for "back-drop" regulation that applies only if firms do not participate in trade association programs, such as those described below with respect to industry funding of municipally operated blue-box programs.

In a similar manner, a fundamental constraint exists on the ability of trade associations to lobby governments on environmental policy. This flows from the fact that not all the member firms in a given industrial sector will necessarily have exactly the same interest with respect to a given environmental policy issue. Kelley (1991) gives an example from the American environmental policy process leading up to reauthorization of Superfund legislation in 1986. The ability of the National Solid Waste Manufacturers' Association to lobby on the issue was limited by the fact that the Association represented groups of firms with different economic interests and, accordingly, competing policy interests: "early in the 1980s member firms with waste treatment capacity found they were pitted against member firms with landfill capacity on regulatory issues" (Kelley, 1991: 117). The former, of course, were more favourably disposed toward regulatory requirements that wastes be treated before being placed in landfills. In this case, the first group of firms finally left the Solid Waste Association and created a new trade association, the Hazardous Waste Treatment Council, so that they might have a lobbying instrument that would pursue only their own particular policy interest.

The existence of such differing policy interests within a given sector means that the larger firms, which have the resources to do so, will often lobby governments independently, rather than simply leaving the task in the hands of their trade association. Firms in a position to do their own lobbying, either through their own public-affairs department or by hiring paid lobbyists, must decide for each new political issue whether they will act alone or not. In general terms, the nature of their political objective decides the choice. When they share the same objective as the other firms in their sector they work through the trade association, but when they are in political competition with those firms they will lobby alone (Brooks and Stritch, 1991: 225).

Usually the larger firms in a given sector, which pay the bulk of the costs of operating the trade association, will have a predominant voice in setting the political objectives pursued by the trade association (Watson, 1999). Although Kelley (1991) has examined the subject in the US context, no research has yet been done on the internal politics of trade associations in this country, such as the Canadian Association of Petroleum Producers or Canadian Chemical Producers' Association, which determine the targets and intensity of their lobbying efforts.

Notwithstanding these constraints, both upon their ability to play a quasi-regulatory role and to forge consensus among member firms on lobbying priorities, trade associations are an important element in the process of environmental politics. Environmental regulators to a large extent rely upon them for technical expertise, a position of dependence which tips power in the direction of the association. Although the resources they deploy, both in terms of annual budgets and numbers of staff (direct employees and staff seconded from companies for special tasks), do not seem to greatly exceed those available to environmental organizations, they possess the enormous political benefit of elite-level access. As discussed below, in the 1980s environmentalists began to gain at least some marginal access to the environmental policy process, through multi-stakeholder consultation. Also during that period they began to be hired as political staff to environment ministers. That kind of access pales, however, in comparison with trade association hiring practices: "trade associations are renowned for giving high paying jobs to former bureaucrats and politicians" (Brooks and Stritch, 1991: 224).

Establishment of PA Consulting Firms

The perceived need by business in the 1970s to devote more resources to political activity meant that a new market was created for public-affairs consultants. In the US, such firms had existed throughout the twentieth century. Perhaps the best known of them, the US firm Hill and Knowlton, was created in 1904 (Miller, 1999). Although undoubtedly individuals with government contacts had been hired as paid lobbyists before then, the first Canadian companies were not established until the early 1970s (Sawatsky, 1987). Those companies, Executive Consultants Ltd. and Public Affairs International (PAI), did not directly lobby on behalf of clients but instead gave them information on internal workings of government and advice on the best way to make their case. By the 1980s, however, the lobbying industry was candid about the fact that it was "selling political influence, not just policy expertise" (Brooks and Stritch, 1991: 229). Firms lobbying Ottawa on environmental policy began to make greater use of lobbyists such as Hill and Knowlton in the late 1990s (Macdonald, 1999: 6), but the role of public-affairs consulting firms in the environmental policy process has not yet been researched.

One fascinating glimpse, however, is provided by the journalist Jennifer Curtis (1999), who has provided an account of the political fight between the gasoline and automotive industries over the additive MMT, manufactured by the US firm Ethyl Corp., in the mid-1990s. The additive had been banned in the US until Ethyl, through litigation, overturned the EPA regulation. The Canadian federal government sought to impose a similar ban in 1995; however, lacking sufficient evidence of toxicity, it did not do so under CEPA but instead through legislation prohibiting import or interprovincial trade (Curtis, 1999; Hoberg, 2000; McKenzie, 2002). Because it believed that MMT interfered with the proper working of its pollution-control devices in automobiles, that industry supported the ban. Ethyl used Hill and Knowlton, which had purchased PAI in 1989, to help its lobbying effort to block the bill; the auto industry used Government Policy Consultants (GPC) to work for its passage (Curtis, 1999). Hill and Knowlton fought a delaying action as long as possible, by giving ammunition to the opposition parties, but also worked to develop a Plan B, a NAFTA court challenge. GPC and the Canadian Vehicle Manufacturers' Association, for their part, established a bootlegger-Baptist alliance with groups like the Sierra Club (Curtis, 1999: 70). The trade bill was passed in early April 1997, and Ethyl immediately filed a $250-million court challenge, under Chapter 11 of NAFTA. In 1998, the federal government capitulated, repealing the trade ban and settling with Ethyl by means of a $13-million (US) payment in damages (Curtis, 1999). Curtis does not tell us the size of the consulting fees paid to the winning and losing lobbyists.

Broad-Based Business Associations
Two of the national organizations that speak for business as a whole, the Canadian Chamber of Commerce and the Manufacturers and Exporters Association, have roots going back to the nineteenth century. In the politicized atmosphere of the 1970s, however, they were seen by business leaders as adequate for lobbying on sectoral interests, but not for giving capital as a

whole the political voice it needed (Langille, 1987). Motivated by the direct intrusion of government into the economy represented by wage and price controls imposed in 1975, a group of CEOs, led by the chair of Imperial Oil, came together to create the Business Council on National Issues (now the Canadian Council of Chief Executives). They explicitly modelled the new organization on the Business Roundtable, established in the US in 1974.

Like sectoral trade associations, from the outset the BCNI has faced the basic problem of conflicting political objectives held by different member firms, complicating the development of a single, clear policy stance. In the case of energy policy, which the BCNI took on as a priority issue in the early 1980s, Langille's research reveals that the oil and gas industry point of view prevailed as the Institute worked privately with representatives of the Alberta, Ontario, and federal governments to broker an agreement on post-NEP policy (1987: 61-64). Other positions it has taken, such as support of free trade or shrinking the size of government, represent business interests at a more generalized level. In terms of environment, in the 1990s it supported the paradigm of sustainable development, translated by business to mean increased efficiency alone, as discussed in Chapter Five. In 1994, it advocated voluntary programs, rather than regulation, to address climate change (BCNI, 1994). As stated in Chapter One, it later joined the other two broad-based associations and other business actors in the effort to prevent Kyoto ratification. More research is needed, however, before anything definitive can be said about the role of broad-based associations in environmental politics.

As the 1970s drew to a close, new issues — most significantly toxic chemicals, symbolized by Love Canal, and acid rain, symbolized by dying lakes — were rekindling the environmental activism and public support of the 1960s. For Canadian business representatives, however, environment was still only one issue among many. Their problem was government as a whole: "business as a whole in Canada was arguing as the 1970s ended that the regulatory burden of government had to be lifted through regulatory reform. By this they meant primarily a lessening of costly social, including environmental, regulation" (Doern and Conway, 1994: 110).

As we shall see in the following chapter, the pro-business Mulroney government elected in 1984 was certainly sympathetic to such calls, but the evolution of environmental politics was such that even that government began to increase, rather than decrease, environmental regulatory pressure. By then, environment had emerged as a dominant issue, instead of just one among many, requiring a specific political response by business. Before turning to that story, however, I give a brief analysis of the events up to 1980, using the three lines of inquiry that form the structure of this work.

SUMMARY

Political Interest Sought

If the pulp-and-paper industry is representative, and there is no reason to believe it is not, the regulated firms were given full access to the decision-making process by which standards were set. Indeed, given the lack of expertise on the part of regulators, standard-setting could not have been done without the benefit of their technical expertise. We can assume that in all cases the regulated industries took advantage of that access to press for standards that would result in the least possible internalized cost. However, none sought to fundamentally change or block the regulatory programs applying to them.

Profitability appears to have been the only factor influencing business political objectives respecting environment during this period. There is no evidence that environmental legitimacy was a concern during this initial period. It was not until the following decade that some business firms and sectors gave the first clear signs that they had become convinced they needed to take action to restore the legitimacy lost with the rise of environmentalism. As we have seen, however, the more general subject of the legitimacy of business as a whole very definitely *was* on the minds of members of the business community, both in this country and in the United States. The loss of prestige and political power and the associated expansion of the regulatory state in the 1960s were subjects of considerable concern, leading to the increased attention paid to business-government relations documented above. During the 1970s, however, business representatives did not single out their environmental management for particular political action. It was seen as being only one aspect of their larger problem of a critical society and activist government.

Strategies Used to Achieve that Interest

It would appear that private negotiation was the only strategy used during the 1960s and 1970s. There were no instances of outside lobbying, nor of policy interventions intended to block or fundamentally change the policy objective. Nor were there any direct dealings with environmentalists. None of these strategies, which became so apparent in the decades following, were employed during these early years.

I would argue that this was because there was no *need* for any strategy other than private negotiation with regulators. Regulators were only making minimal demands, to which firms could readily adapt. This suggests, I argue, that business political strategy, particularly when it is reacting to government policy rather than reaching out to influence policy *de novo*, is determined more by the nature of the external threat than by any factors internal to the firm. Although no such action was taken in the area of environmental policy, business did engage in outside lobbying during this period, intended to give business a louder voice in the public debate, through the creation of the Business Council on National Issues in 1978. As we have seen, the threat during that decade was seen to be government in general, and it was that perception which elicited the political response of creation of the BCNI. In subsequent decades, when environmental regulators had achieved sufficient political power to seriously threaten profitability, that threat too elicited other political strategies.

Success in Achieving that Interest: Political Power

Finally, what can we say about business political power during this period? I would argue it was very much present. Business, it is true, had not been able to prevent the establishment of environmental law in the 1960s, but then it had made no real efforts to do so. That had been part of the larger process in which the power of business relative to both governments and those calling into doubt corporate legitimacy declined during that decade, leaving business on the defensive in a number of regulatory areas. But as we have seen, as the environmental regulatory system came to be implemented in the 1970s, business did not seem particularly weak in its dealing with the new environment departments. When firms such as those in the pulp-and-paper sector engaged with environmental regulators, during private negotiation of standards and timetables for their implementation, they clearly were able to significantly influence and to delay the policy to which they were subjected. It was not until the 1980s that any significant amount of power slipped out of the hands of the regulated firms and into those of the environment departments and their allies in the environmental movement.

CHAPTER FOUR

Increasing Regulatory Pressure, 1980-1993

The era of increasing pressure on business is marked at the beginning by a commitment given by the federal government to act on the issue that dominated the first part of the decade, acid rain, and at the end by the election of the Chrétien administration, which ran on an environment platform but then proceeded to implement the deregulatory agenda of the 1990s. In August 1980, Canada and the United States signed a Memorandum of Agreement that set forth their joint intent to take common action on transboundary air pollution, most notably acid rain, the new issue that was to dominate news media reporting on the environment during the coming decade. The Canada-US Air Quality Agreement was eventually signed, after many twists and turns in the domestic politics of each country, in 1991. The next year, the United Nations Conference on Environment and Development, in Rio de Janeiro, in which Canada was a full and active participant, represented a new high-water mark for attention to the policy issue of environment, both globally and within Canada. Not surprisingly, the issue figured prominently in the election platform of the Chrétien Liberals, who would go on to form the government in November 1993. Once elected, however, few of those promises were kept. Federal environmental policy, soon followed by that of the provinces, made a U-turn away from steadily increasing action on environment. That story is told in the following chapter. Here, we examine the ways in which business performed as a political actor before that sea change, during the period when environmentalists and regulators began to flex some political muscle for the first time.

The first five years of the decade were dominated by the single issue of acid rain. The 1985 program is without doubt the most successful environmental policy action to date, an example of coordinated action by the federal government and seven eastern provinces which more than met its policy objective. The policy role played by Inco, the firm at the centre of the issue, is described below. From that success, the federal government went on to take a series of actions that marked its return as an active participant in the policy arena. In 1987, Canadian federal officials played an important role in negotiating the Montreal Protocol to the Convention on Ozone-Depleting Substances which in turn is seen by analysts as the most successful international policy to date (Macdonald, 1991; Benedick, 1991; Porter, Brown and Chasek, 2000). The next year, federal legislation was amalgamated into one act, the *Canadian Environmental Protection Act*, with much publicity given to the addition of increased fine levels. A few years later, the Mulroney government used CEPA to impose a new round of regulatory controls on pulp-and-paper mills discharging dioxins (as discussed below, similar controls were also imposed by BC, Alberta, Ontario, Quebec, and New Brunswick). That same year also saw the federal government play a role on the international stage with respect to the emerging issue of climate change, when Canada co-hosted with the World Meteorological Organization and the United Nations Environment Program the Toronto Conference, which effectively started the process of international policy development. In 1990, the two levels of government again cooperated, this time on a plan to reduce pollution in the form of smog (which has proved to be a much more difficult issue than was acid rain). In 1991, the Mulroney government announced its Green Plan for Environmental Protection and in 1992 devoted considerable resources to participation in the Rio conference and then made sure that Canada was the first country, in December of that year, to ratify the Framework Convention on Climate Change which had been signed there.

Table 4.1 provides a summary listing of these federal and provincial policy actions.

Table 4.1 Policy Evolution, 1980-1993

1980 Canada-US Memorandum of Intent on acid rain
       Trudeau government National Energy Program
1985 national acid rain program; unilateral Ontario regulation of Inco
1986 Ontario MISA program
1987 Brundtland Commission report
       report of the National Task Force on Environment and Economy
       Montreal Protocol on ozone-layer-depleting substances
1988 Toronto Conference on climate change
       Canadian Environmental Protection Act
1990 CCME NOx/VOC Management Plan
1991 Mulroney government Green Plan
1992 Rio conference, followed by Canadian government ratification
       of UNFCCC
1993 Chrétien government elected

GOVERNMENTS EQUATE ENVIRONMENT WITH ELECTORAL SUCCESS

The basic factor leading to increased regulatory pressure on business during the 1980s was the growing political strength of the environmental movement. Few data are available, but it is clear that the number of organizations, membership in them, and financial support from Canadian citizens were all increasing during this period. New issues, such as acid rain, stratospheric ozone-layer depletion, toxic chemicals in drinking water and, toward the end of this period, climate change were being forcefully brought to the attention of governments by a social movement which had become skilled at gaining news media coverage. Nor yet were the long-established issues, such as forestry clear-cutting practices, urban smog, and solid-waste disposal wanting for local citizen-group or professional ENGO advocates, to make sure they did not disappear from either the front pages or policy agendas of governments. What Paehlke (1997) has described as the "second wave" of popular support for environmentalism was gaining strength throughout the decade.

For the first time, in 1984, environment was a prominent issue in an election campaign. In that year the Mulroney government was elected on a platform that included a written promise, given to the Canadian Coalition on Acid Rain, that it would put in place a Canadian acid-rain program, regardless of whether the Americans acted, within six months of taking office. That promise was kept, and what has traditionally been seen as the pro-business Conservative party administration went on to establish a track record of environmental policy action superior to that of either the Trudeau government it had replaced or the Chrétien government which followed it. Similarly, environment figured for the first time in an Ontario election in 1985; the David Peterson Liberal government, urged on by its minority-government partner the NDP, proceeded to take far more vigorous action than any previous government of that province. Environment was also a factor in the next federal elections. Although the 1988 election centred on the free trade issue, the Mulroney government featured its environmental track record as an important part of its election platform. As mentioned above, the Liberal Party also paid considerable attention to the issue in its Red Book, the platform on which it ran in 1993.

This prominence of the issue during elections shows clearly that during this period, political parties and governments were beginning to think that action on environment might be linked to electoral success. In consequence, an issue that had been relegated to junior ministers became something approaching a senior cabinet post, and environment department budgets began to increase accordingly. The formula given by Mitchell (1997: 219) for an eclipse in business power — "when policymakers assess that the business position detracts from rather than contributes to public support" — was at least in part achieved.

Most directly relevant to the regulated industries was a change in the way governments went about implementing environmental law. The "abatement" approach, in which pollution was characterized as a technical, apolitical issue, to be addressed cooperatively by firm and regulatory officials who shared a common language of science and engineering, was being supplemented by an "enforcement" approach, based in a culture of criminal-law enforcement. The Enforcement Branch of the Ontario Ministry of the Environment was established as a new unit separate from the abatement branches and staffed by former police officers, able to draw upon the services of technical expertise for inspections and lawyers for court prosecution of non-compliance. In Ontario, total fines levied by the courts for environmental offences rose steadily, increasing five-fold from $605,668 in 1985-86 to a high of $3,663,095 in 1992 (Project for Environmental Priorities, 1999). Federal prosecutions rose from a total of 13 in 1988 to a high of 45 in 1992 (thereafter to fall back to 10 in 1998), following the same trend, even though by and large the federal government left enforcement to the provinces: "Complete Canadian figures are not available because many provinces do not publicly reveal environmental-enforcement activities, but, based on the available data, it likely that charges against polluters in Canada peaked in 1992" (Mittelstaedt, 1999).

This change in enforcement practices clearly shows the degree to which industry was being subjected to new regulatory pressures. We now turn to some of the ways in which firms and sectors responded to this new external threat.

NEGOTIATED ADAPTATION: INCO AND ACID RAIN
The International Nickel Company of Canada (Inco) was created in 1902 in New Jersey, through a merger of the Orford Refinery, located in that state, and the Canadian Copper Company. Shortly afterward it was purchased by J.P. Morgan and Company, but by the 1970s it had become a truly transnational corporation. The firm's primary product has always been nickel, smelted from rocks mined in the Sudbury area, the major demand for which has come from governments, for use in armour plating of weapons. It originally operated a refinery in Wales, but in 1916 it built a refinery in Port Colborne, Ontario, and later the refinery that still operates in Sudbury. In 1956, Inco discovered nickel in Manitoba and built a refinery there and then in 1973 began operations in Indonesia (Macdonald, 1997).

Throughout the period of Inco-MOE negotiations examined here, from the late 1960s to 1985, the firm said publicly and repeatedly that it would make investments only in pollution controls that could be justified on financial grounds, through cost savings achieved by increased efficiency. The other major Ontario smelter, Falconbridge, had modernized in the 1970s and thus had much lower sulphur-dioxide emissions per unit of production. The challenge facing regulators was to find the right combination of carrots and sticks that would induce Inco to undertake a similar modernization, in effect making capital investments in this country, rather than Indonesia. At the end of the day it did so, spending more than $500 million between 1985 and 1994 and thereby achieving both major pollution reductions and significant annual cost savings. Regulatory pressure was clearly one factor inducing the firm to spend on efficiency and pollution reduction, but that pressure was in parallel with the basic economic strategy of the firm, which had always been to cut costs by reducing sulphur wastes. Like the pulp-and-paper industry with respect to wood waste, Inco had been working to reduce its sulphur waste, for economic reasons alone, from the early years of the century. Regulation clearly influenced the *timing* of the firm's modernization and accompanying pollution-reduction strategy, but never challenged Inco's basic economic interests. This, I suggest, is why it consistently responded to regulatory pressure by negotiated adaptation, rather than policy intervention.

In 1970, Inco became subject to a control order requiring that it build the celebrated Sudbury tall stack and then, by 1978, bring emissions down to roughly 250,000 tonnes per year. It complied with the first requirement but not the second, and in the summer of 1978, after quiet discussions with the firm, the Ontario MOE rescinded that requirement. By that time, the environmental movement had sufficient political strength to turn that action into a major embarrassment for the government, ultimately resulting in the resignation of the minister.

In 1980, as the acid-rain issue was gaining prominence and Canada and the US were negotiating their preliminary agreement, MOE re-opened negotiations with Inco, hoping to impose a new initial limit and to force the firm to do engineering studies of process changes that could lead to a significantly lower limit. Inco responded in several ways, none of them cooperative. On July 18, 1980, it informed the Ministry in writing that it deemed the proposed regulatory action to be beyond the constitutional powers of the province and that it would defend that position in the courts. The Ontario Minister, Harry Parrott, stated a few weeks later that "[a]s we examined this document, it became clear that a lengthy, legal battle was a possibility" (Macdonald, 1997: 155). At the same time, Inco sought to enlist the federal minister of mines, whose riding was located in northern Ontario, as a political ally (Macdonald, 1997: 156). Perhaps more valuable, in terms of the political pressure the firm was able to bring to bear on the Ontario ministry,

Inco was able to arrange a private briefing to make its case directly to members of the Ontario cabinet (Macdonald, 1997: 156).

The result of this conflict, following the normal pattern, was a compromise. MOE imposed a new regulatory limit in 1980, but it was no more stringent than what the firm already planned to meet in any case, through efficiency improvements. The ministry dropped the demand that the company undertake and submit studies on further abatement options. Instead, it appointed a task force to do the engineering studies, without Inco participation. (The company, nevertheless, proceed to conduct its own private, parallel studies.)

At the same time, the Ontario ministry was negotiating with Ontario Hydro, the other major source of acid-rain emissions in the province. Those discussions culminated in 1981 in a regulatory requirement, previously agreed to by Ontario Hydro, to cut emissions substantially by 1990. With those two regulatory programs established for Inco and Ontario Hydro, the province lost its appetite for further action and instead spent the next couple of years engaged in private diplomacy with the federal government and other provinces, seeking to convince them to weaken the Canadian national objective of a 50-per cent cut, contingent upon parallel American action (Macdonald, 1997a). The federal government periodically made noises about directly regulating Inco, but this was never a real possibility. Meaningful regulatory pressure on the firm did not re-appear until 1984, by which time environmentalists were successfully pressuring Ontario to take further action.

The task force studying Inco options reported publicly in December 1982, announcing that its studies showed emissions could be significantly reduced for a capital cost in the neighbourhood of $500 million. By that time Inco was well launched on its own studies, done privately at a cost of $26 million and not part of the work done by the task force. An internal MOE document dated April 19, 1983, gave this view of the regulator's understanding of what Inco might accomplish:

> Inco has developed and commercially tested a new nickel smelting process which has the potential to reduce sulphur dioxide emissions from the nickel smelter by 75 per cent. These changes may cost Inco more than $500 million for a new nickel smelter. (Macdonald, 1997: 219)

At a private negotiating session with MOE staff in the summer of 1983, the firm conceded that a reduction in the order of 75 per cent was technically feasible, but in the absence of any real pressure from MOE officials refused to make any firm commitment to do so (Macdonald, 1997: 221). Here we see another instance of the firm's relative political power stemming not only from its own motivation and agency action but also from the degree to which the regulator is willing to force the issue.

By that time the federal government, as always more ready to use the spending instrument than any regulatory tools, was developing plans to give the smelters funding for modernization, as had been done a few years earlier for the pulp-and-paper industry. Although other smelters in Manitoba and Quebec eventually took advantage of federal funding for modernization and pollution reduction, Inco never did. The firm consistently refused to trade money for a commitment to act. On December 20, 1983, environmentalists with the Canadian Coalition on Acid Rain (CCAR) met with Inco officials, offering to help Inco lobby for financial assistance from the Ontario and Canadian governments. The company refused the offer. Minutes of the meeting, prepared by an Inco official, give this record:

> The meeting closed with CCAR officials attempting to get a clear commitment from Inco to embrace their help and the financial help of government. No such commitment was offered. Inco left a clear message that we were committed to the task of finding cost-effective ways of further reducing emissions but were not at a decision-making stage at this time. (Macdonald, 1997: 239-40)

Eventually, by the fall of 1984, Inco agreed in private meetings with regulators that it would bring emissions down to 350,000 tonnes per year. That figure formed the basis for Ontario's contribution to the overall national program announced by the Mulroney government in March 1985. For its part, Inco publicly announced the objective the next month, in April 1985, presenting it as a voluntary action, based in good will and a desire to help governments achieve the national goal. This goal of 350,000 tonnes per year was a considerably less stringent standard than the 75-per cent reduction that had been discussed privately with regulators in the summer of 1983.

The national program was some 300,000 tonnes short of the 50-per cent reduction goal, a fact that was glossed over by the federal government, eager to show the Americans that Canada was acting and thus had a moral justification in pressing for comparable action in that country. Since Ontario was responsible for roughly half the eastern emissions, at least half of that shortfall can be attributed to the inability of MOE regulators to press the two major sources, Ontario Hydro and Inco, to make greater cuts.

That changed in June 1985, when the David Peterson Liberal government took power, having forged an agreement with the NDP to defeat the minority Conservative government that had been elected earlier in the year. That Ontario election, it will be recalled, was the first in which the environment had featured as a pivotal issue. Further action on acid rain was an important part of the Liberal-NDP agreement, and the new environment minister, Jim Bradley, immediately acted by re-opening negotiations with Inco. At a meeting on July 16, 1985, Bradley proposed the firm cut emissions to 150,000 tonnes. Inco officials, according to an MOE official present at the meeting, were "very, very concerned" that such a standard was being suggested (Macdonald, 1997: 281). The firm responded with an offer to move forward the date for meeting the 350,000-tonne limit, previously agreed to, and to conduct studies exploring the feasibility of a 175,000-tonne limit. No agreement was reached between MOE and Inco. In November, Bradley prepared to take to cabinet a proposed regulation for 150,000 tonnes. Prior to the cabinet meeting, however, that figure was leaked to the news media by an unknown source. It is not clear if the source was Inco itself, engaging in a rare instance of outside lobbying (Macdonald, 1997: 219).

Regardless, the firm certainly moved to exercise political power through its normal mechanism of private communication with government. On the morning of December 4, 1985, the day cabinet was scheduled to consider the proposed regulation, Inco Chair Charles Baird and President Donald Phillips met in private with Premier David Peterson, reportedly over breakfast at the Sutton Place Hotel. As a result, according to an MOE official, the Premier "got cold feet" and the issue was deferred at cabinet (Macdonald, 1997: 293). Another meeting between MOE and Inco officials was held, and eventually a compromise target of 265,000 tonnes was agreed to, approved as a regulatory requirement by cabinet, and announced on December 17, 1985 as part of the Ontario Count Down Acid Rain Program (Macdonald, 1997: 293). This time, company officials did not try to present the target figure as a voluntary contribution, but instead said they would have to spend time determining how to meet the new regulatory standard. As noted, they did so by the target date of 1994 and achieved considerable efficiency savings in the process.

Throughout these negotiations with environmental regulators, from 1980 to 1985, Inco consistently followed only one policy interest: delaying and weakening the regulatory controls imposed upon it, in order to minimize their impact on profitability. It used only the tactic of closed-door negotiations, with almost no recourse to advertising or other forms of outside lobbying. That may have been because it did not need to, since for the most part it achieved everything it wanted at the private bargaining table from 1970 to 1985. The December 1985, Ontario regulation appears to have been the one time the firm was forced to do something it actively resisted, but even then it was able to use private political power to avoid the lower target sought by the Environment Minister.

The one puzzling aspect of the story is the firm's apparent lack of concern for legitimacy, despite Inco's high visibility throughout the policy-development process. As discussed below, in more recent years Inco has engaged in the same green corporate-image advertising as have many large firms. It displayed no such behaviour, however, while in the heat of the political battle. This is in comparison with the chemical industry, which, as discussed below, went to great lengths in its bid for renewed legitimacy at approximately the same time, without being subjected to anything like the same immediate regulatory pressure.

The explanation for the difference likely lies in the nature of the external threat faced by each. While it is true that the chemical industry in the mid-1980s, when it was developing the legitimacy-seeking Responsible Care program, was not faced with short-term regulatory action, it was clearly, in its own words, worried about loss of its social licence to operate. As with some of the industry concerns over the lost legitimacy of the 1960s, the sector felt it was facing a threat not just to profitability, but to its very survival. Nothing written by Inco officials at the time gives any indication that they perceived themselves to be faced with a comparable threat. Nobody was calling for a ban on nickel as a product, and in any case the regulatory goal of reducing sulphur emissions was in accordance with the market strategy the firm itself had been pursuing for many years. It seems safe to assume that Inco did not actively court legitimacy at the time because it did not feel it needed it. In later years, when it was running corporate-image advertising, it did not face any greater threat, but instead was participating in the general business effort to regain the legitimacy lost during the 1980s.

THE MOTOR-VEHICLE INDUSTRY

Because regulation of products, as opposed to pollution emissions, falls largely in its domain, the federal government necessarily played a regulatory role in issues related to motor-vehicle design: fuel efficiency (then seen as a conservation issue, now central to climate change) and pollution in the form of nitrogen oxides emissions contributing to both acid rain and urban smog. Although they also have a jurisdictional mandate potentially covering product design (Boyd, 2003), in practice the provinces typically regulated motor vehicles only once they had been sold and were in use. British Columbia and Ontario have both implemented "drive clean" regulatory programs, requiring that owners limit emissions through regular vehicle maintenance. This is one of the few sectors, accordingly, that is directly regulated by Ottawa.

Since Canadian motor-vehicle manufacturers function in an integrated North American market, Canadian regulation of their product design has always closely followed US policy. It, in turn, is largely influenced by California policy. That state has a large enough population and economy to ensure it a voice in American federal politics. Cities like Los Angeles suffer from the same kinds of geography-induced wind inversions as do Mexico City and Vancouver, meaning that smog generated by motor vehicles has always been a major political issue in the state. Finally, the motor-vehicle industry does not have a major presence there, meaning that the California state government can take regulatory action without the same concern for political consequences found in other jurisdictions (Grant, 1995). Therefore, to at least some extent a pattern has developed whereby California takes the lead in regulating environmental aspects of motor-vehicle design, Washington follows, and Ottawa follows Washington (Simmons, 2002; VanNijnatten and Lambright, 2002).

In 1982, the Canadian Parliament passed the *Motor Vehicle Fuel Consumption Standards Act*, but the law was never brought into force due to lobbying by motor-vehicle manufacturers (Boyd, 2003: 88). Instead, in one of the first instances of voluntarism as a policy instrument, the federal government entered into an agreement with the industry whereby the latter would "voluntarily" meet the 1978 US Corporate Average Fuel Efficiency Standards (CAFE) standard of 8.6 litres per 100 kilometres (27.5 miles per gallon) in this country, in the absence of any legally binding requirement to do so. The US policy had been developed in the face of bitter resistance by the American industry, which had "threatened to close down assembly lines rather than subject their companies to a fine of up to $10,000 for every car failing to meet the standards" (Bryner, 1995: 102). In that country, policy was eventually set through compromise. In terms of the industry political action here, although no research has been done on the issue, it seems reasonable to make two suppositions. First, we might assume that the Canadian industry was following the usual pattern of offering voluntary behaviour change in order to pre-empt more stringent regulatory standards. Second, although more research would be needed to verify this, it may be that the industry did not engage in a comparable political intervention here because the Canadian industry and trade association knew that the significant battles were being fought in Washington, and that Canadian policy would largely be determined by their outcome.

In 1985, as part of its acid-rain program, the federal government announced it would phase in US standards governing nitrogen oxide emissions. That announcement was made again by the federal minister in 1989, and then a further commitment to coordinate motor-vehicle smog-related regulation was made in the 1991 Canada-US Air Quality Agreement. As with the case of fuel efficiency, however, the federal government then relied on voluntary action, accompanied by what seems to have been a credible regulatory threat, rather than law. In 1992, the Canadian government and the industry entered into a voluntary agreement, committing the latter to meet US pollution-emission standards. As discussed below, in 2005, as part of climate-change policy-making, the federal government offered sufficiently credible threats that it would regulate, and thus induced the industry to agree to "voluntarily" improve fuel efficiency by 25 per cent.

POLICY INTERVENTION: SOFT-DRINK INDUSTRY FUNDING OF BLUE-BOX PROGRAMS

By the early years of the twentieth century the sale of sweetened, flavoured, carbonated water had become a major industry in the United States and Canada. Coca-Cola was originally sold only at soda fountains. It was not until the invention of the refillable glass bottle in the 1890s that the product could be purchased in that container and taken home. For some time after that, the manufacture of the syrup was a separate industry from that of the bottlers, who sold the bottled drinks to local retailers. Both the product, mostly water, and the glass container were heavy, which meant the economics of transport limited each bottling operation to a circumscribed local area (Vestal, 1993).

The cost of each bottle, as a proportion of total product cost, was sufficiently high that it made economic sense for the soft-drink industry to attempt to recover bottles, wash and refill them, instead of buying new ones for each unit of product sold. This was done by means of a deposit-refund system, operated by retailers. By the 1960s, however, technological change in the tin-can manufacturing industry had removed that basic incentive. Metal containers, even if used only once, were sufficiently cheaper than glass bottles that it became economically preferable for the soft drink industry to use them instead of refillable glass bottles.

As well as eliminating the need to transport and wash the containers, cans gave the industry the benefits of lower weight and less bulk, each of which reduced transportation and storage costs. The industry, accordingly, followed its market interest and began to sell an increasingly large portion of its total product in metal cans, intended to be thrown away by the consumer, rather than glass bottles that were to be returned for a refund of the deposit. The *degree* of that market interest is indicated by two things. The first is that by 1999, by which time a significant portion of soft drinks in Canada were sold in less expensive tin cans, packaging represented 35 per cent of total industry production costs (HRSDC, 2005). This is many orders of magnitude higher

105

than the costs of managing pollution impacts for resource and manufacturing industries, which were estimated above to be 5 per cent or less of total annual operating costs. Second, the cost difference between cans and refillable bottles was also significant:

> As automation techniques improved, the logic of the shift to non-refillables became more and more compelling for the industry. By 1983, it was estimated that the cost of filling and distributing non-refillables cost [sic] soft drink companies was four to five times less than filling, distributing, collecting and refilling glass containers. (McRobert, 1994: 77)

That cost differential is only partially explained by differing costs of the two containers — many fewer workers are needed to operate can-filling machinery, per unit packaged, than is the case if bottles are used (McRobert, 1994: 103).

This powerful industry incentive was augmented by the fact that the switch to lightweight tin cans meant that decentralized bottling operations were no longer dictated by the economics of transporting the product. The large companies, such as Coca-Cola and Pepsi, proceeded to buy up independent bottling operations, replacing them with centralized operations which filled throw-away cans and transported them over longer distances than had been possible before (Vestal, 1993; McRobert, 1994).

All of these factors mean that the economic motivation of the industry was many times greater than that of other sectors. While the subject of regulatory action in the soft-drink industry was the beverage container, one of the two central elements of the production process, other sectors were asked only to make changes to their relatively much less expensive pollution management. This greater regulatory threat seems the most likely factor in explaining the fact that the soft-drink industry did not quietly follow the examples of the pulp-and-paper and smelting industries and negotiate with regulators an adaptive compromise. (I am assuming that the motor-vehicle industry, because policy was essentially made in the US, represents yet another set of business motivations. Like the soft-drink industry, it faced a regulatory threat aimed at its product, rather than its pollution, and thus had a greater incentive to intervene in the policy process. In its case, however, the political battle was fought south of the border.)

As was the case for other industrial sectors, the post-war emergence of environmental values posed a new threat for the soft-drink industry. In the 1960s, pollution in the form of "litter" on sidewalks and highway shoulders became an issue of concern. Another aspect of what later came to be known as the solid-waste issue was the new concern over the "throw-away society" and "planned obsolescence." The amount of garbage generated by an increasingly affluent society was coming to be equated with another issue of concern, namely depletion of natural resources such as metals and wood. The nascent environmental movement, concerned about such issues, paid particular attention to the throw-away metal containers that were being introduced by the soft-drink industry.

Environmentalists had become politically strong enough by the early 1970s to pressure some US state governments and Canadian provinces to take policy action on the issue. By 1972, BC, Alberta, Oregon, and Vermont had all introduced "bottle bills," the exact provisions of which varied but which all shared the use of law as the policy instrument of choice to bring about the desired behaviour change on the part of the soft-drink industry: to return to selling its product in refillable glass bottles. Ontario followed suit in 1976, amending its *Environmental Protection Act* and then using that new legislative authority to require stores to offer soft drinks in refillable as well as non-refillable containers, with an accompanying deposit-refund system. The amended legislation, if implemented, would have required an eventual complete phase-out of non-refillable containers. No regulations were drafted, however, since MOE and the soft-drink industry entered into a voluntary agreement whereby the industry would ensure that 75 per cent of its total sales were in refillable containers (McRobert et al., 1990).

The industry did not comply with these regulatory demands but instead first attempted to ignore them, which was made easy by the fact that regulators never seriously tried to enforce them. It then took political action in the form of a major campaign, carried out in a number of Canadian provinces, to convince regulators to abandon the policy objective of re-use and instead accept the less ambitious goal of container recycling. By and large, the industry was successful, although some provinces still have in place policies intended to encourage re-usable containers through deposit-refund systems. In Ontario, the jurisdiction examined here, the industry was able to completely reverse the 1976 policy.

As it engaged in that decades-long political campaign, the soft-drink industry found itself at the centre of events that unfolded through a complex mix of related solid-waste policy fields, involving at various times all three levels of government whose policy thinking was strongly influenced by examples in the US and Europe, and a kaleidoscopic variety of shifting alliances amongst relevant business interests. That story need not be told here, but it is necessary to explain the basics of the "3Rs" hierarchy of waste-management options, since it is that policy which the soft-drink industry has managed to significantly change.

The attempts in the early 1970s by newly established environmental regulators to reverse the market evolution of the past decades toward disposable soft-drink containers were not taken as part of any larger, coherent solid-waste policy effort. Although never completely coherent, such a larger policy framework did emerge, however, in the years that followed. By the late 1970s, regulators were moving to significantly improve legal standards governing the design and operation of solid-waste landfill sites. These efforts, designed to reduce the risk of pollution leaching from landfills into drinking-water supplies had the effect of restricting garbage-disposal capacity, both because existing, polluting landfills were required to close and because the process for gaining regulatory approval for new sites had become much more stringent. Throughout the industrialized world, "not in my backyard" conflicts over the siting of new garbage dumps became common. As their disposal options became narrowed and prices rose, municipalities, charged with responsibility for handling residential and some portion of commercial and industrial solid waste, came to see the value in reducing the total annual flow of garbage. That interest was augmented by the growing strength of the environmental movement, which demanded that both municipal and provincial levels of government do more to reduce landfill pollution and to conserve the wasted resources being poured into them in the form of thrown-away products.

Out of these two factors—a growing shortage of places to put waste and growing pressure from environmentalists—emerged by the early 1980s a consensus on the 3Rs hierarchy of preferred options: (1) Reduction (not generating waste in the first place) being most preferable, followed by (2) Re-use (designing the product so it can be used repeatedly, rather than being thrown away, e.g., collecting, washing, and refilling the beverage container), with (3) Recycling (collecting the product and then offsetting some need for raw materials by feeding all or part of it into a manufacturing process) coming in third. Product disposal, of course, was the option of last resort (setting aside the still vexed question of whether incineration, possibly with energy recovery, should be used as a disposal method). The shift to throw-away containers in the previous decade meant that the soft-drink industry was completely at odds with this articulation of solid-waste policy.

Ontario formally adopted the 3Rs as the basis for its solid-waste policy in the early 1980s, thus privileging re-usable bottles over recyclable cans. The stand-off between the industry and Ontario regulators continued, however, for almost a decade after the 1976 legislative action and accompanying voluntary agreement, during which time the portion of soft drinks sold in refillable glass bottles continued to erode (McRobert, 1994). It might have continued indefinitely, were it not for the evolution of solid-waste policy during that period, as municipally operated curbside recycling programs came to be established in North American cities. Once householders only had to carry a box of recyclable materials to the end of the driveway, rather than transport it by car to a recycling depot some blocks away, residential participation rates became high enough to make recycling a viable component of overall solid-waste policy. Such programs, however, added significantly to municipal waste-management budgets. It was thought in the early 1980s, as curbside recycling programs were being established, that that problem might be addressed through revenues generated by the sale of recycled materials. Logically, this meant that solid-waste policy should have worked to increase market demand for recyclables, thus both offsetting raw materials and providing revenues to fund recycling collection programs. This could have been accomplished through economic instruments such as surcharges or taxes on raw materials, regulatory requirements for recycled content in paper and other products, or government purchasing policies favouring recycled-content products. Such policy is beyond the jurisdictional reach of local governments but certainly could have been implemented by provinces or the government of Canada. Although a few half-hearted efforts were made, the senior governments never moved into the policy field in a meaningful way.

Instead, the question of how to fund curbside recycling programs was left at the local level, giving leverage to the soft-drink industry, drawing in a number of other business actors, and ultimately eclipsing all other aspects of 3Rs policy. Without such policy measures, the only significant source of revenue from the sale of recycled materials was aluminium. Unlike other materials in the waste stream, such as glass or wood fibre, aluminium alone could attract sufficiently high, dependable sales prices to contribute in a meaningful way to funding recycling programs. Thus both the steel industry, which made the soft-drink cans used in Ontario, and the aluminium industry, which wanted to move into that market, had a direct economic interest in soft-drink container policy.

By the early 1980s, the soft-drink industry was beginning to move from its defensive policy stance to venture forth into more aggressive forms of policy intervention. This was done, in Ontario, by offering to trade funding for municipal curbside recycling in exchange for relaxation of the provincial refillable sales ratio requirements. This meant that from the outset the industry was locked into triangular negotiations with the two levels of government. The first experimental curbside recycling program was initiated in Ontario in 1981, and the following year the aluminium company Alcan offered to provide financial support for such programs. In 1983, Alcan joined the glass and paper industries in providing funding for a second pilot program. After extensive negotiations with both the industry players and environmentalists, in 1985 the newly installed Liberal government of Ontario dropped the regulatory target for refillable sales from 75 to 30 per cent. The soft-drink industry, in exchange, promised to fund a portion of capital and initial costs of municipal recycling programs (McRobert, 1994).

Thus we find the same Ontario government, in the same year, 1985, treating two industrial actors in a completely opposite manner. Inco was forced to make environmental management improvements that it had actively resisted. The soft-drink industry, on the other hand, was given a *relaxation* of its environmental management requirements. How do we explain the difference? In large part, the difference resulted from the fact that Inco adapted to pending new policy, while the soft-drink industry intervened to change it. Coca-Cola and the other soft-drink firms, facing a more costly regulatory demand, took interventionist action in the form of offering to fund curbside recycling, in a way Inco never did.

But the accompanying failure of regulators to actively enforce the refillable sales quota was also a factor: "To many senior officials in the Ontario government, it seemed unbelievable that significant MOE investigative and prosecutorial resources were, at least in theory, devoted to prosecuting soft drink companies for violations of Regulation 687/76 while corporations dumping toxins into the Great Lakes or open dumps were left untouched" (McRobert, 1994: 89). Again we find an instance in which the relative power of the business actor flows largely from the degree of motivation of the regulator. The soft-drink industry had the political power to carry out this successful policy intervention largely due to this factor.

Another explanation lies in the nature of the two issues. Acid rain was the most visible issue of the day, and the Ontario government was under strong pressure from environmentalists to act. Re-usable versus refillable beverage containers, on the other hand, was not a hotly debated topic. Furthermore, environmentalists in Ontario were divided on the soft-drink issue, in a way they were not on acid rain, with many groups supporting the relaxation of the refillable sales ratio in exchange for an opportunity to launch curbside recycling. The calculations of electoral advantage made by the Ontario government were obviously very different for each issue.

By 1990, business had provided $20 million toward the cost of such Ontario programs, the bulk of that coming from the soft-drink industry. At that time, 18 per cent of total soft drinks were sold in refillable containers, meaning industry was out of compliance with the 30-per cent requirements. Revenues sufficient to offset municipal blue-box programs had not materialized and local governments were complaining about the fact that per-tonne recycling costs were on average $190, compared with the cost of $80 to collect and dispose of a tonne of garbage (Winfield, 1993). The soft-drink industry continued to use this municipal demand for additional subsidy as a bargaining chip for relaxation of the refillable sales ratio requirement, while at the same time trying to convince the other industries generating materials that ended up in the blue box to contribute a greater share of the total business subsidy. In 2002, with the full support of the industry, the Ontario government enacted the *Waste Diversion Act*, which provided the legislative framework for industry and local-government sharing of curbside recycling costs. A phase-out of non-refillable pop containers, the objective of the 1976 legislation, was history.

This does not mean, however, that successive Ontario governments had previously abandoned re-use as a beverage-container policy goal. In 1989, the government imposed a five-cent surcharge on imported beer sold in non-refillable containers. In 1992, the Rae government increased the "beer-can levy" to ten cents. Why was policy moving in one direction (recyclable cans) for soft drinks and another (refillable glass bottles) for beer? The answer lies in the lobbying efforts of the Ontario beer industry, which was using the fact that it operated a viable deposit-refund system to keep American beer, sold in cans, out of their market (Macdonald, 1996). The two sectors, soft drinks and beer, both lobbied for environmental policy that would further their profitability interests, and both were successful.

THE CHEMICAL INDUSTRY'S SEARCH FOR SOCIAL LEGITIMACY

The chemical-industry response to environmental regulation was different from both the negotiated adaptation of Inco and the successful policy intervention undertaken by the soft-drink industry. For those sectors, as we have seen, the policy objective flowed directly from the market interest and was limited to a desire to delay or weaken forced internalization of cost. The case of the chemical industry in the 1980s, however, is more complex, because the desire for legitimacy loomed so much larger in the motivation of the large firms in the sector.

Political actions by the smelting and soft-drink industries, and also by the chemical industry itself when it lobbied against proposed CEPA amendments in the late 1990s, can accurately be described as "tactical" — movements made in the face of the enemy. In those instances, the sector was engaged in specific negotiations with regulators over short-term, incremental policy that threatened profitability. Nor was the search for legitimacy a major factor. The political action taken by the chemical industry in establishing the 1986 Responsible Care program, however, was "strategic" — action taken to counter a longer-term threat that was not yet fully recognizable. That external threat was a loss of legitimacy in the mind of the public, comparable to that suffered by business as a whole in the 1960s.

When it took this political action, the sector was not facing any immediate regulatory threat, nor was government yet the primary audience in whose eyes the sector so desperately sought renewed legitimacy. As described below, the large chemical firms did not spend their time and financial resources generating technical policy briefs to be read by environment officials. Instead, they worked to improve their environmental performance and at the same time deluged the Canadian public with magazine and newspaper advertising, relying on imagery rather than text, to show a caring, humane industrial sector, fully committed to giving society the benefits of chemicals, while shielding it from their potential harm. Like AT&T eighty years earlier, the chemical industry, fearful for its survival, desperately sought to show Canadians that it possessed a corporate soul.

Coleman gives a succinct picture of the industry as comprising three sub-sectors: "basic chemicals (industrial organic and inorganic chemicals); chemical materials, formed from these basic chemicals (synthetic resins, fertilizer chemicals such as potassium); and chemical products, manufactured in turn, out of the intermediary materials (drugs, paints, perfumes, plastics and so on)" (Coleman, 1988: 203). Another picture of the sub-sectors into which the industry is divided is given by the trade associations that together form, with the CCPA, what the latter refers to as the Chemical and Allied Industries Group: the Canadian Plastics Industry Association, the Canadian Fertilizer Institute, the Canadian Paint and Coatings Association, the Rubber Association of Canada, the Crop Protection Institute, the Canadian Association of Chemical Distributors, and the Canadian Manufacturers of Chemical Specialities Association (CCPA, undated a). In their dealings with government, these other associations allow the CCPA to play a lead role, in part because the large firms are well represented on the boards of all the associations (Coleman, 1988: 206-07).

The industry is located primarily in four provinces: British Columbia, Alberta, Ontario, and Quebec. It consists of both large, visible firms, such as Dow Canada, which are owned by transnational parent firms, and smaller firms. This difference in firm size seems to have been a more significant factor influencing political action of the industry than is the case for other sectors examined in this chapter. The CCPA was created in 1962, with an office established in Ottawa. In the mid-1970s, the CCPA was influential in establishing the Business Association Interchange, a monthly meeting of trade-association officials, often attended by politicians and bureaucrats, to exchange current information on the inner workings of the federal government (Sawatsksy, 1987: 181-84).

Chemical pollution, of course, has been a matter of public concern since the 1960s. It is subject to three distinct environmental regulatory regimes: (1) approval of new pesticide products and regulation of pesticide use; (2) regulations intended to reduce the likelihood of large-volume, single-incident, accidental spills and leaks, either in the plant or during transport, and comparable regulation intended to reduce low-volume, chronic pollution emissions; and (3) regulation by means of the Canadian Environmental Protection Act, which is directed not at plant operations but at chemical substances, many of which are sold as products, which must gain regulatory approval before they can be manufactured, and some of which have been banned. Pesticide regulation is not included in the story told here.

Like all other sectors, the industry first became subject to environmental regulation in the late 1960s and early 1970s, during which period it still had a relatively benign image. In the decades immediately after the war, the industry engaged in public-relations activity intended to demonstrate how important chemicals, and the new wonder-product they had brought into being, plastics, were to technological and economic progress and to "better living" in general. In the US, which moved to regulate before Canada, the industry engaged in private negotiation to stall or weaken proposed regulation and to publicly discredit attacks such as Rachel Carson's *Silent Spring* (Markowitz and Rosner, 2002).

Moffet and his colleagues, quoting the CCPA itself (Bélanger, 1990) give this picture of how, by the late 1970s, the view of chemicals as a positive contribution to society and the relative obscurity of the industry were beginning to change:

> In 1977, the explosion of a chemical factory in Seveso, Italy, marked the first of several high-profile and extensively reported accidents that rapidly undermined public confidence in the industry and led to demands for stricter government regulation. In the words of the CCPA President, "we went from being an 'invisible industry' to one under a microscope. Our employees found themselves being stigmatized simply because they worked in the chemical industry." (Moffet, Bregha and Middelkoop, 2004: 178)

A few years after the Seveso accident, the publicity given to hazardous wastes buried in Love Canal, New York, irretrievably blackened the image of "chemicals." The deaths caused by an accidental leak from a Union Carbide plant in Bhopal, India, in 1984 did similar harm to the public view of the industry's ability or willingness to guard against chemical risk. Publicity stemming from the deaths caused by the Bhopal accident had a deleterious impact on Union Carbide stock prices and sales revenues, and the shock waves spread from that company throughout the industry. That company and many others immediately put in place new internal management controls for handling chemicals, and responsibility for environmental safety moved up the organizational chain of command.

113

The industry in Canada and other countries was very aware of this increasing loss of public confidence and the attendant likelihood of another round of regulatory action by governments. Jean Bélanger, former president of the CCPA, has said that in 1984, "we had just been told by a public opinion poll commissioned by us, that the chemical industry was secretive, that we knew about the risks but didn't tell anyone, and that basically we didn't care" (1991: 3). King and Lenox (2000: 3), writing about the American industry, cite this polling data in that country: "From 1980 to 1990, favorable opinion about the industry fell from 30 to 14 per cent, and unfavorable public perceptions of the industry grew from 40 to 58 per cent." And Gunningham, writing about the chemical industry on a global basis, puts the issue this way: "In the long term, the chemical industry's very poor public image is likely to result in a loss of public support, a regulatory backlash, extreme difficulty in persuading communities to accept new chemical installations in their locality and a host of other problems..." (1998: 161). He quotes an industry spokesperson as saying, in 1992, "Businesses can only survive whilst they have society's acceptance for their activities. Once that acceptance is lost, there is only one way to go" (161).

In Canada, following the 1977 Seveso accident, the CCPA developed a set of guiding principles for the handling of toxic chemicals, which were circulated to member companies in 1978 (CCPA, undated b). Over the next seven years, particularly after the 1984 Bhopal accident, that policy was considerably elaborated, but it kept the same name and was then publicly launched in 1986. The Responsible Care program along with its logo of cupped hands shielding chemical molecules, presented by means of full-page newspaper and magazine advertisements, was intended to achieve the related political goals of restoring industry legitimacy and pre-empting further regulatory controls.

The external threat of declining public confidence leading to new regulatory controls, which had become acute with the 1984 Bhopal accident, posed two problems for the industry. The first was the industry's realization that it would not be possible to change public perceptions purely by marketing and communications strategies, with no attendant behaviour change on the part of the industry. Gunningham cites a senior executive who commented during the 1980s that chemical companies "[could not] just advertise their way out of it" (1998: 160). The other problem was that the large, visible firms, even after deciding they had to implement the second option, were faced with a collective-action problem. They could not restore their own legitimacy purely on the basis of their own behaviour change, since publicity surrounding any one company tarred all firms in the sector with the same brush. Moffet and Bregha, with reference to the Canadian industry, describe the problem this way:

Opinion polls commissioned by the industry showed that the public did not discriminate among companies; the actions of one company tarnished the industry as a whole. Large companies such as Dow Canada realized as a result that only a concerted approach would restore public confidence in the industry. (1999: 69)

Bélanger (1991: 2) gives the same picture:

In 1984, a number of events occurred which made us reflect further on our commitment and several key decisions were taken. Firstly, we realized that we were vulnerable at our weakest link, that is, any member company that did not commit itself. And so it was decided that signing the commitment to Responsible Care would become a condition of membership in the CCPA.

While the industry was forthright in stating that its need for renewed legitimacy was the primary motivation for introducing the Responsible Care program, other factors were undoubtedly involved. Another motivation, which is common to other environmental management systems, such as the ISO 14000 program, is a desire to reduce environmental liability by ensuring the availability of a due-diligence defence to prosecution (Solway, 1997). Another benefit comes from the fact that this reduced liability may help reduce insurance costs. In at least one instance, the cost of environmental liability insurance has been reduced for Responsible Care participating companies (Cutter Information Corp., 1998).

Finally, it seems reasonable to assume that firms in the chemical industry introduced the program because they genuinely felt they *should* act in a responsible manner. Changing corporate culture has to be a part of the explanation. The men and women making corporate decisions undoubtedly wish to be seen, and to see themselves, as "doing the right thing." Immediately after the Bhopal accident, the CEO of Union Carbide, Warren Anderson, ignored the advice of his lawyers and flew to the site of the accident and there publicly admitted liability (Piasecki, 1995: 22). Admittedly, the company then engaged many lawyers over the course of the next decade to contest lawsuits in the Indian courts, but that does not deny the reality of his first, human, response.

The Responsible Care program, which has since been put in place by the chemical industry in many countries around the world, is a self-regulatory system which requires that member firms implement specified management procedures to reduce risks of accidents and pollution. It does not specify any numerical standards governing environmental management, as do government regulations, nor does it require that member firms be in compliance with law. Nevertheless, there seems little doubt that the program has brought about meaningful improvements in environmental performance of CCPA member firms (Moffet, Bregha and Middelkoop, 2004). But how did the program fare in terms of the other goals of those who put it in place — restoring legitimacy and forestalling punitive new regulation?

The best that can be said about the first objective is that public distrust has not worsened during the time since the program was put in place and that Responsible Care may be at least partially responsible. The absence of any accidents on the scale of Bhopal may also be responsible. Polling done by the industry does not, however, show any significant improvement: "Although Responsible Care may have helped arrest the precipitous decline in trust that marked the early to mid-1980s, CCPA polls continue to reveal low overall levels of public confidence in the industry" (Moffet, Bregha and Middelkoop, 2004: 191).

In terms of pre-empting regulation, however, the program has been much more successful. Although, again, it is impossible to precisely allocate causality amongst the program and its use in associated lobbying done by the industry and other factors, the fact remains that the industry fears of the 1980s never materialized. Quite the contrary — as discussed in the next chapter, the 1990s saw a reversal of the trend toward increasingly coercive regulation witnessed during the 1980s, as governments moved from law to voluntarism. In 1988, the federal government put in place the *Canadian Environmental Protection Act*, but the next major federal regulatory initiative to have direct implications for the chemical industry was the Accelerated Reduction/Elimination of Toxics (ARET) Challenge program. In that case, chemical industry participation was purely voluntary. The industry itself claims that its social intervention of the 1980s helped to stave off some regulatory measures in the following decade: "CCPA officials credit Responsible Care with the government's increased willingness to consider voluntary commitments in lieu of regulations for specific issues such as benzene emissions from chemical manufacturers" (Moffet, Bregha and Middelkoop, 2004: 189).

THE SECOND ROUND OF PULP-AND-PAPER REGULATION

As the 1980s progressed, the second wave of popular support for environmentalism grew, bringing with it the second round of regulatory demands for action on toxic effluents, this time centred upon the substance dioxin. Greenpeace USA, by then a multi-million-dollar organization, was the first to carry out an effective campaign to put the issue on the policy agenda. In this country, Environment Canada had been monitoring dioxin levels in herring-gull eggs for some years prior to 1987, the year when dioxin was publicly linked to pulp-and-paper mill effluent through release of a US EPA study. This was followed by considerable scientific controversy over which of the variety of toxic substances in mill effluent caused the most harm and which could best be used, for regulatory purposes, as a marker for control of overall toxic effects (Harrison, 1996b; Harrison and Hoberg 2001, 2002; VanNijnatten, Leiss and Hodson, 1997). Although different approaches were used, and standards, based on the ratio of subject toxic pollutants to pulp production, varied, by the early 1990s Canada, BC, Ontario, and Quebec had imposed new, legally binding controls on mill effluent.

As it had in the 1960s, the industry did not intervene in the policy process to block or fundamentally transform this latest regulatory threat. Prior to the enactment of any regulatory requirements specifically focussed on dioxin, in 1988 the industry took the relatively inexpensive step of reducing emissions of the substance by changing bleaching agents: "These [industry] researchers also found that this process could be prevented by substituting chlorine dioxide for molecular chlorine in the bleaching process, which sparked a widespread movement toward chlorine dioxide substitution in the pulp and paper industry" (VanNijnatten, Leiss and Hodson, 1997: 4). Following what was by then becoming the norm for manufacturing and resource industry trade associations, in 1989 the CPPA publicly released an environmental statement, committing member companies to principles of sound environmental management, although no specific actions or objectives were included (CPPA, 1989). This contrasts with the first round of regulation. Twenty years earlier, when it first negotiated environmental standards, the trade association had not generated any such document intended to give an air of legitimacy. The sector then moved from principles to action. In 1991, the CCPA released a plan to virtually eliminate, subject to economic conditions, persistent, bioaccumulative substances from mill effluent (VanNijnatten, Leiss and Hodson, 1997: 9).

While it was engaged in this effort to regain environmental credibility in public eyes, by changing both its behaviour and image, the industry was also privately negotiating with government regulators in order to weaken the pending standards. Writing in 1990, Bonsor stated, "Kraft mill operators are lobbying hard for a limit of 2.5 [organochlorines] kg per tonne, whereas environmental groups are pushing for a limit of no greater than 1.5 ..." (177). The most notable instance of industry lobbying occurred in British Columbia in 1990, when the provincial environment minister prepared to publicly announce a new regulatory standard of 1.5 kilograms per tonne. Using the same tactic practised by Inco in 1985, industry lobbyists at the last moment went over his head and convinced the premier, Bill Vander Zalm, to instead adopt a standard of 2.5 kilograms, leading to the resignation of the minister (Harrison, 1996b: 490).

In 2003 the trade association, now named the Forest Products Association of Canada, stated in its annual report that the industry had spent $6 billion since 1990 on eliminating chlorine as a bleaching agent and installing external, secondary treatment facilities on all mills (FPAC, 2003: 5). The significance of this roughly half-billion dollars in spending each year over twelve years is indicated by comparison with the $2-billion profit in 2002, which was described as "not a stellar year" (FPAC, 2003: 8), due in part to the "$3.1 billion negative impact" caused by the rise in the Canadian dollar relative to the American dollar (FPAC, 2003: 6). The regulatory threat posed by this second round of regulations was real and significant, but not dire in comparison to other things affecting the economic fortunes of the sector. The industry could also be confident that its competitors in the United States and Scandinavia were being asked to absorb comparably stringent internalization of costs. Finally, it is safe to assume that the cost would have been higher, had the industry been in full compliance with regulatory standards. In a study published in 2000, the Sierra Legal Defence Fund used government data to publicly document widespread non-compliance throughout the 1990s (Clancy, 2004: 125).

As previously stated, the response of negotiated adaptation achieved through private negotiation with regulators was the same as that practised by the same industry in the 1960s and by Inco in the early 1980s. What is different from both is the far greater concern displayed by the pulp-and-paper industry for its public image. It appears this is not limited to the Canadian industry. After years of doing battle with Greenpeace and its allies, while negotiating with governments successive rounds of new regulatory controls, it is fair to say that the industry is now fixated on its environmental image.

Writing in 1998, Diesen summarized the opportunities and threats facing the global industry, giving a total of seven factors in the two categories, only one of which was not directly related to environmental impacts of the industry. He predicted that paper demand would continue to increase because it is made from a renewable resource, trees; that this resource absorbs carbon dioxide and thus contributes to climate change policy; the product can be recycled; and the modern pulp-and-paper process is so efficient that it "does not require outside energy" (Diesen, 1998: 15). The first two threats he listed resulted from a lack of perceived legitimacy with respect to environment:

In 1996, the paper industry faced the following main threats: (1) The poor image of the industry as an old, smokestack industry with high environmental emissions in air, water and soil. (2) The public belief that the forest industry is responsible for cutting rain forests and old northern forests.... To improve its image in forest and forestry issues, the industry faces a number of challenges. If these questions are not resolved, the image of the industry and its methods of securing sources of raw material for production will be in question. This would put the future of the whole industry in grave jeopardy. (Diesen, 1998: 16-17)

Only the third threat listed, namely a decrease in demand for newsprint due to increasing usage of electronic news media, was not related to environmental image (Diesen, 1998: 16). As was the case with the concerns expressed in the 1970s, quoted above, we again find the suggestion made that loss of legitimacy might literally lead to the death of the industrial sector.

In the same way, the 2003 Canadian trade association annual report is couched entirely in terms of environment. The highlights page starts with the usual data on total production and employment but then quickly moves to give summary data on reductions in water use and air pollution, movement to renewable energy sources, and increases in the use of recycled fibre (FPAC, 2003: n.p.). The introductory letter from the FPAC president, Avrim Lazar, a former Environment Canada official, and chair, Russell Horner, CEO of Norske-Canada, makes only one reference to economic performance and even that is linked to environment, when we are told that recent capital investments have made the industry "more globally competitive and benefit the environment and Canada's rural economy" (FPAC, 2003: n.p.). Literally all the other words in their letter are devoted to touting the many ways in which the pulp-and-paper industry is "implementing arguably the most ambitious sustainability agenda ever undertaken in Canadian industry" (FPAC, 2003: n.p.)." The annual report itself does review, in the usual glowing terms, economic performance during the past year, but something like half the space is devoted to environmental performance. Fifteen years earlier, by contrast, the 1988 trade association annual report started by claiming that in the past year pulp-and-paper industry exports had "helped make Canada a great and successful trading nation" (CPPA, 1988: 1) and then devoted the remainder of the report to economic performance with virtually no reference to environmental impacts, even when discussing chemical pulping and bleaching.

There is no doubt that in the interval between 1988 and 2003, the industry considerably increased the time, energy, and money it devotes to its environmental management. But there also was a significant improvement in environmental performance between the late 1960s and 1988. Why was that effort ignored in the 1988 report and talked about to the exclusion of all else in 2003? In the next chapter I discuss the emergence of corporate-image advertising in the 1990s and argue that it was part of a successful effort by business to regain the legitimacy and political power lost to environmentalists in the 1980s. The fixation upon environmental image documented above, compared to the earlier disregard, is another piece of evidence in support of that argument.

ADAPTING TO MULTISTAKEHOLDER CONSULTATION

We now turn from examination of political action by specific firms and sectors in the middle years of the 1980s to the response of business as a whole to a change in the environmental policy development process, which represented another threat to business interests. The advent of multistakeholder consultation, a process by which representatives of government, business, the environmental movement, and other interests discussed policy options in an open, public forum in an effort to achieve consensus, was a marked change from previous practices. From the advent of the regulatory system, environmental policy had been developed by means of private negotiations between regulators and firms (Thompson, 1980; Macdonald, 1991; Cotton and McKinnon, 1993). Not only to bring those discussions into public view, but also to invite environmentalists to fully participate, would seem to be a threat to the political power of business akin to any of the new regulatory initiatives of the decade. But in fact, the threat never materialized. Business showed a remarkable aptitude for the tactic that Wilson, in his analysis of B.C. forestry policy (1998), describes as "talk and log" — to engage in seemingly endless multistakeholder discussion without in any way being forced to deviate from original market strategies. The failed threat of multistakeholder consultation is for that reason an important element in our effort to understand the political power of business in the environment arena.

VanNijnatten's definition of multistakeholder consultation (MSC) sets out the basic threat to business power:

> MSC gathers together all the parties to, for example, an environmental dispute — multiple levels of government, different administrative agencies, industry and environmental interests — with the specific purpose of facilitating consensus (not necessarily unanimity) on how to balance environmental and economic requirements. In such an arena, all parties are expected to participate on an equal basis and the preemptive power of traditionally stronger interests is likely to be diminished. (1996: 5)

Such a process of consensus-based discussion of potential policy-development pathways is different from a traditional white-paper consultation process, in which governments seek advice but do not engage in ongoing discussion. Nor is it the same thing as arbitration, in which parties in conflict seek a compromise because they prefer that to a more expensive method of settling the dispute, such as court litigation (VanNijnatten, 1996). Finally, it must also be distinguished from environmental assessment, another planning process which also gives citizens and environmentalists more access to decision-making, but which is more litigative in nature and which is used almost exclusively for siting and planning specific projects, such as a highway or waste dump, rather than government policy.

Doern and Conway (1994: 112-16) tell us the process was initiated in 1984, when Environment Canada hosted a series of government-business-environmentalist discussions, using the services of the Niagara Institute, a think tank with a previous background in facilitating management-labour discussion. The consultative process was then adopted by almost all provincial and federal environment departments, being used most notably by the 1987 National Task Force on Environment and Economy, for the Waterfront Remedial Action Programs (WRAPS) initiated by the IJC in the late 1980s, the National Packaging Protocol development process, initiated by CCME in 1989, and the development of the Mulroney government Green Plan in 1990. The process was institutionalized in the form of round tables on environment and economy, advisory bodies made up of business, government, and environmental representatives, established by virtually all of the provincial and federal governments as part of Canada's response to the 1987 publication of the Brundtland report. (All of the provincial round tables have since been disbanded, but the federal body, The National Task Force on Environment and Economy, still exists.)

Some analysts suggest that the government's motivation was to respond to criticisms that the traditional regulator-firm process lacked legitimacy "by opening up the decision-making process to environmental interests" (Stefanick, 1997: 101). Certainly environmentalists were happy to participate, since they had been pressing for access to the firm-regulator discussions from the outset. Adoption of environmental assessment procedures in the 1970s had not been the answer, since they usually did not apply to private planning or siting decisions and litigation, because of the nature of the Canadian court system, offers few opportunities to influence policy. Multistakeholder consultation seemed in the mid-1980s to give environmentalists a policy voice in accordance with their growing political power. The fact that pro-business governments intent on deregulation, such as the Harris government that was elected in Ontario in 1995, did not engage in such multistakeholder consultation suggests that the process does in fact enhance the power of environmentalists relative to business. (When the Harris government set out to review environmental regulations in the fall of 1995, as part of the larger exercise in reducing the "red tape" that imposes cost internalization upon business, it consulted only with business interests. Environmentalists, such as the Canadian Environmental Law Association, were not contacted until much later and a public discussion document was not released until July 1996.)

Thus we have no difficulty in understanding why the greens participated

— but why did business firms willingly engage in a process in which they were clearly disadvantaged relative to their former privileged status? Research is needed to answer that question, since to the best of my knowledge no business representatives have spoken publicly on their motives for participation. I offer here three speculative hypotheses. The first is that while public consultation worked to the disadvantage of the firm as a whole, it benefited the public-affairs units that had been established during the preceding decade. It was officials of those units who represented the firm in consultative discussions, which meant, since governments had decreed that multistakeholder consultation was now a necessary part of the policy process, that their importance to the firm increased. Presumably this meant they became a voice within the firm, urging continued participation in this new forum. Second, and more important, business really had no choice but to participate, since failure to take a seat at the table, there to argue that policy be developed slowly and carefully, with full cognizance of its impact on economic well-being, would have been unthinkable. No organization can allow the precise nature of external threats to be discussed by others without taking full advantage of every opportunity to participate in that discussion. Finally, consultative dialogue never really resulted in a loss of political power for business because the locus of government decision-making was never fully transferred there. Nor, presumably, were the lines of private communication between firms and regulators shut down just because both were also engaged in a concurrent public dialogue.

Analysts at Queen's University, in a 1996 study of the ARET consultative process, offer this comment on the fact that governments do not transfer true policy-making power to multistakeholder processes: "although you cannot expect government to promise to abide by any consensus reached by a multistakeholder group, it is reasonable to expect a commitment from government to respond (in writing) to any agreement reached by the group" (Environmental Policy Unit, Queen's University, 1996: 8). Although they do not discuss the point further, the logic of democracy means that no other conclusion is possible. The need for democratic accountability, which at the end of the day rests only with elected governments, means governments have never ceded full policy-making powers to courts or arm's-length regulatory tribunals. Nor could they do so to unelected consultative groups. Certainly governments acted on a number of the consensus recommendations that came out of consultations such as those listed above. At the end of the day, however, multistakeholder groups never rose above the status of advisory bodies, the kinds of sounding boards governments had been using right from the initial establishment of environmental regulation in the early 1970s (Boardman, 1992).

Certainly that was the case with the multistakeholder round tables established by all provinces and the federal government to develop recommendations for policy implementation of the concept of sustainable development. In 1990, Howlett stated that round tables "exist simply as advisory bodies to government and have in no way affected environmental decision-making or administration, both of which remain in the traditional political-corporate realm" (cited in Stefanick, 1997: 118). As noted, all the provincial round tables were disbanded in the 1990s and the only one remaining, the National Task Force on Environment and Economy, does not pretend to be anything more than an advisory body. Throughout the 1990s, climate-change policy was developed through multistakeholder consultation. The voice given to environmentalists by the process never resulted in imposition of regulatory pressure upon relevant industries. Multistakeholder discussion has done nothing to change the basic dynamic of environmental politics, nor to threaten the access of business to the real governmental decision-makers.

EMBRACING SUSTAINABLE DEVELOPMENT
Lafferty and Meadowcroft provide a concise summary of the way in which sustainable development has come to be the dominant conceptualization in the field of environmental policy:

> Over the past decade the idiom of sustainable development increasingly has come to frame international debates about environment and development policy making. Catapulted to dominance by the report of the Brundtland Commission in 1987, sustainable development was formally endorsed as a policy objective by world leaders at the Rio Earth Summit [formally titled the United Nations Conference on Environment and Development] five years later. It has been absorbed into the conceptual lexicon of international organizations such as the World Bank and the OECD; been accorded its own global secretariat in the form of the UN Commission on Sustainable Development (CSD); and achieved near-constitutional status in the European Union through its incorporation in the Maastricht and Amsterdam treaties. Around the globe political leaders and public administrators now routinely justify policies, projects, and initiatives in terms of the contributions they make to realizing sustainable development. (2000: 1)

The concept did not emerge from domestic environmental policy circles, in Canada or elsewhere. Instead, it developed during the 1980s in the global arena, as the concept of "development" as the solution to third-world poverty came to be challenged by increasing awareness of associated environmental impacts. As Hajer (1995) has pointed out, "It is undisputed that the Brundtland Report, *Our Common Future* (1987), is to be seen as a sequel to the Brandt

Report *North-South: A Programme for Survival* (1980) and *Common Crisis* (1983) and the report *Common Security* (1982) of the Palme Commission" (99). As such, it represented a compromise: development would still be the solution, rather than a radical transfer of wealth from north to south, but it would be a different *kind* of development.

Perhaps because it did not grow out of the environmental dialogue, sustainable development is concerned only with human welfare. Unlike environmentalism, it is not grounded in a recognition of the moral rights of other species. Nor, of course, does it recognize the other tenet of environmentalism, namely limits to growth (Carter, 2001). The environmental movement accepted this dilution of its original position as part of its evolution and deradicalization during the 1980s: "The environmentalists of the 1980s were less radical, more practical, and were much more policy-oriented" (Hajer, 1995: 93). Perhaps inevitably, as environmentalists gained influence and at least some access to negotiating tables they weakened their original political stance. Since business at the same time was coming to admit the need for improved environmental performance, sustainable development came to represent the compromise between the two camps.

As it had with the Stockholm Conference in the early 1970s, Canada made a significant contribution to the work of the Brundtland Commission. Maurice Strong was a member of the Commission, and another Canadian, Jim MacNeil, was Secretary General. Canada was one of only four countries that the Commission visited during its tenure. Even before the Commission reported, this country established a federal-provincial task force on environment and economy, with significant business and environmentalist participation. The task force reported in 1987, and its major recommendation — institutionalization of multistakeholder consultative policy development through the creation of advisory Round Tables on Environment and Economy — was quickly adopted by federal, provincial, and some municipal governments. The Mulroney government established a new think-tank, the Winnipeg-based International Institute for Sustainable Development, and placed sustainable development as the core goal of its 1990 Green Plan. But to what extent has this rhetorical dominance of the concept brought about changes in the actual practice of environmental regulators in Canada?

The term figured prominently in the 1993 Liberal election platform and, after it was elected, the Chrétien government added the words "sustainable development" to the title of the parliamentary environment committee, created the position of Commissioner of Environment and Sustainable Development, with a mandate to audit and annually report on federal environmental policy, and asked all government departments to prepare plans for achieving sustainable development within their sphere of operations (Toner, 2000). In the 2000 budget, the federal government allocated $100 million to a newly created Sustainable Development Technology Fund.

However, these actions, and similar ones taken at the provincial level, have not brought about any significant changes in environmental policy. Citizens and environmentalists have not been given any increased access to policy decision-making; indeed, the sustainable development Round Tables, before they were shut down, were "working far from the limelight" (Toner, 2000: 59). Nor has government organization changed in ways that can bring about a resolution of the problem of environment as a horizontal issue. The federal environment and resource departments still function in their silos, relying on traditional interdepartmental committees to coordinate their work with that of industry, trade, agriculture, and other departments (VanNijnatten and Macdonald, 2003).

The central goal of the 1987 federal-provincial task force — integration of environmental and economic decision-making — has not been achieved. The Chrétien government created a task force in 1994, which recommended changes in tax policy to remove perverse subsidies for unsustainable behaviour, but no action has resulted (Toner, 2000: 63). The concept of sustainable development has been incorporated into federal legislation, but only in a limited and largely symbolic manner (Winfield et al., 2002). Boyd (2003) notes that 24 federal departments, four corporations, and five provinces and territories had developed sustainable-development plans as of 2003, but they represent a "hodge-podge" with no coherent set of common priorities and with almost none making any reference to ecological limits and the finite nature of the environmental infrastructure that supports human life and economic activity (297-98). Adoption of the discourse of sustainable development has had virtually no impact on government regulatory actions in the realm of environmental policy, certainly in no way comparable to the funding increases and shift to enforcement-based law in the 1980s, or to the funding cuts and shift to voluntarism of the 1990s. That does not mean, however, that is has not been significant for the regulated industry. The new conceptualization, replacing "limits to growth" with "development," allowed business to move from being seen as part of the problem to part of the solution. Sustainable development offered business a cloak of legitimacy.

What part did business play in this redefinition of the problem and its solution? Although the precise extent to which business support, amongst other factors, accounts for the current dominance of the concept cannot be precisely delimited, it is possible to document the enthusiasm with which the Canadian business community, like that in other countries, endorsed the prescriptions of the 1987 Brundtland Commission report. Canadian business played a prominent role in the work of the National Task Force on

Environment and Economy. Inco vice-president Roy Aitken acted as co-chair, and Dow Chemical, the Canadian Petroleum Association, Alcan Aluminium, and the Canadian Chamber of Commerce were included in its membership. Canadian business played a major role at the 1992 UN Conference on Environment and Sustainable Development and assisted in the creation of the World Business Council on Sustainable Development. The term became prominent in the environmental mission statements that almost all firms began to develop at the time.

Business was already working to improve its environmental performance and to advertise that fact: the first two strategies for regaining legitimacy. Reframing the problem as a need for sustainable development allowed it to implement the third, changing not only the external image of its actions, but also the norms by which those actions were judged. Frankel (1998: 48-49) gives this description of the latter strategy:

> How could business feel good about its role, yet dodge the sustainable-development bullet [of cross-cutting societal change]? The solution that emerged over the years—and it emerged organically, not as a result of a specific conscious process—was to cut sustainable development down to a more manageable size. Third-era corporate environmentalism sent "sustainable development" through a semantic and conceptual sausage-grinder, whence it emerged as the more palatable "eco-efficiency."

A 1999 analysis of the World Business Council on Sustainable Development illustrates the point: "For WBCSD...eco-efficiency is a defining concept and one the organization spends considerable time and effort in refining and promoting" (Najam, 1999: 69). Najam quotes a 1996 statement by Livio DeSimone, CEO of 3M and in that year chairman of WBCSD: "Business... used to be viewed as a primary source of the world's environmental problems. Today, it is increasingly viewed as a vital contributor to solving those problems" (66).

Sustainable development was the grand compromise of environmental politics, comparable to the capital-labour compromise of the 1950s. It allowed business to come in from the cold.

RELATING TO ENVIRONMENTALISTS: HUGS AND SLAPP SUITS

By the early years of the 1990s, the political power of Canadian environmentalists was at its height. For a few brief years, they were exercising more direct influence on federal and provincial government policy than they ever had before, or have since. Not surprisingly, the regulated firms that hitherto had either ignored them or interacted with them only indirectly, through lobbying, marketing or consultative discussion intended to counter their influence, began to engage with them directly. That engagement took two forms, one benign and the other adversarial. Understanding the factors that led firms to either of those positions is necessarily part of our larger subject.

The benign response consisted of direct dialogue with environmentalists concerning the firm's environmental performance, separate from government-initiated policy discussions. As the 1990s wore on, a number of such "business-NGO partnerships" emerged in different parts of the world. In Canada, the most celebrated example was the creation of the New Directions Group. The Group has existed since 1990 as a loosely structured network of senior business managers and ENGO executive directors (New Directions Group, 2005). It had its origins in three-way discussions in the summer of 1990 amongst an academic, a business person, and an environmentalist, which then led to a day-long meeting attended by 24 representatives of the two camps, on December 1 of that year. Dow Chemical Canada and Noranda Forest Inc. were two of the companies involved from the outset.

Discussions continued and the group adopted "zero discharge" as the first substantive issue it would address. The term is used in the Great Lakes Water Quality Agreement and has, along with other terms such as "virtual elimination" and "sunsetting," been at the centre of the policy dialogue surrounding demands that certain chemicals be completely removed from the manufacturing process. Working together, the business and environmental representatives wrote and then released in September 1991 a short, direct document, *Reducing and Eliminating Toxic Substances: An Action Plan for Canada*, which does not differ markedly from the kinds of policy positions being advanced by the environmental movement at the time. It calls upon the federal government to do two things: establish a national inventory of toxic substance emissions and implement a program for both the "phase-out" of some substances and the "reduction of toxic emissions" of others (New Directions Group, 1991). Both were to be done through policy development by what was then the norm of multistakeholder group negotiations.

The federal government acted on both recommendations, establishing an emissions-reporting program and the ARET Challenge program. As discussed in the next chapter, however, the 1994 ARET program differed substantially from the vision of the 1991 joint Action Plan, since the former focussed only on emissions, not sunsetting, and relied purely upon voluntary action, with no legislative or fiscal incentives for firms to participate. Six firms co-authored the Action Plan: Nova Corporation of Alberta, E.B. Eddy Forest Products Ltd., Noranda Inc., Dominion Textiles Inc., The Bluewing Corporation, and Dow Chemical Canada Inc. (New Directions Group, 1991). The business actors involved with the development of the ARET program, by contrast, included broad-based associations, trade associations, and a wealth of regulated firms; business focussed on that program in a way it never has on the New Directions process. Furthermore, since the environmentalist, aboriginal, and labour groups all withdrew from the ARET process in September 1993 and Environment Canada played a passive role throughout (Environmental Policy Unit, Queen's University, 1996), it is perhaps not surprising that the hard-hitting substance of the 1991 Action Plan had been attenuated by the time it emerged as a government-industry program three years later.

The only other substantive document produced since that time by the New Directions Group was a set of criteria for the design of voluntary programs (New Directions Group, 1997). As discussed in the next chapter, such a document serves primarily to legitimize voluntarism as a policy instrument, and thus it is another contribution to the 1990s process of relaxing regulatory pressure on business. Just as the 1991 joint document could easily have been authored by environmentalists alone, so could the 1997 joint document have been authored solely by a body such as the Canadian Chemical Producers' Association. The contrast between the two documents highlights the reversal of political power that took place during that six-year interval. Since then, the New Directions Group has continued to exist, with funding from Suncor Energy, Alcan, Noranda, Dow Chemical Canada, and Inco (New Directions Group, 2005), but it has had no discernible impact on either government policy or firm environmental management.

SLAPP Suits

The term "strategic lawsuits against public participation" (SLAPP) was coined by two American lawyers who in the late 1970s first encountered the phenomenon of legal action taken by corporations against their critics (Pring and Canan, 1996). Pring and Canan define SLAPPs as lawsuits claiming damages caused by public comments made by individuals or organizations with respect to an issue of public debate. Such legal action has the effect of moving the policy debate from the policy forum into the courts, where the greater financial resources of the corporations filing the suits give them an advantage over their citizen critics. Pring and Canan state that the practice had its origins in the citizen activism of the 1960s but did not become common until the 1980s. They describe the situation in the US, as of 1996, in this way:

> Both individuals and groups are now being routinely sued in multimillion-dollar damage actions for such "all-American" political activities as circulating a petition, writing a letter to the editor, testifying at a public hearing, reporting violations of law, lobbying for legislation, peacefully demonstrating, or otherwise

attempting to influence government action. And even though the vast majority of such suits fail in court, they often succeed in the "real world" by silencing citizens and groups.... (1996: 1-2)

The first Canadian suit was launched in British Columbia in 1992 by MacMillan Bloedel, seeking damages from the Galiano Conservancy Association in connection with the Association's lobbying of local government against the firm's land-development plans. The Association was represented by the Sierra Legal Defence Fund, and the suit was dismissed after a year in court (Tollefson, 1994). Logging companies launched similar legal actions in connection with the Clayoquot Sound controversy during that same period. But the most visible case has been *Daishowa v. Friends of the Lubicon*. The Friends initiated a consumer boycott of the firm's paper products in 1991, after Alberta gave logging rights for land claimed by the Lubicon Cree and Daishowa responded with a lawsuit in 1995. The firm lost in an Ontario court, launched an appeal, but then abandoned the action in 2000 (Environmental Mining Council of British Columbia, 2005). It would appear that the tactic has been used most commonly by western forestry companies, as part of BC's rough-and-tumble logging politics, and has not been adopted by the resource and manufacturing industries examined here.

The same explanation seems to hold for another method used to reduce the political power of environmentalists: the creation of "astroturf" groups to give the appearance, like the plastic turf in sports stadiums, of public, grassroots support for a policy position favoured by business (Beder, 1997: 32-35). Yet the tactic of funding the creation of new citizen groups that will argue publicly with environmentalists seems to be limited to western forestry industries. There, the BC Forest Alliance was launched in April 1991, funded by 13 forest companies and relevant labour unions. The Alliance hired Burson-Marsteller Ltd. of New York to develop a media campaign on BC forestry regulation (Emery, 1991). There is no evidence that the tactic has been used by other sectors in other parts of the country.

SUMMARY

Political Interest Sought
In the cases of both acid-rain policy and the second round of regulations imposed on pulp-and-paper mill discharges to water, the policy objectives of the relevant firms did not extend beyond delaying or weakening the standards imposed. The soft-drink industry, on the other hand, began an active campaign in the early 1980s to change the environmental policy objective from container re-use to recycling. As discussed, this difference in objectives

can best be explained by the very different nature of the two regulatory threats. The first two industries were asked only to curb their pollution emissions, something they had been doing even before the advent of modern environmentalism and could continue to do at a relatively low cost. The demand that the soft-drink industry go back to using refillable bottles, on the other hand, was a threat to profitability several orders of magnitude larger. While its first policy response in the 1970s was a negotiated compromise (the agreement that only 25 per cent of the product would be sold in metal cans), it never complied with that agreement and soon afterward began actively working to change policy.

As well as this example of policy intervention, we also witnessed during this period the first clear signs of a search for environmental legitimacy. Few sectors were as candid as the chemical industry in admitting this objective, but others, as we have seen, such as pulp and paper, had come to share this interest. In particular, it would seem that this was the reason for business to participate actively in the process leading to the adoption of the paradigm of sustainable development.

Strategies Used to Achieve that Interest

Private negotiation with regulators continued to be the norm throughout the period, as witnessed by the ability of regulated firms to go over the head of the environment minister and successfully lobby the provincial premier for weaker standards in Ontario in 1985 and BC in 1990. Although firms actively participated in the new forum of multistakeholder consultation, they did not lose access to the private ear of environment ministers and their regulatory officials.

Far more important than multistakeholder consultation were the new strategies intended to regain environmental legitimacy. The chemical-industry trade association used two strategies to that end. First, it did what it could to bring about improvements in the environmental management of its member firms, to bring their behaviour more closely in line with the newly prevailing societal values. Second, it packaged and sold that behaviour by publicizing the Responsible Care program, spending considerable funds on paid advertising intended to change the *image* of the industry's environmental management. As we shall see, many other sectors followed the chemical industry's pioneering lead in the following decade, making significant improvements in their environmental performance, while at the same time using paid advertising in the hopes of receiving full public credit for that behaviour change.

The Responsible Care program was not, however, an attempt to use the third of the strategies for regaining legitimacy set out by Suchman (1995) and other organization theory analysts—changing the norms by which one's legitimacy is judged. The chemical industry became involved in such an effort a decade later, as it worked to kill still-born the emerging policy norm of sunsetting whole classes of chemical products. In the 1980s, however, it was accepting of the currently used benchmarks for measuring environmental behaviour, particularly with respect to accidental chemical spills. Nor did any other sector develop a specific policy initiative explicitly intended to regain legitimacy by this means. This was the strategy used by all sectors in more general terms, however, as they embraced the new paradigm of sustainable development.

As discussed, reframing the environmental problem and its solution by adoption of that paradigm represented the grand compromise between the two previously polarized worlds of business and environmentalism that took place in the late 1980s. As with any compromise, both sides gave ground. Business accepted the fact that environmental concerns were real, were here to stay, and had to be acted upon. Mainstream environmentalists, for their part, gave up the radical elements of their ideology, namely limits to growth and bioequity.

That may seem like an equal trade, but the associated benefits accruing to each side were far from equal. As we have seen, sustainable development has provided no benefits for environmental policy in terms of the specifics of standards, policy instruments, government resources or organization. The basic concept of integrating economic and environmental decision-making met its match in the 1990s with the problem of climate change, an overarching issue touching all elements of society and the economy and one which, unlike pollution, was debated in terms of its impact upon overall economic growth. Such an issue is tailor-made for the paradigm of sustainable development. That close fit, and the fact that the paradigm is subscribed to by all sectors—government, business, and environmentalists—would lead one to expect policy success. But we have found exactly the reverse: government action on climate policy in Canada has to date resulted only in policy failure.

Success in Achieving that Interest: Political Power

The political power of the regulated industries, relative to that of environmental regulators, declined significantly from 1970s levels during this period. Sectors such as smelting, pulp and paper, and various manufacturing industries were less successful in achieving their goal of delaying or weakening the imposition of new regulatory standards. Although they still had the power to influence those standards, which meant that in almost all cases new regulatory requirements imposed during the period were the result of compromises between firms and regulators, the fact remains that those standards *were*

131

imposed. The traditional brown-industry sectors were on the defensive. Other sectors, such as electronics and agriculture were for the first time being drawn into the regulatory ambit. Not only were the resource and manufacturing industries forced to accept new requirements for improved environmental performance, those and existing standards were being enforced with a degree of coerciveness never seen before. As set out above, prosecutions, convictions, and resulting fine levels all increased steadily, reaching a peak in roughly 1992. Business was dancing to a new tune.

The one exception to this trend in the history narrated above is the Ontario soft-drink industry. In that case, the policy intervention mounted by the industry, through contributing to the cost of curbside recycling, had resulted in a weakening of the refillable-container sales-portion standard — from 75 per cent in 1976 to 30 per cent in 1985. As discussed, this can best be explained by the existence of a highly motivated industry, a divided environment movement, and a lack of motivation on the part of regulators, in part stemming from the low salience of the issue.

The concluding analysis in Chapter Six discusses possible reasons for this decline in political power. Essentially, I argue that the growing political power and legitimacy of environmental organizations meant that politicians sensed a new electoral dynamic that resulted in increased resources and powers for environment departments. Imposing stiff fines on polluting firms, despite their contributions to one's political party, began to seem like good politics. As we shall see, however, there were limits to this new-found government willingness to act. Electoral advantages were never decisive. More important was the fact that just like business, governments could regain environmental legitimacy not only by changing their own behaviour in this way, but also by giving the *appearance* of meaningful action. In the 1990s, government funding cuts and a refusal even to consider effective policy instruments such as a carbon tax were masked by multistakeholder consultation and voluntary programs. We turn to that story in the next chapter.

CHAPTER FIVE

Relaxing Regulatory Pressure, 1993-2000

Although the events narrated here go up to the release of the Martin government's climate-change policy document in the spring of 2005 (Canada, 2005), the period between 2000 and 2005 is addressed only in terms of the business defeat in the very public battle fought over Kyoto ratification, coupled with its victory in the private negotiations with the federal government afterwards. This is because the term "relaxing regulatory pressure" can most properly be applied to the period beginning with ARET, the first major voluntary program, and the first reductions in environment-department budgets and ending with the Walkerton deaths from polluted water in May 2000. The Harris government, which along with that of Ralph Klein had spear-headed the drive to environmental deregulation, responded to the Walkerton event with stepped-up inspections and prosecutions, meeting a crisis in perceptions of its environmental legitimacy by falling back on the coercive policy instruments of the late 1980s. In the years since 2000, federal and provincial governments have restored some portion of environment-department budgets and gone some steps back toward active enforcement of environmental law. It is still too early to know, however, whether this marks a true turning point for environmental policy, comparable to those of the early 1980s or early 1990s. Accordingly, this chapter provides a comprehensive treatment only of events up to the end of the century, with climate policy after that date added as a coda.

This is done, as was the case in the two previous chapters, by first sketching the evolution of policy over the entire period. The business role in the turn to deregulation is then examined, which leads to the conclusion that while the regulated firms were happy to benefit from that policy reversal, it would be a mistake to attribute it primarily to the agency power they exercised by lobbying governments. The following section documents the continued effort of business to gain environmental legitimacy throughout the 1990s. Three stories are then told briefly: the apparent failure of two industrial sectors to pursue policy goals that would have contributed to their profitability, and the battles of CEPA in 1999 and Kyoto in 2002. The chapter concludes with summary analysis, which paves the way for the concluding analysis presented in Chapter Six.

POLICY EVOLUTION

The Rio conference of 1992 marked the apogee of the political power of the environmental movement, both in Canada and other countries. At the international level, governments had negotiated agreements on long-range transport of pollutants, the stratospheric ozone layer and, at Rio, on both biodiversity loss and climate change. The year before, in 1991, Canada and the US signed the Air Quality Agreement, after both countries had implemented domestic acid-rain programs, thereby promising to take further action on that issue and on other transboundary air issues, most notably smog. Within Canada, environmental law was being actively enforced, successful regulatory initiatives on issues such as acid rain, the ozone layer, and toxic substances from pulp-and-paper mills had been put in place, and the relative position of environment departments within their federal or provincial government enhanced by both increased budgets and the fact that they were now headed by ministers who had clout at the cabinet table.

As Canada moved toward the 1993 election, the governing Progressive Conservative Party, under Kim Campbell, prepared to defend a credible environmental record, while the Chrétien Liberals prepared a Red Book promising significant further advances. At the time, no one could have predicted that the years ahead, which seemed so full of promise, would in fact see a fundamental reversal of environmental policy — from a steady increase to a relaxation of the regulatory pressure on industry.

This was the most profound change of direction for environmental policy since the system of laws, government departments, and various mechanisms for inter-governmental coordination was first established in the late 1960s and early 1970s. Ever since then, environmental policy-making had moved steadily in one direction, toward *increases* in the level of environmental protection collectively provided by municipal, provincial, and federal governments. In the mid-1990s, however, beginning with the Ralph Klein government in Alberta and quickly followed by the federal government, Ontario, Quebec, and other provinces, that policy direction was reversed. The size of environment departments was reduced by anywhere from one-third to two-thirds; environmental laws and regulations were amended, reducing the standards of care they imposed upon regulated industries; and governments began to use the policy instrument of voluntary programs, rather than law, to achieve new environmental objectives. All of this added up to a reversal of the movement of environmental policy since the 1960s —

in the mid-1990s, Canadian governments began to *decrease* the level of environmental protection they provided.

Climate change dominated the policy agenda, just as acid rain had a decade earlier. The National Action Program on Climate Change was unveiled by the federal and provincial governments in 1995 and presented as evidence of Canadian action on the issue at the first meeting of UNFCCC parties in Berlin that year. The major policy initiative contained in the plan was the Voluntary Challenge and Registry (VCR), accompanied by ÉcoGESte, a comparable plan in Quebec that also relied on voluntary action. Canada committed to a new policy goal in 1997 at Kyoto and ratified that protocol to the 1992 agreement in 2002. The federal government stated at the time it would replace voluntarism with law as the principal climate-policy instrument, but as of 2006 that had not yet been done. Furthermore, the Martin government in 2005 reduced the total share of greenhouse gas emission reductions to be provided by large industry. A strong threat of regulation, however, was used in that year to convince the auto industry to agree to a "voluntary" 25-per cent reduction in carbon dioxide emissions from motor vehicles.

Other forms of pollution were addressed by the voluntary ARET program of 1994, and various efforts were made to implement a national program on nitrogen oxides and volatile organic compounds. In 2001, Canada and the US signed the "smog annex" to the 1991 transboundary air treaty, committing themselves to further action. The federal government took regulatory action in 1998 to reduce sulphur levels in gasoline, but at approximately the same time was forced to abandon its attempt to ban the additive MMT. In that same year, the two levels of government reached agreement on the Canada Wide Accord on Harmonization, an effort to improve policy coordination that was seen by environmentalists as a retreat by the federal government from the policy field it had moved back into in the late 1980s (Winfield, 2002). During this time, following the much-publicized Clayoquot conflict of the early 1990s, British Columbia moved to strengthen forestry regulation in that province. For the most part, however, the provinces were all engaged in varying degrees of deregulation and, with the exception of drinking water after 2000, took few new regulatory initiatives. Table 5.1 provides a summary listing of the major policy events in this period.

Twelve years after the Rio conference marked the high point of political power, American activists, faced with the undeniable fact of their impotence on the climate-change issue, began debating the "death of environmentalism" (Shellenberger and Nordhaus, 2004). Writing two years earlier, the analyst Jeremy Wilson offered this assessment of the political strength of Canadian environmentalists: "Despite all of its strengths and accomplishments, though, the movement has failed to bring about the kind of changes that most ecologists of the 1980s and early 1990s agreed were required by the end of the millennium" (2002: 62). We now turn to the question of how responsibility for the policy reversal of the 1990s can be allocated amongst lobbying pressure by business, environmentalism's loss of power, and the larger flow of ideas and government financing which were the context for environmental politics during that decade.

Table 5.1 Policy Evolution, 1993-2006

1993 NAFTA signed, Commission on Environmental Co-operation created
1994 voluntary ARET program
      Alberta Department of Environment budget cut by 30 per cent
1995 federal-provincial National Action Program on Climate Change, VCR
      Alberta establishes Regulatory Reform Task Force
      Ontario establishes Red Tape Commission
      Paul Martin deficit-reduction budget
1997 Kyoto Protocol negotiated
1998 federal and provincial environment department budget cuts, 30-65 per cent
1999 House of Commons approves amended CEPA
2000 federal-provincial climate-change Business Plan
      Canada and US negotiate smog annex to Air Quality Agreement
2002 House of Commons ratifies Kyoto Protocol
2005 reduction of total greenhouse gas emissions required by industry

THE BUSINESS ROLE IN DEREGULATION

This section examines the role of business in the variety of different policy developments of the 1990s which, taken together, add up to a lessening of regulatory pressure. This new deregulatory agenda had two major components: the drastic cuts made in environment-department staffing levels, which significantly decreased their ability to influence the environmental performance of regulated industries, and a conscious, publicly announced decision — particularly on the part of far-right governments such as Klein in Alberta and Harris in Ontario, but also in other governments such as the social-democratic Parti Québécois in Quebec — to make regulatory standards less onerous for industry and thereby contribute to economic growth. Two other policy initiatives further contributed to the lessening of regulatory pressure that took place in the 1990s. The first was the decision to supplement law-based regulation with voluntary programs, and the second was the attempt to improve coordination of federal and provincial policy, known as "harmonization."

Budget Cuts and Red-Tape Reviews

Boyd gives a concise summary of federal and provincial budget reductions throughout this period. The Environment Canada budget was reduced from $800 million in 1988 to a low of $550 million in 1998 — roughly a 30 per cent cut. The provinces cut deeper: Newfoundland and Quebec reduced their environment-department funding by 65 per cent between 1994 and 1998, Ontario by 43 per cent from 1995 to 1998, BC by 35 per cent from 1995 to 2000, and New Brunswick and Alberta by 30 per cent from 1994 to 1998 (Boyd, 2003: 239-40).

These environment-department cuts were part of the larger reductions in the size of government made during the 1990s. The rationale for spending reductions, enunciated most visibly by then-finance minister Paul Martin in connection with his 1995 budget, was the need to move away from the annual deficits that had become traditional since the 1970s, to return to the practice of balanced budgets and then to start to pay down what had become a massive accumulated debt. Janice MacKinnon (2003), finance minister for Saskatchewan from 1993 to 1997, presents an excellent picture of the financial crisis facing Saskatchewan and all other Canadian provinces as they found themselves hurtling toward the "debt wall." Because accumulated debt had become so high, interest payments were absorbing an increasingly greater portion of total spending, requiring more revenue, which could only come from tax increases or yet more borrowing. The limits to borrowing as a revenue source that are evoked by the phrase "debt wall" come from the fact that eventually credit-rating agencies would downgrade a government's rating, meaning that it could only borrow more at even higher interest rates. MacKinnon describes the gut-wrenching debates within her NDP government (similar to those in the Rae government in Ontario prior to its 1995 defeat) as MPPs raised in a left-wing tradition argued that the solution was not to cut spending, but instead to increase corporate taxes. For whatever reason, governments of all political stripes chose not to; all cut spending, rather than increase taxes.

The argument that government borrowing was not sustainable had been made by business actors such as the BCNI for years previously. It resonated with individual Canadians, perhaps because they equated government debt with the limits they knew they faced on their own borrowing ability. Very quickly, however, the rationale for spending cuts shifted from the somewhat abstract subject of deficit and debt to the new reality of tax cuts. In provinces such as Ontario, after 1995, spending had to be reduced because the Harris government had been elected on a platform of cutting taxes, which it proceeded immediately to implement. The result, even after draconian spending reductions, was that annual deficits continued far longer than would have been needed, had tax revenues remained constant. That fact was ignored, as was the problem of deficit and accumulating debt as the original rationale for spending reductions. Individual citizens had sympathized with that rationale, and did so even more in the case of tax cuts, re-electing the Harris government in 1999. This phenomenon of a right-wing government, from which one would expect fiscal prudence, cutting taxes, and ignoring the resulting debt increases has been displayed most visibly by the Reagan and George W. Bush administrations in the United States.

Leaving aside the question of whether such policies are a deliberate attempt by pro-market forces to gut the basic capacity of the state, we need here only point to the fact that spending reductions suffered by environment departments were significant, probably greater than those imposed on any other parts of government. Ultimately, the environmental movement simply did not have the political power to protect its client department when the going got tough.

Can either overall government downsizing or the disproportionate reductions suffered by environment departments be attributed to business pressure? Certainly the former can, since it had been publicly advocated by business leaders for years. Nor was business shy about first ruling out tax increases and then advocating tax reductions, pointing to the need to maintain a competitive position relative to the United States. No such public calls were made, however, for disproportionate spending cuts in environment. Whether such private messages were being given to governments must remain an open question in the absence of empirical data.

I would suggest, however, that more important than specific business lobbying, to the extent it did take place, was the overall reduction in the priority given to environment by governments in the mid-1990s. Jean Charest, environment minister under Brian Mulroney and later premier of Quebec, has noted that environment was less significant in the federal elections of 1993 and 1997 and the Quebec election of 1998 than it had been in previous elections (Corbeil, 2005). That loss of priority status was symbolized by the return to the practice of appointing newly elected MPs as ministers, something that had been standard in the 1970s. Sheila Copps and Ruth Grier were senior ministers in the Chrétien and Rae governments, but their successors, such as Christine Stewart and Brenda Elliott, simply did not have the political stature needed to protect their departmental budgets in the process of overall government reduction. Provincial governments gave more priority to health and education spending, in response to public attitudes, than to environment.

Voluntarism as a Policy Instrument

The term "voluntarism" is used here to refer to government initiatives intended to bring about improvements in the environmental performance of the firm, without putting in place either financial incentives or legally binding requirements. The term "voluntary" is somewhat misleading, since analysts agree that the effectiveness of such programs is directly related to the threat made by governments, implicitly or explicitly, to mandate such behaviour change if it is not "voluntarily" forthcoming (Gibson, 1999). For many years, confronted by new social problems such as violence on television, governments have called upon relevant societal actors to regulate their own activity before taking any other policy measures. As we have seen, when environment first came on the policy agenda, the threat of coercive regulation was so far-distant that voluntary behaviour change was an essential part of the policy effort. That initial regime was, however, based in law. Voluntary programs with no accompanying legal component did not become significant until the 1990s. (As discussed above, the 1982 voluntary agreement by the auto industry to meet US fuel-efficiency standards had been accompanied by passage of the federal *Motor Vehicle Fuel Consumption Standards Act*, although the law was never enacted. The same holds true for the 1976 Ontario soft-drink industry voluntary agreement.)

During the latter part of the 1980s, as it was being used with an increasingly heavy hand, the critiques of "command and control" law-based regulation had multiplied. For a brief period, the alternative market-based approach of economic instruments, including such things as pollution charges and tradeable permit systems, was in vogue. Economists and other analysts pointed to the superior economic efficiency of market instruments, since they give incentives for those with the lowest per-unit reduction cost to reduce the most, thus minimizing the overall cost of achieving a given pollution reduction goal. Writing at the beginning of the decade, Doern made the case this way.

> In the 1990s, market approaches must be utilized to a far greater extent as a complement to regulation. This is because market approaches—the use of tradable pollution permits, taxes and charges—can achieve environmental goals as well as, or better than, an exclusive reliance on traditional regulation but at less overall social cost. (1990: 1)

Governments studied economic instruments (Canada, 1992), but at the end of the day made little use of them. No Canadian government has put in place a true trading system, with a legally binding cap on total emissions. Taxes or charges have been used only in a few instances, such as the Ontario beer-can levy, discussed above, or some municipal garbage-bag pricing schemes. Howlett attributes this failure to the deficit-reduction climate of the 1990s:

In the case of market-based financial instruments, declines in government fiscal capacity and the political emphasis placed on fighting the deficit led to their quick demise. This was most readily apparent in the failure of numerous such proposals contained in the 1990 federal Green Plan to be seriously implemented. (Howlett, 2002: 35)

I suggest below that this decline in fiscal, and therefore regulatory, capacity led governments to endorse voluntarism (as does Howlett in the article cited above), but it is difficult to see why a lack of cash would induce governments to turn away from revenue-generating instruments. Calls to dedicate such revenues for environmental protection have always been resisted by finance departments, but it is difficult to believe they would object to unfettered cash flows from pollution taxes. It is more likely that governments were deterred by business resistance. Olewiler (1990) documented business distaste for environmental taxes: "firms vigorously oppose pollution taxes, which would make many of them worse off" (198). Motor-vehicle manufacturers, with the support of labour, successfully opposed a 1992 proposal that Ontario increase its tax on less fuel-efficient vehicles (Macdonald, 1996). A few years later, the European Union did not institute a proposed carbon-based tax as a climate-policy instrument because of industry resistance (Carter, 2001).

Although governments failed to implement economic instruments, despite studies showing their potential effectiveness, without doing any prior study they moved quickly to embrace voluntary approaches. The model followed was the 1991 US EPA 33/50 challenge program, intended "to induce firms to voluntarily reduce their emissions of 17 high priority toxic chemicals" (OECD, 2003: 44). The program goal, which gave it its name, was a 33-per cent emission reduction by 1992, followed by a 50-per cent reduction by 1995. In that same year, as discussed above, the environmentalist-corporate New Directions Group published the discussion paper that led to the development of the ARET program. Environment Canada convened a multi-stakeholder group to develop the program, but by 1993, when it had become apparent it would apply only to emissions, and not to chemical inputs, and would be voluntary, environmentalists refused to participate (VanNijnatten, 1999). With the concurrence of Environment Canada, the program was then initiated in 1994 as a "challenge program" comparable to 33/50, which invited firms to participate but gave no motivation, other than moral suasion, to do so. Also in the early 1990s, Environment Canada entered into a voluntary partnership with the food and beverage industry, referred to as the Canadian Industry Packaging Stewardship Initiative, in which commitments were made to reduce the quantity of packaging that ended up as solid waste

(Labatt, 1997). The department then went on to negotiate a series of voluntary agreements with automobile-assembly and parts-manufacturing firms (Environmental Commissioner of Ontario, 1996: 31).

During this period, provincial governments were also negotiating such voluntary agreements, which usually took the form of a codified, formal, written memorandum of understanding setting out, in more or less precise terms, the environmental management objectives to be achieved. Despite the existence of such a written agreement, firm participation is still very much voluntary, since no penalties for non-compliance are included in the agreement and the agreements do not have the same legal effect as a contract. They must be distinguished, accordingly, from the policy instrument of a "covenant," which does have the binding nature of a contract.

The provincial and federal governments together relied upon the challenge program model for the VCR/ÉcoGESte as the major component of the 1995 national climate program. Use of such a voluntary program had been recommended in June 1994 by the multistakeholder Climate Change Task Group and then, as mentioned above, was endorsed by the BCNI in a report released in July of that year:

> We believe that a voluntary industry program must form a cornerstone of Canada's national action plan on climate change.... A voluntary program offers flexibility to industry to develop lower cost options and explore the potential for innovative new technologies. We believe that it will be the most effective route to achieve both Canada's environmental and economic objectives. (BCNI, 1994: covering letter)

Why did governments adopt voluntarism as a policy instrument in the 1990s? More specifically, to what extent was this major evolution in environmental policy the result of lobbying pressure by the regulated industries? Analysts have advanced three explanations for the adoption of this new policy instrument: (1) governments came to recognize the limitations of law-based regulation and for that reason adopted what they believed would be a more efficient and effective instrument; (2) it was part of a larger trend in regulatory methods; and (3) they had little choice, since budget cuts precluded adoption of any new law-based programs. I discuss each of these briefly and then return to the fourth possible explanation, given above, namely lobbying pressure by business.

Webb (2004: 4-5) points to a number of the problems attendant upon command-and-control regulation, such as the cost of developing and enforcing standards, jurisdictional constraints, inadequate government funding, and adversarial relations with industry and then says that these explain the move to voluntarism: "In apparent recognition of these limitations, and of the potential value of other approaches, governments and scholars have begun in recent years to recognize the role of other techniques, including use of non-governmental voluntary code and standards approaches." Cohen (2004: 36) also points to the limitations of law to explain the turn to voluntarism: "Perhaps 20 years ago, many Western governments began realizing the model was breaking down. Law as a solution to social ills became increasingly expensive." He argues that economic instruments are similarly deficient because, like law, they require governments to set standards and pay the cost of implementing them: "economic instruments still required public bureaucracies to monitor and ultimately to enforce the standards" (36). This explains, he says, the fact that "Today we seeing a rapid evolution of regulation towards private rather than public institutions" (36).

To be credible as explanations for government motivation, such arguments need to be based in evidence of government studies of the inadequacies of law and economic instruments. That evidence, however, does not exist. Economic instruments were extensively studied by federal and provincial governments, as noted above, but no comparable studies were done on voluntarism. Another problem with this argument is the fact that law in fact clearly *was* an effective instrument. The significant improvements in firms' environmental management that took place in the late 1980s and early 1990s coincided with the increasingly stringent enforcement practices discussed above. A survey of firm motivations, done in 1996 by the accounting firm KPMG, found that environmental managers pointed to regulatory pressure as the most important factor influencing environmental performance (Boyd, 2003: 244). In the absence of data showing law to be ineffective or, regardless, that governments *believed* it to be ineffective, the explanation that governments were simply moving to a more effective instrument is not credible.

VanNijnatten and Boardman (2002: xii) suggest that governments moving to voluntarism were "propelled by mounting debts and encouraged by New Public Management advocates." The latter phrase refers to the concepts of "responsive" (Ayres and Braithwaite, 1992) or "smart" (Gunningham, 1998) regulation. The argument is that governments can increase the effectiveness of their limited regulatory resources if they apply them more selectively, using more resource-intensive coercive approaches where most needed, and less expensive self-regulatory approaches in other instances. That such thinking had permeated environment departments is illustrated by the 1996 Ontario Ministry of Environment discussion paper, which carried the former term into its title "Responsive Environmental Protection." Although the document has a heavy overlay of Harris government "cutting red tape" discourse, it does take increased regulatory effectiveness and efficiency as its central themes. It seems reasonable to conclude that this changing regulatory style was part of the explanation for this evolution of policy instruments (Wood, 2003; 2006).

Doern (2004: 68) argues, however, that the second factor cited above, "mounting debts," was the most important: "the severity of public sector budget and personnel cuts in the last decade is one of the key factors why voluntary codes and other types of 'reinvented regulation' are being advocated." A study done by the Environmental Commissioner of Ontario also lists "reduced government resources" as one factor motivating governments (1996: v). These explanations seem reasonable, given the budget cuts of the 1990s. The cost to Environment Canada of administering the ARET program from 1991 to 2000 was approximately two million dollars, far less than would have been the cost had the department used CEPA to impose legally binding standards (OECD, 2003: 30).

While changes in regulatory styles and funding cuts seem to be part of the explanation, business lobbying pressure must also be included. The 1996 study by the Ontario Environmental Commissioner pointed to that factor: "In addition, business interests have become increasingly vocal in the arguments that existing regulatory requirements in Canada impose non-productive costs on the affected firms, act as deterrents and barriers to innovation, investment, and job creation, and thereby undermine competitiveness" (v). Although the studied neutrality of the language means one must do some reading between the lines, ten Brink, writing primarily about European policy, gives a similar picture of the factors leading governments to voluntarism:

> Voluntary environmental agreements (VEAs) are increasingly being looked to as a possibly appropriate instrument to help address environmental problems covering a broad range of pollutants and natural resources. Interest has developed in the context of increasing concern in the 1990s that command-and-control legislation and regulation can be too burdensome and that the use of economic instruments, such as environmental taxes, can be too costly for industries in a rapidly globalising market. (2002: 14)

The terms "burdensome" and "costly" certainly suggest a business role in the move to voluntarism. He becomes more explicit, though when he refers, amongst other factors generating the shift, to "the more ideological interest of 'rolling back the state': in other words, reducing the amount of public administration" (14).

In the case of ARET, there is no doubt that voluntarism was used at the direct behest of industry. As discussed, the original proposal by industry and environmentalists was for a law-based program. After environmentalists left the task force developing the program, the final choice of instrument was made by the remaining group, consisting only of business representatives and Environment Canada officials. Without environmentalists in the room, business had the dominant voice and it spoke in favour of voluntarism. Similarly, BCNI publicly advocated the climate-change Voluntary Challenge before it was implemented. Other evidence of business lobbying for voluntary instruments comes from Dwivedi and his co-authors. On March 31, 2000, they examined 17 companies and nine trade associations listed on the Industry Canada Sustainable Development Strategy website. They found that various policy positions were espoused, but that they had one thing in common: "All these associations prefer a voluntary approach to changing current environmental practices" (Dwivedi, et al., 2001: 91).

Although it is clear that business was lobbying in favour of environmentalism, there simply are not enough available data to conclude that this was the primary factor influencing government actions. The most we can say with certainty is that it was one factor, along with changing norms respecting the role of the state, regulatory fashions, and reduced budgets. Nevertheless, unlike the overall reduction in size of governments and disproportionate reductions of environment departments, we do have here a clear indication of business agency power influencing, along with other factors, environmental policy.

Whatever was motivating governments, there is no doubt that voluntarism constituted a relaxation of regulatory pressure. Firms were under no requirement, financial or legal, to change their environmental behaviour, and many chose not to do so. Webb and Clarke (2004: 337), using EPA data, give this picture of participation in the original 33/50 program: "Over the life of the program, 7,500 companies were invited to participate, of which nearly 1,300 responded (13 per cent) with commitments and their facilities reported more than 60 per cent of the 1988 releases and transfers of 33/50 chemicals." They note that amongst the 500 largest, the participation rate was much higher, standing at 64 per cent. That close to two-thirds of the large firms responded and that those participants represented two-thirds of total targeted pollution certainly shows a new attitude on the part of American business. But the fact remains that one-third of the large firms did *not* participate. For them, there was no regulatory pressure at all.

Results of the Canadian ARET program are similar. Not all firms participated, a small number of the firms participating contributed the bulk of the reductions reported under the program, and it is far from certain that the existence of ARET was the factor that caused those reductions. A draft Environment Canada study of the program stated that "[o]ther factors such as regulations, modernization and business decisions were considered to be more important in the decisions made by industry about the management of toxic substances" (2000: 10). An OECD study (2003: 29-30) gave this finding:

> To what extent are the achievements a result of the program/agreement? Impossible to disentangle.... it is very difficult to say to what extent—if any—the voluntary approach contributed to environmental improvements beyond what would have taken place in any case.

That same study of the effectiveness of voluntary environmental programs in all OECD countries came to this conclusion:

> While the environmental targets of most—but not all—voluntary approaches seem to have been met, there are only a few cases where such approaches have been found to contribute to environmental improvements *significantly different* [emphasis in original] from what would have happened anyway. Hence, the environmental effectiveness of voluntary approaches is still questionable. (14)

Voluntary programs applied only to those firms that chose to participate, and even for those the program was not the major factor motivating improved performance. There is no disputing the fact that voluntarism was a relaxation, or perhaps more accurately a complete removal, of regulatory pressure. As Cohen points out, it is a move from reliance on public to reliance on private institutions for protecting ecological health. Such a move inevitably means that return on investment—private rather than public benefit—becomes the dominant criterion used in making environmental policy decisions. The point is nicely illustrated by the following story.

In the late 1990s, the Dow chemical plant in La Porte, Texas, conducted studies of potential "pollution prevention pays" changes in its manufacturing process. One opportunity to benefit both the environment and the firm's profitability was identified: changes to waste-stream processes would allow the closing of the firm's on-site hazardous waste incinerator. As Greer and Sels note, "The investment would pay for itself somewhere between 15 months and five years.... Estimated savings are $1 million a year" (1997: 422A). Nevertheless, the Dow plant did not proceed with the project. Why not? That decision was made because the funds necessary to make the engineering changes could generate a higher rate of return if used elsewhere:

> The project was considered for implementation twice by the urethane business group within Dow Chemical and was put off both times because other, more financially attractive business opportunities were given higher priority. Had EPA

required that Dow reduce these waste streams ... the rate of return of the project would have been irrelevant to Dow's decision making. However, because these were voluntary opportunities, they were considered in the same way as other business opportunities. To succeed, these opportunities had to do more than reduce waste and save money; they needed to be superior to other options for capital investment. (Greer and Sels, 1997: 422A)

One might argue that the problem here was an insufficiently green corporate culture. Had the internal values of managers in the urethane business group been different — or, perhaps, had the decision been left to those in the company who wrote Dow's green public-relations literature throughout the decade — the firm would have chosen the less attractive investment option, in order to provide the attendant environmental benefit to society. But even in that case there is another problem, in that a decision on pollution that affects society as a whole is being made privately, with no accountability and no voice given to that society. The move to the ineffective and unaccountable instrument of voluntarism in the 1990s, for whatever reason, constituted a major shifting of political power from regulators to firms. The basic dynamic of government dependence upon those who make private investment decisions was extended into the area of environmental protection.

The Harmonization Initiative

The Harmonization Accord signed by the federal and provincial governments in January 1998 constituted the third element in the pattern of deregulation, in that it signalled a retreat of the federal government from the environmental protection role it had first taken up under the Trudeau government in the late 1960s, discarded, and then begun to play again under Mulroney in the late 1980s. Inter-governmental negotiation of the Accord began in 1993, prompted primarily by provincial resistance to the renewed federal activity in what the provinces saw as their jurisdictional backyard (Harrison, 1999; Winfield, 2002). The Accord succeeded in restoring federal-provincial harmony, since it guarantees the federal government will not act unilaterally and will, in effect, defer to provincial policy-making in cases of conflict. Again we ask the question, what role did business play in bringing about this policy initiative?

Political scientists have studied the influence of the existence of two levels of government upon industry lobbying, suggesting that a federated state like Canada provides more opportunities for access to policy decision-makers than does a unitary state (Brooks and Stritch, 1991: 177-80). They have paid less attention, however, to the question of whether a given industrial sector would rather be regulated provincially or federally. The "race to the bottom" theory would suggest that industry prefers provincial regulation since that gives the opportunity to play off one province against another (Harrison 1996b). As discussed, however, environmental management costs are not a large enough portion of total firm costs to give a significant incentive to move to a pollution haven. It would seem that policy-makers are as likely to race to the top as to the bottom, as occurred with the new pulp-and-paper standards in the late 1980s, weakening the supposition that industry has in all instances a strong preference for provincial regulation (Olewiler, 2006).

The "crazy quilt" theory suggests industries that operate in a number of provinces, or countries, prefer not to be faced with a wide variety of standards and regulatory procedures and thus, one might expect, would prefer federal regulation, or at least a strong federal role in coordinating provincial efforts. Certainly the motor-vehicle industry has been willing to voluntarily comply with federal standards, provided they are harmonized with those in place in the United States. By the same token one would assume that business would prefer harmonization of standards amongst Canadian governments. Harrison (1999: 130) says this was the case: "regulated interests were fearful that overlapping regulatory authority would lead to delays and duplication." Winfield (2002: 127) gives a similar picture: "Representatives of business and industry were also supportive of the initiative, with the mining sector being particularly aggressive in its promotion of the harmonization of federal and provincial environmental assessments."

The one study that has been done of business participation in negotiation of the Accord, however, shows that such concerns were not the major preoccupation of firm officials. Based on a study of submissions made by both environmentalists and business during the process, Fafard (2000) found that the former had a very clear preference for federal regulation, combined with distrust of the ease with which business could influence provincial governments. No such clearly stated preference was found, however, in the opposing camp. He found that business called for reduced overlap and supported the harmonization objectives, but did not rule out a strong federal role. More interesting, jurisdiction was not the major item addressed by the business briefs, despite being their purported subject:

> However, considered overall, the submissions by firms and organizations representing business were not concerned, in the first instance, with federal and provincial roles. Rather, the message that repeatedly comes through is the need to simplify regulation, in some cases, deregulate, and allow for voluntary regulation and compliance. (Fafard, 2000: 92-93)

It seems fair to conclude that during the 1990s business was far more interested in which policy instrument regulators used than they were in the question of whether it was used by a federal or provincial official.

GREENING THE CORPORATE IMAGE

During this period, the search by the large, visible firms in Canada and other countries for an image of environmental legitimacy accelerated. The first of the three strategies set out above, changing one's own behaviour, proceeded apace. Although the primary motivation may have been increased regulatory pressure, the fact remains that sectors such as pulp and paper, chemicals, steel, smelting, and motor-vehicle manufacturing made significant progress in reducing the environmental impacts of their pollution. At the same time, the two other strategies came fully into play. Advertising intended to convey a particular image of the corporation itself, as opposed to one of its products, underwent a fundamental change. Where previously firms had wished to connote images of security, stability, and economic growth, they now began to present themselves as lovers of nature. The third strategy, working to redefine the environmental norms by which the firm is judged, was also fully pursued as the terminology of "sustainable development" came to appear in corporate mission statements, public reports, and advertisements.

Writing in 1992, Howlett and Raglon reported on a survey of 500 print advertisements that appeared between 1910 and 1990. They found that making connections between positive images of nature and the product being sold was an advertising method used throughout the period: "In 1910 the Burnham and Morril Company advertised canned codfish as 'fresh from the ocean to you' while Heinz Ketchup assured readers it was 'nature's best'" (62). They argue that because nature has throughout the twentieth century conveyed such positive images as "fresh" and "natural" it has always been used to sell products, but only when the values of environmentalism began to move into the realm of dominant social ideas did firms try to associate those images with that of the corporation itself:

> What the survey does reveal as 'new' in the 1990s is the desire of companies to create corporate images which are environmentally friendly or benign. This contrasts sharply with efforts to construct or manipulate public images of business from earlier decades which were more likely to associate business with the 'leading edge' of consumptive, nature-defying, modernity. (54)

Two examples illustrate their point. Marchand has documented the way in which corporate-image advertising of the 1880s and 1890s in the United States often focussed upon the physical manifestation of the firm—the factory complex within which the manufacturing process took place. Pillsbury, Jell-O, and the Bradley Fertilizer Company all proudly displayed paintings of their massive, modern buildings to project images of "size, stability, efficiency, or cleanliness" (Marchand, 1998: 29-30). Compare those with five corporate-image advertisements contained in the November 2005 issue of *The Atlantic*. There are no pictures of factories, smoke, or even, for the most part, human beings. Weyerhauser (9) gives us a watercolour of trees and water and assures us "we're making sure the forests we care for will be an endlessly renewable resource for the paper we produce"; bp: beyond petroleum provides only one graphic image, its new "helios" logo (discussed below) and text saying it is "reducing our footprint" and looking for "solutions to global warming" (21-23); Dow provides a picture of a woman gazing contentedly at steam rising from her mug of coffee and talks about ways in which it is "recovering waste heat...to produce additional power and steam" (39); Chevron provides graphics and text showing rising global energy demand, daily oil consumption, geological oil searches and what appear to be happy African children and tells us it is "committing over $100 million every year on renewable energies, alternative fuels and improving efficiency" (47); finally, Altria, the parent company of Kraft Foods and Philip Morris, like Weyerhauser, provides an image of green trees and tells us "in order for our companies to continue to be in business they need to strive to meet the expectations of Altria's shareholders, their consumers, regulators and society" (55). This historical comparison over a 100-year period shows that the two sets of firms are engaged in exactly the same activity: using graphics and text in advertisements to convince the reader that the corporation, above and beyond its products, is a legitimate member of society. What is different is that by the 1990s legitimacy flowed not from images of industrial production but from images of nature and, particularly for the oil companies, from the message that while they might be part of the problem, they are also a necessary part of the solution. What Greenpeace (1992) referred to as "Greenwash" and Welford (1997) as "highjacking environmentalism" was in full swing.

During the mid-1990s, by which time climate change had became established as the dominant environmental issue, two of the major transnational oil companies engaged in major efforts to transform their corporate image. British Petroleum and Royal Dutch/Shell were established in the early years of the twentieth century, based on oil discoveries in the Middle East and South-East Asia. Both diversified during the oil crises of the 1970s and then, twenty years later, along with all others in the oil and gas sector, became the object of a powerful environmental critique. Because of that lost legitimacy, and because after a series of mergers the company was looking for a new identity common to all parts of the corporate empire, BP in 2000 launched itself into a "re-branding initiative" (Miller and Muir, 2004: 197). Miller and Muir describe the firm's objective: "Firstly, and most significantly, BP wanted to redefine its role in society: to be a constructive, positive force — a new company in an old industry" (2004: 197). It attempted to do this by changing both its image — adopting the new name "bp: beyond petroleum" and changing its logo from the familiar shield to one that embodied nature itself: super-imposed white, yellow and green petals, giving an image of both the sun and a sunflower — and its behaviour. The latter consisted of "acknowledging the reality of climate change and the potential we hold to help resolve an issue of which we are part.... [and] Setting targets, and progressively reducing the emissions from our products and our operations...." (Miller and Muir, 2004: 198). As is often the case, the firm's CEO, Lord John Browne, was fully candid in admitting that this was done in a bid to regain legitimacy and that he equated legitimacy with survival: "BP's sustainability — its ability to continue to thrive and grow through times of great uncertainty, beyond anything we can predict — depends upon maintaining the confidence of a whole range of different groups" (quoted in Miller and Muir, 2004: 199).

Shell's effort to regain legitimacy was prompted by two events in 1995: the successful campaign by Greenpeace to prevent it from disposing of the *Brent Spar* oil-drilling rig by deep-sea disposal, and the controversy surrounding its operations in Nigeria and the execution of activist Ken Saro Wiwa. Firm managers believed there was a direct connection between these two legitimacy crises and financial performance:

> In 1995 the market value of the Royal Dutch/Shell Group of companies fluctuated dramatically as investors reacted negatively to the two crises. Shell's managers recognized that the company's business results depended heavily on Shell's reputation, not only with the investment community, but also with the general public, the media and even activists. (Fombrun and Rondova, 2000: 78)

Beginning in 1996, Shell began a major research effort, through surveys and focus groups, to determine the extent and nature of damage done to its legitimacy and to develop plans to restore it. One interesting finding was that both the 1995 events and the 1989 *Exxon Valdez* accident had had negative financial repercussions, not only for the two firms involved, but for the oil and gas sector as a whole (Fombrun and Rondova, 2000: 85). As discussed, this is exactly the same problem that Canadian chemical companies faced in the 1980s: a legitimacy problem that no one firm acting alone could solve. More research is needed to determine why this led to a collective-action response by the chemical industry, Responsible Care, but did not in the case of the oil and gas industry. There, we saw instead a splitting within the ranks, as firms such as BP and Shell worked to restore their environmental image, while others, such as Exxon, stayed the course (Rowlands, 2000).

Unlike BP, Shell did not change either its name or its logo, and it seemed to focus more upon internal communications and activities. It adopted a new statement of core purpose— "Helping People Build a Better World" — and launched an internal communications strategy to present this to employees (Fombrin and Rondova, 2000: 91). As Klein notes, "Shell has looked deep into its corporate psyche and has focus grouped and deconstructed itself into a pulp. It has put its employees through a kind of New Age-consultancy boot camp..." (2000: 386). It also, however, engaged in new external communications efforts, centred on its work in the areas of sustainable development and human rights. *Globe and Mail* business writer Eric Reguly gave these comments on the 1999 release of Shell's sustainable development guidelines:

> A $25-million media campaign will deliver the message to the world.... Over 42 glossy pages that appear to have been designed by Vogue magazine, the reader is told that, contrary to public opinion, Shell is run by a bunch of tree-caressing sweeties, veritable Mother Teresas of the biosphere.... (1999: B2)

He went on to discuss comparable use of the sustainable development image in other sectors:

> The concept of sustainable development is catching fire in other industries. Mining, forestry and natural gas companies talk about it now as if it were just another economic goal. Some companies have "SD" departments just like they have "HR" (human resources) or "IR" (investor relations) departments...." (B2)

DEFINING SUSTAINABLE DEVELOPMENT

As discussed above, shortly after the 1987 Brundtland Commission report, business in Canada and other countries embraced the concept of "sustainable development" and began to use the term in mission statements and environmental-protection policies. As we saw, there was a tendency from the outset to define the concept as being synonymous with the pre-existing value of efficiency. Business firms had always worked to reduce waste and had no difficulty coming to refer to that practice as "eco-efficiency." The International Chamber of Commerce (ICC) Business Charter for Sustainable Development, adopted in 1991, clearly set forth what by then had become the two basic messages in the business discourse on sustainable development: the need to integrate economic and environmental decision-making; and the argument that business financial resources and technical and managerial expertise were not a cause of the problem, but instead an essential part of its solution (Macdonald, 2002).

In February 1997, I undertook a small survey to determine how the Canadian signatories to the ICC Business Charter were defining the ambiguous term "sustainable development" in their published literature. That group was chosen on the assumption it represented those Canadian business actors most actively engaged with greening their operations and therefore the ones that had given the greatest thought to how they would define the term with respect to their own operations. Letters were sent to the 46 firms and trade associations that had formally subscribed to the Charter, using a list supplied by the Canadian Council for International Business, asking for readily available, published literature describing current activities with respect to sustainable development. Twenty-five replies were received, as shown in Table 5.2.

Table 5.2 Firms Surveyed, 1997

1) resource and manufacturing, 18: Alcan, Alliance of Manufacturers and Exporters (now the CMEA), Bata Shoes, CCPA, Dofasco, Homestake Mining, Inco, John Deere, the Mining Association of Canada, Noranda Forest, Norcen, Nortel, Ontario Hydro (now Ontario Power Generation), Rio Algom, Stanley Tools, Stelco, Syncrude, Xerox;

2) financial, 5: Bank of Nova Scotia, Canadian Bankers Association, CIBC, Royal Bank, Sedgewick Insurance;

3) other, 2: Orser Consulting (a one-person firm offering environmental management expertise), Southam Press.

Of those companies that replied, fourteen used and at least implicitly defined the term "sustainable development." Another seven did not use the term but had developed an explicitly stated environmental policy, while materials supplied by the remaining four made no mention of either sustainable development or environmental protection. Apparently for that group the fact of signing the Business Charter had not yet resulted in any further action. Some members of the other two groups, on the other hand, provided very impressive pictures of actions taken or being planned to reduce solid wastes, various forms of hazardous waste, energy use or paper purchased. These were presented in terms of specific quantities or percentages, rather than generalities, and showed results already achieved, rather than simply providing promises for future action.

Only one respondent, Ontario Hydro, had defined sustainable development as including an element of social equity (the third leg of the economy-environment-equity stool often used in definitions of sustainable development). Most made reference to the Brundtland dictum of "meeting the needs of future generations," thus including the concept of intergenerational equity. While noting this ethical obligation to future generations of humans, none referred to an ethical obligation to other, non-human species. After this, the most common theme was the integration of environment and economy. The Alliance of Manufacturers and Exporters (1997) said it was working for "enhanced environmental performance to secure a safe and healthy environment and a sound and prosperous economy." The term "balance" was used often: "At Scotiabank we believe the quality of all our lives improves when economic growth is balanced by respect for the environment" (Bank of Nova Scotia, 1997). The Inco (1997) policy stated that "Inco is committed to the concept of sustainable development, which requires balancing the need for economic growth with good stewardship in the protection of human health and the natural environment."

The third most commonly mentioned theme was the "business case" for environmental protection. Usually this meant cost savings through reduced waste or energy use, but it also included such things as innovation to meet future market needs and satisfying green consumer demand. Other themes included full-cost accounting, community responsibility, pre-evaluation of capital spending in terms of environmental impacts, and philanthropy.

In summary, then, we can say that this handful of business actors made two major statements in these public accounts of their environmental management practices. The first is an undeniable commitment, in a number of cases backed up with specific documentation, to reducing the pollution impacts of their operations. The second is the conviction that the goals of environmental protection are fully compatible with, and include, economic growth. Both behaviour change and participation in the reframing of environmental norms associated with the concept of sustainable development were being used as sources of legitimacy.

FAILURE TO TAKE POLITICAL ACTION ON APPARENT SELF-INTEREST

While the 1980s witnessed for the first time firms and sectors sacrificing some degree of their profit interest in an attempt to achieve their second fundamental interest, legitimacy, in the 1990s a new phenomenon appeared: two sectors which apparently sacrificed profit with no attendant legitimacy gains. Each failed to take political action to press governments for environmental policy that appeared, to an outside observer, to contribute directly to their profitability. The first of these, the insurance industry, was exposed throughout the decade to increasing costs as a result of severe-weather events and yet did not lobby for climate change policy. The second was the new-born environmental industry, which has not publicly lobbied for more stringent regulation, even though such policy would increase the market for its goods and services. The cases are significant for environmental politics, since had these industries entered the green political arena, a further fragmentation would have appeared in the business community, and new counter-vailing forces, implicitly or explicitly allied with environmentalists, would have been directed toward environmental policy. Why did they fail to act? In neither case was it a question of trading profit for legitimacy, since in neither case was the environmental reputation of the sector at stake. Nor can a full explanation be found in a corporate culture that instinctively allied itself with other business interests, rather than tree-hugging environmentalists, although that likely is a factor. Instead, we find that each sector *did* in fact take political action, or inaction, in line with its profitability interest.

In 1999, an Insurance Bureau of Canada official noted that costs borne by the sector for weather-related losses were increasing sharply (Brieger, Fleck and Macdonald, 2001: 111), the same point the large European re-insurers, such as Swiss Re and Munich Re, had been making for some time. Hoping to draw both insurers and the renewable energy industry into an alliance against the oil industry, the UK arm of Greenpeace had invited both sectors to a conference immediately prior to the first UNFCCC meeting in 1995. UNEP took similar action, working with Swiss Re and others to establish a forum for discussion of global climate change. Some insurance firms then participated in the Kyoto negotiations. The sector has never become a significant voice in the global negotiations, however, speaking against that of the oil industry (Jagers, Paterson and Stripple, 2005).

Within Canada, the sector was never directly courted by environmentalists, but it did turn its mind to the political issue of greenhouse-gas reductions. In September 1997, while Canada was debating the position it would carry into the Kyoto negotiations in December of that year, Insurance Bureau representatives gave two private briefings, the first to the federal and provincial environment and energy ministers and the second to Liberal MPs (Brieger, Fleck and Macdonald, 2001: 121). In May 1998, the annual Canadian Insurance Congress included a debate on whether the sector should begin to lobby Ottawa for increased action to reduce greenhouse-gas emissions. No decision was made at the meeting and the industry then declined to participate in the climate policy multistakeholder consultations which began that year (Brieger, Fleck and Macdonald, 2001: 121). Nor has it publicly lobbied for emission reductions since.

This does not mean, however, that the sector has been politically inactive. In 1999 it publicly released its plan for increased government action, requiring several hundred million dollars of new spending, to improve the ability of Canadian communities to withstand damage from flooding, strong winds, and other severe-weather impacts. The Insurance Bureau then lobbied governments through presentations to both Senate and House committees in 1999 and 2000 (Brieger, Fleck and Macdonald, 2001: 122). Rather than lobbying for policy to reduce emissions, it has lobbied for policy to increase adaptive capacity. Why?

Interviews reveal that insurance officials did have some qualms about allying themselves with "fringe and radical" environmentalists (Brieger, Fleck and Macdonald, 2001: 123). More important, however, according to those representatives, was the fact that adaptive policy, such as building new flood-drainage systems, would provide direct, immediate financial benefits to insurers, while reduction policy was associated with uncertain science, long time periods, and the fact that Canadian action, by itself, can make little difference to the global problem and therefore the storm-weather damage suffered in this country. Furthermore, it was pointed out, while severe-weather losses had been rising, they still represented a relatively small portion of total financial activity for the sector, in comparison to such things as auto-accident losses (Brieger, Fleck and Macdonald, 2001: 122-23). In the absence of legitimacy concerns, the industry has pursued a political objective that flows directly from its economic interest, in exactly the same way as did the resource and manufacturing sectors when first confronted by environmental regulation in the 1970s.

The same explanation applies to the political inaction of the environmental industry. That sector, made up of firms which sell waste-management and pollution-control goods and services, traces its origins to the onset of environmental policy in the 1960s and ever since has been dependent upon government action to motivate the customers to whom it sells. In fact, according to OCETA, "The environment industry has been characterized as being regulation-driven" (1997: 4). The national trade association, the Canadian Environmental Industry Association (CEIA), was created in 1988, with branches established in most provinces at the same time. The Vancouver annual Global Trade Show was initiated in 1990. Both Industry Canada and Environment Canada were actively working to foster the industry in the early 1990s, as was the Ontario Ministry of Environment within that province. Alberta, Saskatchewan, Manitoba, Quebec, and Nova Scotia have also worked to assist with the development of the sector (Stewart, 1999). CEIA opened its Ottawa office in 1993, with funding supplied by Industry Canada (Redhead, 1998). In 1995, the Canadian industry had annual revenues estimated to be approximately $15.5 billion (OCETA, 1997: 4).

Despite the direct link between government regulation and profitability, the sector has been noticeably absent from the policy dialogue since it came into being. The Ontario Association went through an internal controversy during the late 1990s CEPA review, as some member firms objected to what they saw as public statements being made by the Association which came too close to environmental activism (Redhead, 1998).

Only once, to my knowledge, has there been a news media report of lobbying activity on the part of the environmental industry. In February 2000, the CEIA met with officials in the Prime Minister's and Environment Minister's offices, to argue that Canadian regulatory standards governing treatment and disposal of hazardous wastes imported from the US were too lax. "But while environmental groups have long argued that Canada has become a magnet for US hazardous waste, the association's call is one of the few times an influential industry lobby group has made the same complaint publicly" (Mittelstaedt, 2000). The CEIA did not advocate closing the border to waste imports, but instead putting in place "technical solutions" which presumably would, although the trade association did not mention this, be mandated by regulation (Mittelstaedt, 2000).

Although more research is needed to verify this, it seems likely that the sector does not publicly lobby for regulation because to do so would alienate customers and for that reason would be counter-productive. Like the insurance industry, a shared business culture may play some role, but direct economic interest is likely more significant.

THE CHEMICAL INDUSTRY WARDS OFF SUNSETTING

Although by the mid-1990s voluntarism had become established as an instrument used by cash-strapped environment departments, the next policy development threatening the profitability of an industrial sector was the potential use of law — specifically, the review and amendment of the *Canadian Environmental Protection Act*, initiated in 1994. As described in Chapter One, the major problem this posed for the chemical industry was the fact that since Responsible Care was first developed a decade earlier, environmentalists and some government agencies had begun to explore the complete removal of some classes of chemicals from the production process.

Unlike the original calls for chemical pollution control, which came first from a social movement and were then given specific form by government regulators, the concept of complete elimination of some chemicals from the production process originated with environmental professionals. It was one of a series of concepts and principles that were being actively debated by the late 1980s. The proliferation of names leads to confusion. The original term used, dating back to the 1970s, was "pollution prevention," which referred to changes in product design or manufacturing processes so that fewer toxic inputs were required. This was contrasted with "end of pipe" pollution control, which referred to treatment of hazardous wastes to reduce toxicity and improved methods of disposal. A current term, comparable to pollution prevention, is "eco-efficiency," an approach that has been endorsed by business organizations such as the WBCSD.

Writing in 1993, Hirschorn, Jackson and Bass gave this list of terms: "A multitude of terms and phrases define and describe the emerging preventive environmental paradigm. These terms include pollution prevention, source reduction, waste reduction, waste minimization, toxics-use reduction, and clean or cleaner technology" (1993: 125). They go on to define the "preventive" approach represented by all these terms as a reduction in pollution emissions by "measures which attempt either to close material cycles inside the [manufacturing] process or else substitute hazardous materials used in the process with less hazardous materials" (131). Both Environment Canada and the Ontario Ministry of Environment have initiated programs to assist industries wishing to voluntarily move in this direction.

This approach is similar to calls by environmentalists for chemical "bans" or "sunsetting," in that both refer to manufacturing inputs, rather than pollution emissions. They differ, however, in that a chemical ban is aimed at complete elimination, rather than reduction, and calls upon governments to use law to that end, rather than relying upon voluntarism. In Canada and the United States, this demand stemmed originally from the goals of "zero discharge" and "virtual elimination" of persistent, bio-accumulative toxic substances which were set out in the Canada-US Great Lakes Water Quality Agreement (GLWQA), originally signed in 1972 and since amended.

In the United States, in the late 1980s, Greenpeace and other environmental groups launched an advocacy campaign calling for the elimination of chlorine, both in manufacturing uses and as a drinking-water disinfectant. The US chemical industry responded by creating a new lobbying organization, the Chlorine Chemistry Council, described by Fagin and Lavelle (1999: 235) as "a new outfit that chemical manufacturers had assembled to protect yet another product." When the EPA began considering placing limits on the amount of chlorine in drinking water, the Council sent a mailing to 4,000 water providers, members of the American Water Works Association, asking them to lobby against the EPA proposal (Fagin and Lavelle, 1999: 236).

In this country, Greenpeace and other environmental non-profit organizations were making similar demands of the federal government, as described in a June 1994 report on the issue prepared by Jay Palter, a Greenpeace staffer:

In February, seven organizations (Greenpeace, Pollution Probe, Great Lakes United, Sierra Club, CELA, CIELAP, and Société pour Vaincre la Pollution) wrote environment minister Sheila Copps demanding that Canada develop a national strategy for eliminating chlorinated and other persistent toxic substances. To date, Copps and the federal government have failed to respond adequately to this demand. The thrust of their response has been proposals to develop timetables for the phaseout of a mere 13 toxins, although no details have been provided. (1994: 2)

What is more likely to have caught the attention of the chemical industry, however, was the fact that the concept of chemical bans was being advanced by those outside the environmental movement.

One of those voices was that of the International Joint Commission (IJC), the bilateral organization funded and managed by Canada and the US which, among other things, was charged with the task of reporting publicly every two years on the implementation of the 1978 GLWQA by the two countries. In its 1986 report, it suggested that some chemicals may have to be "prohibited or replaced at their source if their intrusion into the environment cannot otherwise be prevented" (IJC, 1986: 31). In 1992 it recommended that a number of specific substances, such as PCBs, DDT, dieldrin, toxaphrene, and mirex, be sunsetted, and it then went on to discuss problems associated with the class of substances associated with use of chlorine: "We know that when chlorine is used as a feedstock in a manufacturing process, one cannot necessarily predict or control which chlorinated organics will result, and in what quantity. Accordingly, the Commission concludes that the use of chlorine and its compounds should be avoided in the manufacturing process" (IJC, 1992: 29). The IJC specifically recommended that governments in Canada and the United States work with industry to "develop timetables to sunset the use of chlorine and chlorine-containing compounds as industrial feedstocks" (IJC, 1992: 30).

Worse yet, from the industry perspective, the Conference Board of Canada, a reputable body generally seen as supportive of business interests, was also raising the issue. In a 1993 report, the Board stated the following:

Most stakeholders in the chemical industry, including business and environmental groups, agree that certain chemicals have proved harmful and they should now be 'sunsetted', or discontinued. There is no formal mechanism now in place to address this issue, and many competing notions of risk assessment and risk management are certain to be addressed. (St-Pierre, 1993: 6)

As mentioned above, the policy dialogue on chemical bans centred on the *Canadian Environmental Protection Act*, which when it was enacted in 1988 included a requirement that it be periodically reviewed and if necessary updated and amended. That process began in 1994, when the Act was referred to Charles Caccia's Standing Committee on Environment and Sustainable Development, which then began a series of public hearings. Canadian environmentalists, working through the Toxics Caucus of the Canadian Environmental Network, submitted a brief in September 1994, recommending the renewed CEPA be used to sunset chemicals. It called for a Sunset Chemical Protocol, which would be used to "phase-out all persistent, bioaccumulative and toxic substances" (Muldoon, 1994).

Caccia had briefly served as environment minister in 1983-84, in the final years of the Trudeau government, and had used his parliamentary seat since that time to add a powerful voice in support of environmental protection. A long-time Chrétien supporter (which cost him his seat when he was ousted by the Martin forces in the Liberal party prior to the 2004 election), he had been appointed chair of the House committee when the Chrétien administration took power in 1993. Two years later, he stayed true to his principles. After public hearings and study of the operation of CEPA since 1988, his committee reported to the House of Commons in June 1995, setting out recommended amendments to the legislation. The news release summarizing that report gave pride of place to these two:

- ban or sunset all persistent, bioaccumulative and inherently toxic substances unless proponent can demonstrate extraordinary reasons
- substances banned or sunsetted by a province or OECD nation would be considered to automatically have that status in Canada as well. (Standing Committee on Environment and Sustainable Development, 1995)

Thus, during the previous decade, calls for regulatory action to ban classes of chemicals had migrated from technicians to the environmental movement, from there to an international governmental body, and thence to a parliamentary committee controlled by a voting majority of Liberal government members. That same government would be deciding on implementation of its committee's recommendation in the near future. The regulatory threat to the chemical industry was far more specific and coming from far more powerful actors than anything seen during the years leading up to the 1986 announcement of the Responsible Care program. Furthermore, like regulation of soft-drink containers, it was a threat to a *product*, rather than to pollution generated during the manufacture of a product. It is fair to say that the Standing Committee recommendation of June 1995 to amend CEPA in order to ban any class of chemicals that had been subjected to a regulatory ban in any OECD nation was the most significant regulatory threat to chemical-industry profitability yet seen. As discussed below, the difference in the severity of the regulatory threat is the most likely explanation for the difference in the industry response. This time, the industry did not spend any time or money developing new voluntary programs or hiring advertising companies to show its benign face to the Canadian public. Instead, it worked in secret, in the back rooms of Ottawa, and devoted its financial resources to hiring paid lobbyists.

The industry trade association was, naturally enough, intimately involved at each stage of the CEPA review from 1994 to 1999. A review of the public submissions it made during that period reveals two major themes. The first was the argument that voluntarism should be the major instrument used by the federal government, with legal instruments such as CEPA to be held in reserve, only to be used if needed. By their repeated references to them, it seems clear the industry was attempting to gain political advantage from the original creation of the Responsible Care program and the subsequent move by the federal government to voluntary programs such as ARET.

The first submission made by the CCPA to the Standing Committee started, as is the norm with industry arguments on environment, by pointing to the economic importance of the chemical industry—the third-largest sector, with annual revenues of $22 billion, employing 31,000 people (CCPA, 1994). Laudatory reference was then made to Responsible Care. The brief then quarrelled with the Porter hypothesis that tough, law-based standards lead to innovation and therefore competitiveness, saying this was "simplistic, not supported by empirical analysis" (CCPA, 1994: 6). Reference was then made to ARET and other federal government voluntary programs, as well as the fact that voluntarism was also coming to be accepted by provincial environment departments, to support the argument that voluntarism should be the first instrument used by governments to manage chemical risks. The brief then recommended adding to the CEPA preamble a statement that environmental protection and economic development are best achieved by a mix of regulatory and non-regulatory instruments and recommended adding a section to the legislation clarifying that regulations would not constrain any voluntary approaches.

The other theme, which came to the fore in briefs submitted after the Standing Committee report of June 1995, was to warn the government of the calamitous consequences that would follow adoption of the chemical bans recommendation. In a letter to the Minister of Natural Resources, dated July 19, 1995, the CCPA called the Committee report "badly flawed" and said, "Taken together the recommendations in the Report would mean that most of the substances used in commerce in Canada today would need to be phased-out; which clearly does not make sense" (CCPA, 1995). It was further argued, in this and other briefs which followed over the next four years, that bans were not based in valid science, that automatically banning a substance banned elsewhere took policy control of chemicals out of Canadian government hands, and that bans were a reversal of existing government policy.

One tactic used by the CCPA to influence the decisions that eventually would be made by the Chrétien government was to work closely with their champions within government, in particular Industry Canada and Natural Resources Canada. On October 16, 1995, the *Globe and Mail* reported on leaked confidential documents stating that the Deputy Minister of Industry Canada was "very concerned" about the economic impact of the CEPA amendments proposed by the Caccia committee, and quoted both departments as saying that voluntary programs "are often effective at a much lower cost than compulsory programs" (Matas, 1995).

The lobbying battle between environmentalists and an array of trade associations went on for four years. In December 1995, the ministers of environment and health tabled their response to the Standing Committee report. The CCPA found that much more to its liking, saying that it reduced "the significant concerns raised in the business community (and their potential for negative impact on investment) that resulted from the tone, excesses and impractical recommendations that were part of the Parliamentary Committee Report" (CCPA, 1996: 4). After more consultations, a revised Act was introduced in the House in December 1996. By 1997, the chemical industry had joined forces with the Mining Association and other sectors to present a common business front. A letter sent by eleven trade associations to the Chrétien government in January of that year pulled out the same argument that had been made continually over the past thirty years: "we account for millions of jobs in communities across Canada" — and, therefore, they might add, their concerns must be addressed (Macdonald, 2002: 80).

That bill, too, died on the order paper when the 1997 election was called and the government then re-introduced another revised version of the Act in March 1998. Generally speaking, the CCPA was in favour of that bill (CCPA, 1998). The bill, however, was then referred to Caccia's Standing Committee. Knowing what would happen now that Caccia again had his hands on the draft legislation, the industry mounted a major lobbying campaign in the winter of 1998-99 to prevent the House of Commons from adopting the recommendations of the Standing Committee. The CEPA Review Industry Group was the name given to the coalition of sectors lobbying in the spring of 1999. Letters and meetings were used to make the industry group's arguments to virtually all MPs. As noted in Chapter One, that political campaign was successful. At the end of the day, the government in the House of Commons voted down the recommendations made by its own Standing Committee.

CODA: THE OIL AND GAS INDUSTRY FAILS TO PREVENT KYOTO RATIFICATION

In 1851, the first oil company in North America was established and, seven years later, the Canadian Oil Company began extracting oil from under-ground reserves at Petrolia, Ontario. In 1908, gas production began near Calgary, while Imperial Oil opened the first Canadian gas station, to serve the emerging motor-vehicle market, in Vancouver. The first industry trade association, the Oil Operators' Association of Alberta, was created in 1926, and a decade later the first Texas-scale oil well in that province began opera-tions in the Turner Valley. The Alberta industry was immediately faced with the same collective-action problem faced by fisheries and all other common-pool resource industries — firms pursuing individual self-interest, with no means of coordinating their actions in an enforceable manner, were pumping out too much oil, too quickly, glutting the market and driving down prices. To solve their problem they turned to the state, and on February 26, 1938, the Alberta Petroleum and Natural Gas Conservation Board came into being with a mandate to regulate oil and natural gas extraction to maximize effi-ciency (Richards and Pratt, 1979).

Although they had come into being as provinces at the beginning of the century, it was only in 1930 that full authority over natural resources was transferred from the federal government to Alberta and Saskatchewan. Neither province felt it possessed the capital or expertise to develop its fossil-fuel resources itself, through a mechanism such as a Crown corporation, and so instead both did what they could to attract industry capital investment. In 1947, when Imperial Oil established the Leduc oil well, the Alberta govern-ment's dependence upon the oil industry, which has existed unchanged to the present day, came into being. Subsequently, the federal government estab-lished its own regulatory body, the National Energy Board, and thereby added the other element to the oil sector's business-government dynamic — an alliance between the industry and Alberta, as both engaged in a political battle with their common enemy, Ottawa. Such a dynamic also exists in the area of climate-change policy.

Because oil has been the dominant energy source over the past century, fuelling not only economic development but also the world's navies, armies, and air forces, the industrial sector has always been a subject of intense inter-est to governments (Roberts, 2004). Not surprisingly, the industry has a much more extensive history of political activity than do the other sectors examined here. Berry (1974) cites Hartschorn, who in 1962 described the basic political problems facing the industry, wherever on the globe it is situated: governments always want a portion of the revenues generated; the product is considered essential, which means in times of emergency, governments will always be willing to regulate it; it consistently faces calls for conservation of the resource, which would entail lost revenue; and it suffers from a lack of public trust and legitimacy. All of those themes are consistently present in Canadian oil politics.

Industry activity is divided between the "upstream" functions of oil and gas extraction and the "downstream" function of petroleum refining to make gasoline, chemicals, and other products. As discussed, regulation of gasoline product design has seen its share of political conflicts. Political action on climate-change policy, however, seems to be the domain of firms in the Canadian upstream industry, and their trade association, which, after a number of transformations, has been since 1992 the Canadian Association of Petroleum Producers (CAPP), headquartered in Calgary. CAPP lobbying efforts are supported by subsidiary industries, such as drilling-well contractors, which have similar market interests. As is the norm in all sectors, large firms such as Imperial both contribute financially to support political activity by CAPP and themselves carry out their own inside and outside lobbying (Berry, 1974).

The industry suffered its first significant regulatory threat from Ottawa in 1973, when the OPEC oil crisis drove up world prices and was seen to threaten Canadian supplies. The Trudeau government began to take policy action on both fronts, moving to regulate exports and prices charged by the Canadian industry and, like Alberta and Saskatchewan, also to tax away some portion of the industry's increased revenues. Berry (1974) has analyzed the political response of the industry. It worked in tandem with Alberta, but had no support from provinces like Ontario. With the exception of the Canadian Chamber of Commerce, most business interests, concerned about their rising energy costs, did not support the industry's position that prices should rise to world levels, without government interference. The industry carried out an advertising program to elicit public support, with the argument that what is good for the industry is good for individual Canadians, and threatened to cut back investment in exploration for new Canadian sources. It was unable, however, to prevent the imposition of a price freeze by the federal government in April 1974. Berry concludes that the industry lost the battle.

A similar battle, fought largely over the same basic issue of division of revenues was occasioned by the Trudeau government's National Energy Program (NEP) of 1980. This involved, first, the question of how much industry revenue would flow into the coffers of governments and, second, how much of that taxation revenue would stay in Alberta and how much go to Ottawa. The industry had not been consulted during the development of the NEP and was stunned by its announcement (Doern and Toner, 1985). The immediate response was an opinion poll confirming its poor public image, followed by a $3-million advertising campaign intended to give the industry increased legitimacy. The central political message was not an outright attack on the NEP. Instead, the industry said it supported the goals of the program but disagreed with specifics. As is often the case in such instances of outside lobbying, the advertisements highlighted the investment and job creation provided by the sector (Doern and Toner, 1985). As well as receiving political support from its subsidiary industries, the sector was able to draw into the political conflict the broad-based business associations, as it later did during the battle over Kyoto ratification. The BCNI (now the Council of Chief Executive Officers) organized private sessions on energy policy attended by premiers and energy ministers. The industry itself presumably also did whatever private lobbying it could in Ottawa, as well as engaging in a public-relations effort to complement its paid advertising. Finally, the industry not only threatened to reduce, but in fact did reduce, some capital investment (Doern and Toner, 1985).

Within a few years of the announcement of the NEP, world oil prices fell significantly, thus removing the basic impetus for the program. The industry then worked closely with the Progressive Conservative Party prior to its taking power in the 1984 election. What is relevant to this analysis is the fact that in both the 1974 and 1980 battles with Ottawa the industry used the same tactics: legitimacy-enhancing advertising coupled with private lobbying. In both cases, despite political support given by Alberta, the industry lost the immediate battle. After the issue had receded from the front pages, however, the industry's political activity was more successful. The Kyoto battle of 2002 was almost an exact replica.

Although climate policy is not centred on export and price controls or governments' share of revenues, it presents a comparable economic threat to the oil industry. That threat can best be conceptualized by making the same distinction between regulation of pollution and regulation of a product that is a central theme of this study. Of the total greenhouse-gas emissions associated with one barrel of oil, 15 per cent result from extracting, processing, and transporting the product and the remaining 85 per cent from its end use (Edwards, undated). The industry, responsible for that initial 15 per cent, has an automatic economic incentive to reduce the quantity of fossil-fuel energy used to produce a barrel of oil for sale on the market, in the same way that all industries have an incentive to lower costs by reducing waste and pollution. Equally automatically, the industry has an incentive to oppose policy measures aimed at reducing the other 85 per cent of emissions generated by those who buy its product, since profitability is directly linked to the total quantity of oil sold each year.

If climate policy were ever imposed in a sufficiently stringent fashion that demand for renewable or other sources sky-rocketed, in order to replace foregone fossil-fuel sources, oil firms might switch investment strategies to capitalize on this new demand and take concurrent political action in support of such a policy. Exactly that behaviour was demonstrated by DuPont in 1987, during negotiation of the Montreal Protocol. DuPont supported development of the Protocol, in part because it would help create a market for the alternatives to CFCs which the company was investigating (Macdonald, 1991: 256). Although some firms such as Shell have increased their investments in non-fossil-fuel sources, no such political dynamic is yet in evidence. Instead, Canadian climate policy from the late 1980s to 2006 has been met with an adaptive response from the oil firms when aimed at their *own* emissions, and an interventionist response when aimed at the emissions of those to whom the industry sells its product.

Propelled by the rising popular support for environmental protection in the late 1980s, Canada was one of the first countries to call for international action on the global climate. The Mulroney government made a unilateral commitment to stabilize emissions in 1990 and then signed and immediately ratified the UN Framework Convention in 1992. Not to be outdone, the Liberals were then elected in 1993 on a platform of reducing emissions, not merely stabilizing them. The federal and provincial governments developed the first national program in 1995, based solely on voluntary participation (the VCR and ÉcoGESte). During the Kyoto negotiations in 1997, Canada accepted a goal of reducing emissions by 6 per cent by no later than 2012. The second national program was announced in 2000, again based solely on voluntarism despite the failure of that instrument to prevent steadily rising emissions during the previous five years.

In 2002, however, as part of the ratification process, the federal government signalled for the first time its willingness to use legally binding controls, in the form of government-firm "covenants," as well as the instruments of voluntary programs and spending on technology development. Ratification, which was bitterly opposed by Alberta, brought an end to any semblance of co-ordinated federal-provincial action, and Ottawa then set out to itself directly impose regulatory controls on industry. As discussed, by 2005, federal government negotiations with the oil and gas and other industrial sectors had resulted in a significant relaxation of the targets for industry reductions (with the exception of the auto industry, which had been induced to agree to a "voluntary" 25-per cent reduction in vehicle emissions), but no law-based regulatory action had been taken. During the fifteen years since making its first stabilization commitment, Canadian policy has been almost completely ineffective, as witnessed by steadily increasing greenhouse-gas emissions (Canada, 2005).

How much of that failure is due to lobbying by the oil and gas industry, and what does that say about the political power of the sector? To answer that question we need to review the political actions taken by CAPP and the oil firms as Canadian climate policy evolved.

Not surprisingly, the industry in Canada and all other countries has been engaged with the issue from the outset. It has fully participated in international negotiations at all stages (as have environmentalists), consistently arguing against meaningful international action (Legett, 1999; Newell, 2000). Within Canada, the industry has also been a full participant in the policy process, both privately and publicly. The industry trade association made a submission to the House of Commons Standing Committee on Environment in 1989 (Canadian Petroleum Association, 1989), and one firm, Imperial, released a discussion paper on policy options in 1991 (Imperial Oil, 1991). In 1994 a number of firms established the Alliance for Responsible Environmental Alternatives. In that same year, as discussed, what was then the BCNI entered the public debate, as it had during the industry's battle against the NEP, releasing a report advocating voluntary business action on the issue as an alternative to regulation.

These public policy initiatives were complemented by the usual quiet Ottawa diplomacy, working closely with its departmental champion, NRCan, in opposition to Environment Canada. During that period while the federal government was preparing its first climate program, the two departments were engaged in internal conflict over the use of regulatory or voluntary instruments (Macdonald and Smith, 1999). The latter were eventually selected, but before then, on January 20, 1995, NRCan and CAPP signed a memorandum of agreement, committing the industry to make voluntary efforts to reduce its own emissions.

The central program in the 1995 federal-provincial climate policy, the Voluntary Challenge and Registry, invited all institutional users of energy, including firms, universities, government agencies, and others to develop plans for reductions in their greenhouse-gas emissions. They were to register them publicly on the VCR website, followed in subsequent years by public reporting on progress made in achieving those goals. Like the Responsible Care program, the VCR was premised on the assumption that peer pressure from other participating organizations could bring about behaviour change comparable to that which could be induced by regulatory pressure from governments. Writing five years after the program was initiated, one analyst concluded that the VCR had "utterly failed to bring about the kinds of emissions reductions that Canada will need to meet its Kyoto commitment" (Bramley, 2000). Ten years later emissions are increasing, not decreasing.

The VCR was successful, however, in giving the *appearance* of action. By its nature, the VCR can be effective only if it is widely publicized, in order to bring peer pressure to bear. That publicity provides legitimacy for both the governments that selected the policy instrument and the participating firms. This is particularly the case for the latter, since it combines some element of adaptive behaviour change with publicity intended to draw attention to that behaviour change. By participating in a program designed to curb their *own* emissions, the industry implicitly gave the message that this was the limit of its social responsibility respecting climate change. The fact that it was a voluntary program meant, as demonstrated by its failure over the next decade, that the VCR was unlikely to significantly reduce demand for the product sold by the industry, allowing the industry to enthusiastically support it (in contrast to the sector's attempt to defeat Kyoto ratification).

The fact that industry performance was measured only in terms of its own fossil-fuel use, rather than other criteria such as switching of investments from oil extraction to renewable energy development, meant that the VCR sent the message, coming from both government and industry, that the former was the only norm by which the oil industry should be judged. As a policy tool, the VCR was ineffective, but as a legitimacy-enhancing tool it was a success.

Throughout the year prior to the third meeting of UNFCCC parties in Kyoto, Japan, in December 1997, climate-change politics in Canada, as in other countries, again became a hot topic. The federal government had to decide what position it would take during those international negotiations and was, of course, subjected to lobbying by provinces, environmentalists, and a variety of industry sectors. In May 1997, a split within the global industry became apparent when the CEO of BP gave his speech, discussed above, stating that the problem was real and that action must be taken. That same year BP withdrew from the international oil-industry lobbying effort, the Global Climate Coalition. Shell withdrew in 1998. Within Canada, a comparable split was identified in the news media, which proclaimed Suncor, Shell, and Petro-Canada as being more willing to cooperate with federal regulators than were Imperial Oil, seventy per cent owned by Exxon, and Talisman (Jang, 1997).

Presumably that split influenced the internal decision-making of the Canadian Association of Petroleum Producers as it prepared to engage in outside lobbying in the fall of 1997. Whatever those internal politics, in a series of full-page newspaper ads in October and November 1997, CAPP made its position clear: the international regime should be expanded to require reductions from developing nations like India and China; the regime should do more to recognize Canada's unique position; Canadian natural gas exports to the US, which reduce the American need to burn more carbon-intensive coal, should be taken into account in setting the Canadian target. The latter point was subsequently taken up and advanced by Canadian diplomats, unsuccessfully, during post-Kyoto international negotiations.

Although both the industry and its ally, Alberta Premier Ralph Klein, had spoken out vehemently at the time that Canada took on the Kyoto commitment, the public debate subsided over the next few years, since it quickly became apparent that the federal and provincial governments had no intention of deviating from their exclusive reliance on the non-coercive instrument of voluntarism. That all changed in July 2001, when Prime Minister Chrétien announced that, since other UNFCCC nations had agreed to reduce the total Canadian commitment by taking into account "sinks" of carbon stored in soil and wood fibre, his administration would, after all, ratify the Protocol. That announcement unleashed the major outside lobbying campaign to prevent ratification, described in the introductory pages above, replete with detailed policy briefs, paid advertisements and public threats by oil firms to rethink their planned investments in the Alberta oil sands. As was the case with the anti-NEP campaign, both the subsidiary oil-extraction industries and the broad-based associations like the Canadian Chamber of Commerce became fully engaged in support of the oil industry. The coalition of anti-Kyoto forces was broader, however, than had been the case in the early 1980s. This time some other provinces, most notably British Columbia, actively supported the Alberta industry position, and Ontario, rather than actively opposing Alberta as it had done previously, stayed mute. As noted, a number of other industrial sectors and broad-based associations joined the coalition effort to block Kyoto ratification.

Nevertheless, as was the case in 1982, the oil industry lost in its bid to derail federal government policy — the Chrétien government ratified the Protocol. Why did the business interests lose the political battle? The primary reason seems to have been changes in the composition of the policy network which occurred in the fall of 2002 (Macdonald, 2003). The first was the exclusion of Alberta and the other opposition provinces from the political arena. Unlike development and implementation of national climate policy, ratification by a vote in the House of Commons was a policy action that could be taken by the Chrétien government alone with no need for provincial participation. At a meeting on October 28, 2002, all the provincial environment ministers signed a statement calling upon the Prime Minister to convene a first ministers' meeting to discuss climate policy, prior to the ratification vote. Chrétien ignored that demand and thus effectively excluded the provinces from the ratification decision-making process.

Second, within the federal government, management of the file moved up from the two lead departments, Environment and Natural Resources, to the Prime Minister's office, reflecting Chrétien's personal commitment to what he had adopted as one of his legacy issues. The oil industry was now engaged in conflict with the Prime Minister himself, rather than only his environment minister, a relatively weak member of his cabinet. Finally, the Liberal back-bench MPs began to speak publicly on the issue, urging the Prime Minister to stay the course. This change in the composition of political forces within the arena took place while opinion polling was showing that public support for ratification stayed constant in the fall of 2002. At the end of the day, the oil industry did not have the political power to prevail.

The fact that the industry lost the public battle over ratification does not mean, however, that it lost the climate-change policy war. Between 2003 and 2005, the federal government negotiated privately with the three major manufacturing sectors being asked to reduce emissions: oil and gas, electricity, and manufacturing. As is usually the case, the forum of private negotiation was a favourable one for the business interests. The threatened use of legally binding measures was successfully delayed until the defeat of the Martin government in January 2006. Furthermore, while the total Canadian reductions necessary to meet the 1997 Kyoto commitment increased (since emissions increased between 2002 and 2005, causing projected emissions for the 2008-12 period to be revised upward) the portion of that total allocated to business *decreased* from 55 to 39 megatonnes (a megatonne, abbreviated as Mt, is one million tonnes of carbon dioxide or equivalent greenhouse gases) (Canada, 2005; Macdonald and VanNijnatten, 2005). Working in private, the relevant business actors convinced the Martin government that other Canadians, not them, should be responsible for almost a third of the total reductions originally assigned to them by the Chrétien government in 2002.

This story casts some light upon the motivations and the extent of the political power wielded by the oil and gas industry. The firms readily adapted to policy aimed only at their own emissions, but intervened to change policy aimed at their product, thus confirming one the central themes advanced in this work. Second, the sector was unable to block ratification, a highly visible process which mobilized other actors and from which the provinces were excluded. Nevertheless, it has been quite successful in private negotiations, thus confirming that business power to influence policy is greatest when it is working behind closed doors. Can the failure of Canadian climate policy to date be laid solely at the door of the industry? Of course not. Many other sectors, institutions, and individual Canadians must share responsibility, along with the lack of power exercised by the environmental movement, in explaining the electoral calculations made to date by Canadian federal and provincial governments. The sector has exercised significant power, but it is not limitless.

SUMMARY

A summary of business political engagement on the environment file since the election of the Chrétien government in 1993 results in a picture completely different from that of the preceding thirteen-year period. Using the same format as the previous two chapter summaries, I briefly summarize here this very different set of findings.

Political Interest Sought

The objective of delaying and weakening standards as they were being negotiated with regulators was much less in evidence during this period, simply because very few new legally binding standards were put in place. As discussed, some sectors were faced with pending new regulation and responded by the traditional norm of negotiated adaptation. Examples include gasoline manufacturers forced to reduce the sulphur content of their product or the agricultural industry faced with the threat of new legal requirements governing manure management. For the majority of industrial sectors, however, the political objective of fundamentally changing or completely blocking new regulatory initiatives, hitherto only attempted by the soft-drink industry, became the new practice.

This attempt to fundamentally change environmental policy, as we have seen, was most widespread in the many instances in which business argued, often successfully, that its participation in new policy measures should be voluntary. Letting each firm decide for itself whether it would or would not implement suggested improvements in environmental performance was the most radical change in the regulatory system since it had been established in the 1960s. Even when industries in the early 1970s had been able to negotiate agreements giving them ten or fifteen years to come into compliance, that regulatory threat still existed, even though deferred, and still carried the moral weight of law. No such explicit, delayed threat accompanies voluntary programs (governments have made only the vaguest noises about introducing regulatory programs if voluntary ones are not effective) and non-participating firms remain members of the community in good moral standing.

As we have seen, beginning in the early 1990s, business took on the radical new political agenda of doing all it could to ensure it never again would be required to comply with any new, legally enforceable environmental standards but instead would only take voluntary action. Beyond that, the specific examples of policy interventions to block or radically alter policy described above can be summarized quickly. They included litigation by the Ethanol company that forced Environment Canada to abandon its MMT regulation under CEPA, elite-level lobbying by the chemical industry resulting in a refusal by the Chrétien government to adopt recommendations made by its own House of Commons committee for amendments to CEPA, and the failed effort to prevent ratification of the Kyoto Protocol in 2002. The reasons why the latter effort failed while others succeeded (even though it was by far the largest political initiative seen to date, as measured by the number of participating sectors and firms) are, as discussed above, the mobilization of their opponents, the fact that their provincial allies could not participate in the policy venue, and the active engagement of the Prime Minister. The latter two factors were exceptional, since environmental regulation (as opposed to foreign policy) is in the hands of the provinces, and prime ministers and premiers have almost always left the issue to their environment minister.

During this period legitimacy became a major political interest of all the large firms

Strategies Used to Achieve that Interest

For the most part, business used the same strategies to achieve this new objective of voluntarism as had previously been used for the more limited objective of delaying or weakening regulation. Private lobbying of governments, accompanied by participation in multistakeholder discussion, remained the norm. The two different strategies—litigation in the case of MMT and large-scale outside lobbying on Kyoto—were isolated examples. The fact that the same method of influencing policy could produce such different results—the move to active enforcement in the 1980s and the adoption of voluntarism in the 1990s—suggests that the explanation for this sea change from the 1980s to 1990s must be found by looking at changes in the political power of the regulatory departments, rather than that of the relevant firms.

Where we do find a change in strategy is in the methods used to gain environmental legitimacy in the eyes of the broader public. The large firms continued to pursue the first legitimacy strategy, greening their operations, which was initiated in the 1980s. The fact that in cases such as ARET and the VCR the voluntary nature of this behaviour change was formally recognized, testified to, and applauded by regulatory authorities added a new sheen of legitimacy. Change occurred, however, in the second strategy. For the first time, advertising was used to project a new, green image of the corporation, above and beyond its products. As discussed, this was a repetition of the corporate-image strategy first used by AT&T almost a century before. Legitimacy enhancement by means of the third strategy, changing the norms by which it was judged through endorsement of sustainable development, continued throughout the decade.

171

Success in Achieving that Interest: Political Power

Here we need only repeat the obvious. The regulated firms regained all of the political power, relative to that of regulators, lost in the 1980s — and perhaps even more. To give the two most significant examples, governments were unable to ban classes of chemicals or to reduce greenhouse-gas emissions. While some new regulatory initiatives were put in place, for the most part governments were unable or unwilling to do more than ask politely for voluntary improvements in environmental performance. As discussed, the most part obvious reason for this drastic reversal of political power in the 1990s was the fact that environment-department budgets were cut roughly in half. Since then, they have been at least partially restored and law remains the basic policy instrument used by regulators. Business power fluctuated upward in this period, but never became totally dominant.

CHAPTER SIX

Business and Environmental Politics

In this concluding chapter, I attempt to pull together the stories presented above, in order to present one coherent view of our subject matter: the interests, strategies, and power of business in the arena of environmental politics. To do that, I first present, in Table 6.1, one overall summary picture of business engagement with environmental politics in this country from the onset of regulation to the present—what might be termed a summary of the three summaries provided at the conclusion of each history chapter. The purpose of the table is to provide a clear picture of the major trends that can be seen when we look back over that entire period. I then turn to the fascinating but elusive question of why those trends emerged, why business political activity has evolved in the way it has. That analysis is organized by means of the three research questions presented in the introductory chapter: What objectives has business sought with respect to Canadian environmental policy? How has it worked to achieve them? And how successful has it been—in other words, how much political power has it been able to exercise? Fruitful areas for further research are briefly discussed in the latter part of the chapter. The book then concludes with a very brief statement of the implications of the analysis presented here for future efforts to protect the ecological health of Canada and the rest of the planet.

Table 6.1 Summary View of Business Political Activity, 1956-2006

1) 1956-1980

Interest

Negotiated adaptation or policy intervention?	no interventions intended to block or fundamentally change policy
Legitimacy interest?	no major effort made to achieve environmental legitimacy

Strategy

Private or public lobbying?   only private

Relations with ENGOs?   ignore

Legitimacy strategy?   none

Power

Why fluctuate?   declined as part of broader change in post-war values, rise of social movements, loss of business legitimacy

Influence on policy?   weaken and delay environmental regulation; part of broader effort in 1970s to roll back the regulatory state

2) 1980-1993

Interest

Negotiated adaptation or policy intervention?   soft-drink industry mounts first major policy intervention

Legitimacy interest?   chemical industry Responsible Care program first major effort to regain legitimacy; sustainable development embraced as part of effort to become part of the solution

Strategy

Private or public lobbying?   mostly private, but advertising of Responsible Care program an attempt to gain public support

Relations with ENGOs?   largely ignore, but some efforts to both cooperate, through multistakeholder consultation, and limited number of attempts to intimidate by litigation

| Legitimacy strategy? | change own behaviour by improved environmental management; first attempts to change image of that behaviour; first attempt to redefine environmental norms through concept of sustainable development |

Power

| Why fluctuate? | declined, due to increasing popular support for environmentalism and politicians' search for electoral benefit |
| Influence on policy? | less than in any other period |

3) 1993-2006

Interest

| Negotiated adaptation or policy intervention? | norm is still adaptation, but witnessed CEPA and Kyoto interventions |
| Legitimacy interest? | a major interest of large firms, through corporate-image advertising |

Strategy

Private or public lobbying?	primarily private; anti-Kyoto advertising was the exception
Relations with ENGOs?	still largely ignored, decline in co-operation, but no major increase in SLAPP-suit litigation
Legitimacy strategy?	all three methods used: improve environmental performance, work to change image and work to change norms

Power

| Why fluctuate? | increased, less due to own efforts than to changes in role of the state |
| Influence on policy? | restored to 1970s level, or higher |

POLITICAL INTEREST SOUGHT

Here we discuss two things: the factors inducing an adaptive or intervention-ist response to regulatory demands, and the fact that a concern for legitimacy was virtually non-existent at the beginning of the historical period and then increased steadily during the 1980s and 1990s.

Negotiated Adaptation vs. Intervention

As we have seen, two sectors — pulp-and-paper and smelting — engaged only in negotiated adaptation without ever mounting major policy interventions. Both were successful in delaying for a decade or more the additional spending needed to meet the regulatory standards imposed upon them, and in both cases government programs for industrial modernization were established that offered a subsidy for some portion of those expenditures. In addition, both sectors successfully negotiated to weaken the level of environmental protection provided by the standards imposed upon them. Neither sector, however, attempted to completely block or fundamentally change the environmental policy to which they had become subjected. Negotiated adaptation was also the initial response of the chemical industry, as it was that of the oil and gas industry, with respect to climate policy, until 2002.

In contrast, three regulatory demands were met by policy interventions intended to eliminate or fundamentally change them: soft-drink container regulation, amendment of CEPA to allow chemical sunsetting, and Kyoto ratification. In the first case, intervention had been preceded by a different response to the same demand, non-compliance, but in the early 1980s the soft-drink industry began its ultimately successful campaign to replace "re-use" with "recycling" as the Ontario government policy objective. The other two sectors had initially accommodated regulatory demands by adaptation and then later were moved to intervene. How do we explain these differences? Why did two sectors only adapt, while the other three adapted to some regulatory demands but intervened to block or change others? Amongst those three, why do we find interventionist responses occurring at different times?

As discussed above, the analysis presented here places explanatory factors in either of two categories: those internal to the firm, summed up by the catch-all phrase "corporate culture," and those outside the factory perimeter, referred to as the "external threat." Discussion here centres upon regulatory demands as the most pressing type of external threat, but the term also includes demands for behaviour change by environmentalists and other forms of societal pressure. We begin, accordingly, by examining whether differences in corporate culture can fully explain these different responses to regulatory demands.

I suggested in the introductory chapter that we find a disconnect when we compare two trends: the greening of corporate culture and the choice of adapting to or attempting to change environmental policy. Publicly expressed attitudes of firm managers, internal organization in terms of size and administrative power of environmental management units, and behaviour in terms of improved environmental management—these have all moved steadily in one direction, namely toward a greener corporate culture. However, we have not seen a corresponding linear evolution of political activity. In no case did a sector start with policy intervention (when corporate culture was least in tune with environmental values) and then move steadily toward negotiated adaptation. This leads to the conclusion that corporate culture is not the major factor explaining choice of political objective when the firm responds to new regulation.

The two cases of the CEPA and Kyoto interventions confirm this view. This is because both occurred very shortly after each sector had negotiated voluntary agreements to improve their environmental performance. In both sectors, it was the *same* corporate culture that first chose to adapt and then to intervene. The soft-drink case is somewhat different, in that it never really did adapt to the demand that it return to selling its product in glass bottles. Although in 1976 it negotiated the agreement for a 75 per cent refillable sales target, it took little action to meet that goal. It is similar, however, in that it was less than a decade later when it was actively working to change policy, by offering to subsidize curbside recycling. For all three sectors, it is simply not credible to believe that corporate culture changed enough, in such a short period, to bring about these changes in political objective.

Is it possible to believe that culture in the pulp-and-paper and smelting industries was sufficiently different from that in chemicals, oil and gas, and soft drinks to explain the fact that only the first two adapted? Undoubtedly, more detailed study would find variances in corporate culture amongst firms in the five sectors and, perhaps, amongst sectors as a whole. At this level of macro analysis, which is not based upon direct empirical study of internal culture, the only such difference was within the oil industry, between the hard-liner firms and those more willing to concede that climate change was a real issue. But those cultural differences were not strong enough to bring about a corresponding change in either economic strategy in the market or, when pressed, political strategy in the case of Kyoto ratification. There is no doubt that differing cultures exist, and that they exert at least some marginal influence on firm behaviour, be it economic or political. However, there is no evidence that pulp-and-paper and smelting cultures were significantly greener and more accommodating than those in the other three sectors.

Rather than internal factors, those differing responses can better be explained by differences in the nature of the regulatory demand that each sector encountered. Demands that threaten the product — soft-drink containers, chemical bans, and total fossil-fuel consumption — have been met with interventionist responses. Demands to abate and better manage pollution, on the other hand, have been met with an adaptive response, albeit only after extensive negotiation. Although they are not the subject of detailed research here, it seems clear that these product-related regulatory demands posed a greater economic threat than did the pollution-related demands. As discussed, expenditure on pollution management might be around five per cent or less of firm capital or operating expenditure, and in many cases those expenditures can be justified on a purely business basis, regardless of regulatory pressure, since they will bring about reduced material input and waste-management costs. Data are not available to allow comparison of those pollution-abatement costs with product-related costs of chemical bans or a Kyoto cap on fossil-fuel emissions, but it seems reasonable to assume the latter would be much higher. Certainly we do know that containers represent something like one-third of soft-drink industry costs and that refillable bottles are four times as expensive as recyclable cans. We can safely assume that regulation aimed at products is a greater economic threat to the firm than is regulation of its pollution.

That leads to the conclusion that policy intervention is stimulated not by internal culture, but by severity of the regulatory threat. Corporate culture has been ruled out for three reasons: because it is unlikely to have changed in a retrograde fashion, from green to brown; because it could not have changed quickly enough to explain the change in objective within sectors; and because there is no evidence of significant differences amongst sectors. The nature of the external threat is preferred as an explanation, because in the three intervention cases examined, regulation was aimed at the product, not at pollution.

This conclusion is in accordance with the assumption, set out in the introduction, that the firm functions as a unitary, rational actor when it engages in political activity. A calculation of cost and benefit will lead the firm to adapt to regulatory demands, provided that the cost of doing so is not too high. Above a certain cost, however, it makes more sense for the firm to attempt to change the nature of that demand. It also fits with the historical trend we have witnessed, whereby business initially ignored or took minimal action to meet the demands of environmentalism and new regulatory standards and then embraced the concept of sustainable development. Business adapted in the 1970s, when the price of doing so was low, but then as regulation became more rigorous in the 1980s it intervened in the broader political debate, pressing for adoption of sustainable development as the societal goal because it was much less threatening than a steady-state economy, for example. Such intervention to change the norms by which a business is judged is, of course, the third strategy to achieve legitimacy discussed in this work.

Profitability and Legitimacy

The findings presented above confirm the view that the firm's search for profitability is the most important factor determining the policy objective it seeks as it engages in the environmental policy arena. We can confidently say that business actors want governments to put in place environmental policy that will have the least adverse effect on their search for profit or, in some cases, positively contribute to it. This proved to be true even in the two instances presented in which sectors seemed, at first glance, not to be pursuing policy directly related to profitability. The nascent environmental industry has from the outset refrained from actively and publicly advocating increased regulation, even though that would boost sales, because to do so would alienate potential business clients and, ultimately, hurt sales instead. The Canadian insurance industry has not joined environmentalists in lobbying for more stringent greenhouse-gas regulation, despite its concerns about increased severe-weather damage payments. To do so would, again, potentially damage relations with clients; moreover, other policy avenues, such as increased adaptive capacity, provide a faster and more direct route to meeting the sector's economic goals. Other sectors, whether adapting or intervening, pursued political objectives that they believed would best contribute to the goal of profitability.

These findings also confirm the view of environmental policy analysts that the search for policy which contributes to profit leads to political conflicts amongst business actors. The conflict between the gasoline and motor-vehicle manufacturing industries over federal smog-reduction policy is one example. Such conflicts may clear the way for "bootlegger-baptist" alliances, such as the support provided by the Ontario beer industry for environmentalists in that province who were pressing for refillable beverage container policy.

Beyond confirming the views found in the current literature, the findings presented here also allow us to expand our understanding of the business interest by adding the search for legitimacy as another political goal that stands beside profit. Such things as the Responsible Care program, the many other large firms and sectors that improved their environmental performance beyond current regulatory requirements, and the emergence of green corporate-image advertising demonstrate clearly the business interest in environmental legitimacy. Should it be seen as a goal distinct from, and potentially conflicting with, the profit objective? Certainly, legitimacy is a pathway to profit and to the political power that can also be used to generate profit. To a large extent it is a self-interested goal. But it is also more than that. Altruism, too, can be seen as stemming from self-interest, since cooperation is often the best way of achieving the individual goal. Nevertheless, it is normally thought of as an attribute of individual humans distinct from purely selfish behaviour. In the same way, I think it helps to recognize the firm's search for political and societal legitimacy as a goal distinct from others it pursues simply because they will contribute to profitability.

How do we explain the trend we have witnessed, whereby legitimacy only became a major goal some twenty years after business was first subjected to the demands of environmentalism? Here, I again compare the relative importance of factors having to do with the internal workings of the firm and those found in its external environment. Unlike the similar analysis made above, however, in this case I conclude that both help to explain this trend.

Throughout this work, we have accepted the argument made by business itself that corporate culture has become steadily greener, keeping pace with that of the surrounding society (setting aside for the moment the question of how business and society have defined "greener"). In this case, therefore, unlike in the adaptation vs. intervention scenario, the trend in corporate greening matches the other trend of increased resources being devoted to the search for legitimacy. As corporate culture increasingly came to accept the values of environmentalism, firm managers, it seems reasonable to assume, increasingly wanted to gain credit in the eyes of external audiences for their improved environmental management. They wanted environmental legitimacy because they themselves had come to accept, to at least some extent, the new norms bound up in that concept.

We find a similar concurrence in trends when we look to the external factors. Business efforts to achieve legitimacy, through such things as increased spending on environmental management, image advertising, and embracing sustainable development, occurred at the time when business was under the greatest regulatory and societal pressure. Business actively worked to gain legitimacy in those ways in response to that heightened pressure, not solely as a result of internal changes in values. Mitchell (1989) makes a convincing case that business in the 1920s adopted a new ideology of corporate social responsibility as a means of defusing external pressure. He also makes the point, however, that by then business had abandoned the notion that it was a purely market actor, with no societal responsibilities. Those 1920s legitimacy-seeking actions stemmed from both corporate culture and external pressure. It seems reasonable to assume that the 1990s search for environmental legitimacy was also stimulated by both sets of factors.

STRATEGIES FOR ACHIEVING THAT INTEREST
What does this historical review tell us about the ways in which business has

sought to achieve its political goals, in terms of both specific policy issues and the larger debate over environment and sustainable development? Following the format of the second research question and subsidiary questions set out in the introduction, I now review three sets of strategic choices made by firms: (1) the question of whether to layer outside lobbying on top of the ongoing process of private negotiation; (2) relations with environmentalists; and (3) means of regaining environmental legitimacy.

Private and Public Lobbying

As we have seen, a major source of the political power of the large firms examined here is the fact that they, unlike environmentalists, have guaranteed access to government decision-makers. The nature of the regulatory process means they are always in detailed negotiation with environment department officials. Thus, the findings here confirm the view found in the environmental policy literature that the essence of environmental regulation is private firm-regulator negotiation (Thompson, 1980; Cotton and McKinnon, 1993). When necessary, they can supplement that with access to the minister or her staff and, as we have seen, when pressed are also able to go over the minister's head, to make their case to the provincial premier. Thus it is hardly surprising that the strategy of private lobbying has always been used, even after the process was expanded to include parallel public discussion through multistakeholder consultation. The question, then, is why business ever seeks to compete with environmentalists on their own turf, by publicly lobbying for public support.

The first point to be made is that in fact they rarely do so. Certainly, business has devoted considerable resources to improving its environmental image in the eyes of the general public, through such things as the Responsible Care program and corporate-image advertising. Much less has been done, however, to garner public support while engaged in private negotiation of specific regulatory measures. Throughout Inco's decades-long process of negotiating acid-rain controls with the Ontario Ministry of Environment, and although it did its best to make its case in the news media, it never used paid advertising to generate public support. Nor did the chemical industry, during the time when it devoted considerable resources to private lobbying on CEPA in the late 1990s. Although this is not a definitive history of outside lobbying, in these pages we find only two instances of this strategy being used: the creation of "wise use" groups in British Columbia in the 1990s, and the public lobbying by the oil- and gas-industry prior to the 1997 Kyoto meeting and again during the campaign to prevent Kyoto ratification in 2002.

This leads to the supposition that such efforts are taken only when firms come to believe that the political power they are bringing to bear in private negotiation is insufficient. Certainly that seems to explain the 2002 Kyoto major outside lobbying campaign. No comparable effort was seen between 1992, when Canada first signed the Rio Climate Convention, and 2001, when for the first time the Prime Minister said that ratification was likely. During that period, it seemed possible that Canada never would ratify, and nothing more onerous than voluntary instruments was being applied to the oil- and gas-sector. The campaign for public support, pointing to the job losses which it was claimed would result from ratification, was initiated only once it had become clear that the traditional method of influencing policy was no longer working. Nor, as we have seen, did the public campaign *replace* private negotiation. During the fall of 2002, the industry was publicly doing what it could to prevent ratification and, simultaneously, privately negotiating terms it could live with after ratification had occurred. No such outside lobbying on climate policy has occurred between 2003 and 2006, as federal regulators and firms have again been negotiating privately. Again, I would argue that this was because it was not needed: business was achieving its political objectives behind closed doors (the decrease in the goal for industry emissions from 55 to 39 Mts, referred to above) and saw no need to step outside.

The conclusion, then, seems clear. Business certainly seeks public approval and support, as do the environmentalists. Unlike them, however, it rarely seeks support for specific policy measures, but instead concentrates on strengthening its public image as a caring, concerned member of society working as hard as any other for environmental protection. When it speaks to government, however, it relies on the strategy that has always worked: elite-level, closed-door discussion.

Relations with Environmentalists

What determines strategy for dealing with ENGOs? Again I can only speculate, but in doing so, as a prelude to the necessary research, I would point to the political power of the environmental movement. When it held only marginal political power, in the 1970s, business ignored it. Only when environmentalists gained power in the late 1980s did the New Directions engagement begin. Not too much should be read into that phenomenon, however, since it involved only some firms and only one part of the environmental movement. To the extent it was significant, I would assume the firm's search for legitimacy, achieved through publicly linking arms with ENGOs, was a primary factor. But then why did other firms risk losing legitimacy by attacking environmentalists, through law suits and funding counter-vailing non-governmental organizations? This too, I would suggest, is a relatively isolated phenomenon in Canada, associated primarily with western forestry politics, and not representative of business political strategy as a whole.

It seems fair to conclude that for the most part regulated industries have not gone out of their way to embrace or attack environmentalists. The firms have provided financial donations to ENGOs, and their public-policy officials have negotiated with them in multistakeholder processes (and happily drunk beer with them in the evenings), but aside from that have largely ignored them.

Legitimacy Strategies

What trends can we identify in the methods used to gain environmental legitimacy? Initially, none of the three strategies we are discussing here was used in the early years, but by the 1990s all three had been brought into play. This seems to be explained by the steadily increasing external pressure, both regulatory and societal, which occurred over that period.

In the 1970s, the large firms improved their environmental performance, but only grudgingly, in response to regulation. Little was done to burnish their image and no alternative vision of environmental values was offered. Presumably this lack of concern stemmed from the fact that environmental legitimacy was only one part of the overall legitimacy loss first experienced by business in the 1960s. Dow, for instance, was attacked in the 1960s for its napalm, not because of possible links to chemicals in breast milk. The 1986 Responsible Care program, the first major, high-profile search for environmental legitimacy, marked a significant change. For the first time, an industrial sector worked to improve its environmental performance in ways not directly related to regulatory requirements, while at the same time making efforts to gain public recognition and credit. Both tactics were then used by other sectors in the years that followed. Once environmentalism became politically strong enough to cast serious aspersions upon the legitimacy of the large firms, they moved to meet those new norms and made sure external audiences knew they were doing so.

Use of the third tactic, seeking to change environmental norms by accepting and promoting the concept of sustainable development, is more complex, since here business was only one participant amongst many in this evolution of ideas. The first two tactics were initiated and largely controlled by business itself. (Even though behaviour change was initially motivated by regulation, "beyond compliance" activity was in the purview of the firm, as of course were the efforts to publicize those activities.) The concept of sustainable development, however, was not invented by business, either in Canada or elsewhere. As we have seen, it came from the very different world of global poverty and development policy, which during the 1980s had had to come to grips with the environmental problems associated with its primary strategy of southern industrialization. The 1987 Brundtland Report was a serendipitous gift for Canadian business, which it immediately put to use, but was not something of its own making.

Nor did it become the dominant mantra solely because of business support. Environmentalists also embraced the concept, since it seemed to be a recognition and legitimation of their claims. The fact that the prescription of sustainable development did not include what analysts see as the two central concerns of environmentalism, limits to growth and bioequity (Carter, 2001), was ignored by the mainstream Canadian ENGOs. In this country and elsewhere, sustainable development represented a grand compromise between business and environmentalism, comparable to the capital-labour compromise of the 1950s. By accepting sustainable development as the way to frame the problem and conceptualize the solution, each side gave something and received benefit in return. Business acknowledged that its environmental performance had to improve, but it received the assurance that the solution to the environmental problem would be found within the context of economic growth based in capitalist values and distributions of power. Environmentalism gave up its radical critique and in return saw its values, albeit in attenuated form, move from the fringe to the centre of the policy dialogue (Hajer, 1995). Governments were quick to endorse the compromise and make sustainable development, at least at the rhetorical level, the expression of their environmental policy goal.

Thus we see that Canadian business intervened in the political dialogue to change the norms by which it was being judged, but only as part of a larger, global process. The fact that the evolution of norms from limits to growth to sustainable development was not initiated or controlled by business is significant for understanding business political power, the subject we turn to next. Despite its dominant political power, business was never sufficiently powerful to independently invent and impose a new definition of environmental protection.

SUCCESS IN ACHIEVING THAT INTEREST: POLITICAL POWER

As noted at the outset, the nature of the subject makes it difficult to speak definitively about political power. Bearing that caveat in mind, in this section I offer some thoughts on lessons that can be learned from this historical review respecting two aspects of business power. These are, first, the factors that might explain changes in that power and, second, the extent to which the political power of business, relative to other factors, explains the evolution of environmental policy in Canada during the past fifty years.

How do we explain fluctuations in the power of business relative to that of environmental regulators? The general loss of business power in the 1960s can be explained by two changes that occurred during that turbulent decade. The first was the rapid expansion of the welfare and regulatory state, fuelled by the steadily increasing tax revenues in that period of unprecedented economic growth. The second was the overall loss of business legitimacy, discussed above. The explanation for the loss of power experienced during the 1980s in the environment policy field has to look to factors specific to that issue, however, since there was no overall dip in business legitimacy at that time. Quite the opposite was the case, in that the business campaign to present government itself as part of the problem, symbolized by the coming to power of Margaret Thatcher and Ronald Reagan at the beginning of that decade, was by then in full swing.

The first such policy-specific explanation must be the growing political power of environmentalists as new problems emerged, seemingly on a daily basis, and as ENGOs grew more skilful at the one game they were able to play, namely outside lobbying through the news media to stimulate public interest. The "second wave" of popular support for environmental action gave environmentalists political power they had never held before. Once that power became sufficient to influence the electoral strategies of governments and parties, regulators received support from the centre of government that they too had never had before. The growing political power of environmentalists meant they were able to muscle their way into at least the outer circle of policy-making, multistakeholder consultation, which tipped the firm-regulator balance even further in the direction of the latter.

Why was that balance then changed so quickly and decisively in the 1990s? The answer cannot be found in a sudden decline in the political power of environmentalists during that decade. Although public support may have declined somewhat after the cresting of the second wave, the Canadian ENGOs were nevertheless well funded by donations throughout the decade (Wilson, 2002). Far more important, I would suggest, were changes in the overall capacity of governments, which reduced the power of environmental regulators. As noted, political leaders to some extent had become disenchanted with environment as an electoral strategy. More important, they had become caught up in the political problem of debt and deficit, with the resulting cuts to environment department budgets described above. Events such as the election of the Harris government in Ontario in 1995 then showed that reducing the size of government, and associated tax levels, could win elections — more so than action on pollution (Schrecker, 2005). Environment departments, with significantly fewer staff and operating as part of explicitly pro-business governments, were simply unable to exert anything like the power they had previously used to influence the environmental performance of the regulated firms.

The point here, like that made above with respect to sustainable development, is that the regulated industries did not by themselves bring about this change in the balance of power. Their own agency power was important, both in improving their own performance and then making sure they got the associated legitimacy gains. The fact that many large firms were in fact making improvements beyond regulatory requirements gave credibility to the notion of voluntary action as a policy instrument. Furthermore, political action by business as a whole, working through organizations such as the former Business Council on National Issues, was in part responsible for the budget reductions of the mid-1990s. But only in part: as described above, former Saskatchewan treasurer Janice MacKinnon (2003) made it clear that governments had dug themselves into financial holes and that their budget reductions were motivated by fear of the higher borrowing costs that would flow from credit-rating downgrades, not external pressure. Like sustainable development, the government debt crisis of the 1990s was a factor that influenced the unfolding of environmental politics but was not something attributable solely to business actions.

Another factor explaining these changes in business power is the set of dominant ideas within which environmental policy was unfolding. In the 1980s, activist, expanding government had a legitimacy that it would lose by the mid-1990s. Moreover, the problem of environment was seen as immediate and unsolved in that earlier decade, while by the 1990s it had been reframed from an issue of toxic health threats to humans, dying lakes, and species extinction to the anodyne and ambiguous concept of sustainable development. The problem had also by then gained connotations of being an issue well in hand. Blue boxes were being collected, "partnerships" had replaced conflict, and, most important, business had seen the light, changed its ways, and was applying its skills and resources to solving the problem.

These explanations for fluctuations in business power lead to the conclusion that the firm's own political activity (agency power) is a less important source of its power than are events and ideas outside its boundaries (inherent, or structural, power). Clearly, agency is one source of power. The actions taken to achieve legitimacy obviously contributed to the mind-set of the 1990s, described above. Further, two instances of private lobbying of premiers, by Inco in 1985 and the BC pulp-and-paper industry a few years later, were effective, as was the ability of Ethyl Corp. to defeat the MMT ban and the chemical industry to defeat the Caccia Committee amendments to CEPA in 1999. The fact remains, however, that industrial sectors like smelting, pulp and paper, and chemicals were forced to accept regulatory standards that they had vigorously opposed. When business as a whole united to stop Kyoto ratification, it was unable to do so (although it has continued to exert considerable influence on climate policy since then). Beyond these policy specifics, the larger trends in environmental politics, such as the shift to sustainable development and deregulation, can be only partially attributed to business action. Business exerts agency power, but the reach of that power is limited, and other factors beyond the control of business are more important for determining the total power, inherent and agency, it can wield at any given time.

This conclusion is directly germane to the second aspect of business power considered here, namely the extent to which it has shaped environmental policy. Here too we find that other factors, beyond business lobbying, have been significant. As we have seen, business succeeded in delaying and weakening pollution regulation, but the regulatory system was put in place and over time made more effective. Regulation of products, such as consumption of fossil fuels, has encountered greater business resistance and been less effective. Other factors, however, also explain that lack of success. The environmental movement has failed to develop a convincing vision of overarching political goals, based in concepts of limits to growth and equity in society and nature that challenge dominant ideas of economic growth as the solution to all problems. Second, we must point to the attractiveness of the neo-liberal vision. Ever-expanding wealth, removing the need for political conflict based in class and providing undoubted benefits in areas such as communication or health care, has, so far at least, delivered what it promised. The rising tide has lifted all yachts, in absolute terms, even though the gap between rich and poor is widening. That vision, and the associated privileging of market over state, gained strength throughout the period we have examined. The failure of environmental policy to address the fundamental issues associated with economic growth and material consumption is only partially due to business influence. Business has certainly influenced environmental policy, but it has not fully shaped it.

WHERE DO WE GO FROM HERE?
This final section offers a few thoughts on how we might build on the initial exploration of the subject presented here. The first part offers suggestions for further academic research. From there, attention turns briefly to what these findings mean for our efforts to protect the environments of Canada and the planet.

Academic Research
The first suggestion, not surprisingly, is that research needs to be conducted in the areas not touched upon at all in this work. The account given here is largely historical, and focussed only on the large, visible firms. As such, it needs to be supplemented by empirical research, through interviews and surveys, of the ways in which business is currently engaging with environmental politics. Furthermore, research needs to be extended to small business and to

sectors not examined here, such as agriculture, electronics, tourism, and financial and other industries. Beyond that, we need more information on the internal decision-making of sectoral and broad-based trade associations to gain better understanding of how they choose their political objectives and strategies. To what extent are those bodies autonomous political actors, bridging differences between regulators and their member firms, and to what extent are they simply the agents of those firms? Do they in fact work more toward the political benefit of the large firms that pay the majority of their costs, to the detriment of smaller firms in the sector?

In terms of the first research question explored here, more empirical research is needed on the question of what motivates adaptation or intervention. I have argued that internal corporate culture is less important than the nature of the external regulatory threat. However, corporate culture seems to play some role and we need to understand it better. Current empirical studies of internal political management, comparable to what is being done now on firm environmental management (e.g., Gunningham, Kagan and Thornton, 2003) are needed. Second, we need a more sophisticated understanding of the *degree* of political interest associated with different regulatory threats. I have made a distinction between regulation of pollution and of products, suggesting that the firm is more motivated to intervene in an effort to change policy in the case of the latter. This leads to the hypothesis that degree of political motivation increases steadily with the perceived cost of proposed regulatory measures. Is there in fact such a close linkage between the two variables?

I have argued that firms seek legitimacy as an interest separate from profitability and are willing to sacrifice some of the latter to gain the former. But *how much* are they willing to see profits reduced in order to gain legitimacy? There must be a limit, but we know little about where it lies. Putting the question another way, how much do they want legitimacy? Enough that they will completely abandon a field of activity such as fossil-fuel production and shift investment into more legitimate activities such as renewable energy? That seems unlikely. Some sectors, most notably the tobacco industry, have suffered an enormous loss of legitimacy but continue to operate and generate profit. It seems there are limits to the legitimacy interest, but we know little about what they are. We also need data on the choice of legitimacy-gaining strategies. Studies comparing firms' spending on environmental management beyond regulatory requirements with spending on corporate-image advertising would tell us something about the priority a firm assigns to each strategy.

In terms of strategy, one question to be examined is what triggers an outside lobby campaign. Beyond that, we need data on the basic mechanics of how such campaigns are run, in terms of financial and staffing resources applied and their deployment. More important, we need to know more about the influence of such public lobbying on the concurrent private negotiating process. Does such an outside campaign in fact succeed in putting extra pressure on regulators?

Most important, however, is the need to look inside this secret world of private lobbying. Who are the targets of lobbying, from mid-level bureaucrats to ministers? How do sectors coordinate their efforts? What carrots and sticks are used? Case-study examination of the internal details of some of the lobbying efforts that have been described here only from the outside would be invaluable. Another area of inside strategy to be examined is political alliances between industrial sectors and provinces, working together in opposition to Ottawa. There are numerous obstacles to gathering information while researching inside lobbying, but since this is the arena in which almost all environmental policy is created, the attempt must be made.

In terms of political power, I suggest, not surprisingly, there is a need to focus on the variable of environmental legitimacy. What is it, how can we measure it, where does it come from, and why does it change? Presumably environmentalists are the most important arbiters, so their values and opinions must be surveyed, but those of government officials, the general public, and business people themselves must also be examined. Legitimacy raises the issue of linkages between social and political power, which in turn leads to all of the theoretical complexities of political power. Whether or not those can be resolved, more study is needed into the ways in which perceived legitimacy in the eyes of different members of the public influences power in the environmental policy arena.

That in turn raises the question of the relative importance of structural, or inherent, power versus agency power. I have suggested that the environmental legitimacy of business was determined in part by factors beyond direct business control, such as the decline in the legitimacy of the state that took place in the 1990s. The study of such structural power, with its many and complex sources, is an enormous challenge. Agency power, on the other hand, could be readily tackled. Getting basic data on the financial and staffing resources that regulated industries devote to influencing environmental policy is a much better starting place.

These are just some suggestions for future avenues of research and there are undoubtedly many others. The basic point is that at present we know very little about one of the most important influences on environmental policy decisions and outcomes. For that reason, no matter what lines of inquiry are pursued, the results are bound to be rewarding.

Business and the Future of the Planet

The modern environmental movement came into being in the 1950s and

1960s, and during the half-century since then has had some impact, but mostly at the margins. Some harmful products like CFCs and leaded gasoline have been eliminated; the environmental impacts from toxic pollution generated by resource and manufacturing industries in the OECD nations and, to a lesser extent, in the southern countries as well have been significantly reduced. However, smog remains an unsolved issue in the industrialized world, and it and other forms of air pollution are steadily increasing in China and other developing countries. More significant, there has been almost no success in addressing the larger, more fundamental problems, such as materials consumption, species extinction or climate change, either in Canada or in the rest of the world. Those problems require behaviour change by business (and all other societal actors, including each of us as individuals) on a scale far greater than any seen to date.

What are the implications of the analysis presented here for the likelihood that business, the most powerful of the societal actors, will change its ways to this extent during the next half-century? Does the picture presented here of the way in which business engages with environmental policy mean it will never happen and that our children and grandchildren are doomed to live in an increasingly polluted, warmer, resource-depleted world, bereft of any large mammals living wild in a state of nature?

The answer is no. The analysis presented here is a cause for optimism respecting the ability of governments to regulate the environmental performance of business. This analysis does not lead to the conclusion that business is an intractable force inherently opposed to all progress on environmental protection and possessed of sufficient political power to be sure none takes place. One could only believe that if one started from the implicit premise that business in all aspects was at heart rigid and unyielding, which is fundamentally false. Exactly the opposite is true. Business, whether defined as capital, the sector, the firm or the individual manager, is at heart nimble, light-footed, and above all adaptive to changes in its external environment. The investors, firms, and individuals who are not able to adapt do not survive in a market of constantly changing technologies and desires. The firm has to be able to make profits from buggy whips one year and then from horseless carriages the next.

But what about adaptation to non-market external change, such as the new societal values of environmentalism? Here, too, business is flexible and adaptive. The analysis in the preceding pages shows that business, at least the large, visible firms, have an interest in legitimacy sufficiently strong that they will trade off some profit to achieve it. Just as it is incorrect to view business as essentially unyielding, the view of business as "pathological" — blind to changing societal norms and completely uncaring about its impacts on society—is a mistaken premise. Business *has* changed its behaviour to fit the new norms of environmentalism, in some instances because doing so is another adaptive road to profit, in others because of superior political power brought to bear by the state, and in yet others because it genuinely does want to do the right thing.

As we have seen, in almost all cases business has adapted to the requirements of environmental regulation, albeit after negotiating to weaken their stringency. This is a cause for optimism, since given sufficient political power exerted by environmentalists and governments there is no reason to think that this trend will not continue in the future. That said, we have also seen that on at least some occasions business has not adapted but instead intervened to influence the demands being made on it. Furthermore, the three interventions examined here seem to have been stimulated by the fact that the firms were facing the greater economic threat of regulation of their products, rather than just their pollution. Beyond those policy-specific interventions, business also intervened, when faced with increasingly onerous, and expensive, changes in enforcement practices, to encourage the sustainable development paradigm. It seems business adapts when the cost of the required behaviour change is low, but intervenes when it is higher. This leads us to conclude that future demands for the kind of large-scale behaviour change needed to address the basic issues referred to above will also elicit an interventionist response.

The question, then, is whether such future interventions are likely to significantly influence policy or the more general framing of the issue. Here, too, I suggest that the analysis presented in these pages does not lead to a pessimistic answer. We have seen that business certainly has the power to influence policy and environmental discourse, but that power is limited. Two of the three interventions examined here, those by the soft-drink and chemical industries, were successful, while the third, the attempt to block Kyoto ratification, failed. The Kyoto battle was by far the most publicly visible of the three, which seems to confirm Smith's thesis (2000) that business is less powerful when fighting high-profile issues that have mobilized counter-vailing forces than when it is negotiating sectoral regulation in private. In future, policy transparency and an engaged environmental movement bringing issues to public attention could limit business power.

Second, we must remember that business did not invent sustainable development, nor was it solely responsible for the fact that it became the dominant paradigm. Environmentalists compromised as well, and both governments and the general public, told they could save the planet at no great cost, readily acquiesced. Business did not have the power to impose by itself the paradigm of eco-efficiency. Whether future such interventions will succeed will depend as much on the actions of others as on the power of business.

So where does this picture of an adaptive actor with major but limited powers leave us? I would make two points. First, we cannot rely on the greening of corporate culture alone as we struggle over the coming decades with the enormous challenges facing the planet. Business does genuinely want to do the right thing, but as we have seen, it has worked very hard to convince itself and all of its external audiences that the proper definition of "the right thing" is increased efficiency and little more. Business went green during the 1990s and voluntarily reduced its pollution impacts, but when asked to absorb the costs associated with phasing out products it balked. The new green culture was proudly displayed in legitimation advertising but it was not strong enough to bring about meaningful change in business practice. Government regulators, asked to achieve the same policy results with only half the financial and staffing resources, had no choice but to accept the business argument that voluntarism might actually be a viable policy instrument. Doing so has given both them and the firms they regulate an aura of legitimacy, but has been of little help in the protection of ecological health. Green corporate culture and business-government partnerships give only the illusion of meaningful action.

This leads to my second point, which is that the answer lies not in the internal values of the firm, but on the external pressure exerted upon it. Business will adapt in a meaningful way, defined as something more than the efficiency enhancement it would have undertaken eventually anyway, only when it is forced to by societal and regulatory pressure. But as we have seen, before doing so the firm will first engage in political battle, in an attempt to stave off or refashion the regulatory demand. Regulators will only be strong enough to prevail in such conflicts if they have the full support of their governments, which in turn are looking to electoral advantage from a populace that is engaged, aware, and unwilling to settle for the easy definition of environmentalism as nothing more than taking out the blue box once a week. As Wilson has stated, "How the Canadian environmental movement will rate on a report card issued in 10 or 20 years will likely depend on whether, building on the successes of their forebears, environmental organizations in the years ahead can discredit the 'we can have our cake and eat it too' notions of environmental modernization that have been so successfully pushed by government, industry and the media in the post-Brundtland, post-Rio world" (2002: 63-64). Business will adapt and find new means of making profits if the society in which it functions and to which it looks for legitimacy presents it with clear, powerful messages of the need to move away from ever-expanding material consumption, end the addiction to fossil fuels, and preserve the continued existence of other forms of life.

The essentially adaptive and legitimacy-seeking nature of business, combined with the fact that there are limits to its political power, is a cause for optimism. In fact, the future of the planet does not rest in the hands of business at all, since it could survive and prosper fifty years from now in a new and very different world, one truly based on limits and equity, and will do so if asked forcefully enough. It would sell different products and services and play by different rules, but it would adapt, thrive, and prosper, just as it has done so many times in the past when faced with changes in its external environment. Instead, that future rests in the hands of those living and working outside the boundaries of the firm, those who own its shares, buy its products, exert social pressure upon it, and vote for the laws by which it must abide. Whether they can muster sufficient will to change not only business but also themselves is, of course, another story.

References

Adkin, Laurie E. (1998). *Politics of Sustainable Development: Citizens, Unions and the Corporations*. Montreal: Black Rose Books.

Alliance of Manufacturers and Exporters (reviewed 1997). *Environmental Policy*.

Amos, William, Kathryn Harrison, and George Hoberg. (2001). "In Search of Minimum Winning Coalition: The Politics of Species-at-Risk Legislation in Canada." In Karen Beazley and Robert Boardman, eds., *Politics of the Wild: Canada and Endangered Species*. Toronto: Oxford University Press.

Anderson, Robert O. (1982). "Foreword." In Joseph S. Nagelschmidt, ed., *The Public Affairs Handbook*. Washington, DC: Amocom.

Atkinson, Michael M. (1993). "Introduction: Governing Canada." In Michael M. Atkinson, ed., *Governing Canada: Institutions and Public Policy*. Toronto: Harcourt Brace Jovanovich.

Atkinson, M.M., and W.D. Coleman. (1996). "Policy Networks, Policy Communities and the Problems of Governance." In Laurent Dobuzinkis, Michael Howlett, and David Laycock, eds., *Policy Studies in Canada: The State of the Art*. Toronto: University of Toronto Press.

The Atlantic 296(4): 21-23.

Ayres, Ian, and John Braithwaite. (1992). *Responsive Regulation: Transcending the Deregulation Debate*. New York: Oxford University Press.

Bakan, Joel. (2004). *The Corporation: The Pathological Pursuit of Profit and Power*. Toronto: Viking Canada.

Baldwin, David A. (1989). *Paradoxes of Power*. Oxford: Basil Blackwell.

Bank of Nova Scotia (reviewed 1997). *The Bank of Nova Scotia's Policy on Environment*.

Bartha, Peter F. (1994 [1982]). "Managing Corporate External Issues." *Business Quarterly* 58: 138-43.

Beder, Sharon. (1997). *Global Spin: The Corporate Assault on Environmentalism*. Dartington Totnes, England: Green Books.

Bélanger, Jean. (1990). *Being Responsible Partners in Canadian Society.* Ottawa: Presentation to the Air and Waste Management Environmental Government Affairs Seminar.

———. (1991). "Responsible Care: Delivering on a Promise." Speech delivered to the first International Responsible Care Workshop, Rotterdam, April 9.

Benedick, Richard Elliot. (1991). *Ozone Diplomacy: New Directions in Safeguarding the Planet.* Cambridge, MA: Harvard University Press.

Benedickson, Jamie. (2002). *Environmental Law.* Toronto: Irwin Law. 2nd ed.

Bentley, Arthur. (1949 [1908]). *The Process of Government.* Bloomington, IN: Principia Press. The Governmental Process: Political Interests and Public Opinion.

Berle, Adolf A., and Gardiner C. Means. (1932). *The Modern Corporation and Private Property.* New York: Macmillan.

Berry, Glyn R. (1974). "The oil lobby and the energy crisis." *Canadian Public Administration* 17(4): 600-35.

Boardman, Robert, ed. (1992). *Canadian Environmental Policy.* Toronto: Oxford University Press.

Bonsor, Norman C. (1990). "Water Pollution and the Canadian Pulp and Paper Industry." In G. Bruce Doern, ed., *Getting it Green: Case Studies in Canadian Environmental Regulation.* Toronto: C.D. Howe Institute.

Boulding, Kenneth E. (1989). *Three Faces of Power.* London: Sage.

Boyd, David R. (2003). *Unnatural Law: Rethinking Canadian Environmental Law and Policy.* Vancouver: UBC Press.

Bramley, Matthew. (2000). *A Climate Change Resource Book for Journalists.* Ottawa: Pembina Institute.

Brieger, Tracey, Trevor Fleck, and Douglas Macdonald. (2001). "Political Action by the Canadian Insurance Industry on Climate Change." *Environmental Politics* 10(3): 111-26.

Brooks, Stephen, and Andrew Stritch. (1991). *Business and Government in Canada.* Scarborough: Prentice-Hall.

Brummer, James J. (1991). *Corporate Responsibility and Legitimacy: An Interdisciplinary Analysis.* New York: Greenwood Press.

Bryner, Gary C. (1995). *Blue Skies, Green Politics: The Clean Air Act of the 1990s and its Implementation.* Washington, DC: CQ Press.

Buchholz, Rogene A. (1998). *Principles of Environmental Management: The Greening of Business.* Upper Saddle River, NJ: Prentice-Hall. 2nd ed.

BCNI [Business Council on National Issues] (1994). *Climate Change: A Strategy for Voluntary Business Action.*

Byfield, Mike. (2002). "A question of sovereignty." *The Report*. April 21.

Cairncross, Frances. (1991). *Costing the Earth*. Boston: Harvard Business School Press.

———. (1995). *Green Inc: A Guide to Business and the Environment*. Washington, DC: Island Press.

Cairns, Alan. (1986). *The Embedded State: State-Society Relations in Canada*. In Keith Banting, ed., *State and Society: Canada in Comparative Perspective*. Royal Commission on the Economic Union and Development Prospects for Canada. Toronto: University of Toronto Press.

Campbell, Monica. (1982). *Profit from Pollution Prevention: A Guide to Industrial Waste Reduction and Recycling*. Pollution Probe Foundation.

Canada. (1992). *Economic Instruments for Environmental Protection: Discussion Paper*. Ottawa: Supply and Services.

Canada. (2005). *Moving Forward on Climate Change: A Plan for Honouring our Kyoto Commitment*.

CCPA [Canadian Chemical Producers' Association]. (undated a). *Canada's Chemical Industry: A Keystone of the Canadian Economy* <http://www.ccpa.ca/splash.asp>. April 2001.

———. (undated b). *Responsible Care: Doing the Right Thing*.

———. (1994). *Submission to the Standing Committee on Environment and Sustainable Development on Review of the Canadian Environmental Protection Act*.

———. (1995). Letter to Minister of Natural Resources, Anne McLellan. July 19.

———. (1996). *Submission on "CEPA Review: The Government Response."*

———. (1998). *Submission by the Canadian Chemical Producers' Association on Bill C-32, Canadian Environmental Protection Act, 1998, to Standing Committee on Environment and Sustainable Development*.

Canadian Petroleum Association. (1989). *Submission to House of Commons Standing Committee on Environment: Subject Global Warming*.

CPPA [Canadian Pulp and Paper Association]. (1988). *Annual Report for the Year 1988*.

———. (1989). "Press Release: The Pulp and Paper Industry of Canada issues an Environmental Statement."

Carroll, William K. (1986). *Corporate Power and Canadian Capitalism*. Vancouver: University of British Columbia Press.

———. (2004). *Corporate Power in a Globalizing World: A Study in Elite Social Organization*. Toronto: Oxford University Press.

Carson, Rachel. (1962). *Silent Spring*. Boston: Houghton Mifflin.

Carter, Neil. (2001). *The Politics of Environment: Ideas, Activism, Policy.* Cambridge: Cambridge University Press.

Cashore, Benjamin. (2002). "Legitimacy and the Privatization of Environmental Governance: How Non-State Market-Driven (NSMD) Governance Systems Gain Rule-Making Authority." *Governance* 15(4): 503-29.

Chase, Steven. (2002). "Kyoto seen to cost billions unless revised." *The Globe and Mail.* April 3.

Chatterjee, Pratap, and Matthias Finger. (1994). *The Earth Brokers.* London: Routledge.

Clancy, Peter. (2004). *Micropolitics and Canadian Business.* Peterborough, ON: Broadview Press.

Clapp, Jennifer. (2005). "The Privatization of Global Environmental Governance: ISO 14000 and the Developing World." In David L. Levy and Peter J. Newell, eds., *The Business of Global Environmental Governance.* Cambridge, MA: MIT Press.

Clement, Wallace. (1975). *The Canadian Corporate Elite: An Analysis of Economic Power.* Toronto: McClelland and Stewart.

Cohen, David. (2004). "The Role of the State in a Privatized Regulatory Environment." In Kernaghan Webb, ed., *Voluntary Codes: Private Governance, the Public Interest and Innovation.* Ottawa: Carleton Research Unit for Innovation, Science and Environment.

Coleman, William D. (1988). *Business and Politics: A Study of Collective Action.* Kingston and Montreal: McGill-Queen's University Press.

Coleman, William D., and Grace Skogstad, eds. (1990). *Policy Communities and Public Policy in Canada.* Toronto: Copp Clark Pitman.

Corbeil, Michel. (2005). "Souvenirs de Rio." *Le Soleil.* November 26. D3.

Cotton, Roger, and Kelley M. McKinnon. (1993). "An Overview of Environmental Law in Canada." In Geoffrey Thompson, Moira L. McConnell, and Lynne B. Heustis, eds., *Environmental Law and Business in Canada.* Aurora, ON: Canada Law Book.

Curtis, Jennifer. (1999). "Big Oil vs Big Auto." *Report on Business Magazine.* March.

Cutter Information Corp. (1998). "Chemical Companies Get Insurance Discount for 'Responsible Care' Participation." *Business and the Environment* IX(2): 9.

Deal, Terrence E., and Allen A. Kennedy. (1982). *Corporate Culture: The Rites and Rituals of Corporate Life.* Reading, MA: Addison-Wesley.

de Silva, K.E.A. (1988). *Pulp and Paper Modernization Grants Program— An Assessment.* Ottawa: Economic Council of Canada.

DeSombre, Elizabeth R. (2002). *The Global Environment and World Politics.* New York: Continuum.

Diesen, Magnus. (1998). *Economics of the Pulp and Paper Industry.* Helsinki: Fapet Oy.

Doern, G. Bruce. (2004). "The Institutional and Public Administrative Aspects of Voluntary Codes." In Kernaghan Webb, ed., *Voluntary Codes: Private Governance, the Public Interest and Innovation.* Ottawa: Carleton Research Unit for Innovation, Science and Environment.

————. ed. (1990). *Getting it Green: Case Studies in Canadian Environmental Regulation.* Ottawa: C.D. Howe Institute.

Doern, G. Bruce, and Thomas Conway. (1994). *The Greening of Canada: Federal Institutions and Decisions.* Toronto. University of Toronto Press.

Doern, G. Bruce, and Glen Toner. (1985). *The Politics of Energy: The Development and Implementation of the NEP.* Toronto: Methuen.

Dwivedi, O.P., Patrick Kyba, Peter J. Stoett, and Rebecca Tiessen. (2001). *Sustainable Development and Canada: National and International Perspectives.* Peterborough, ON: Broadview Press.

Edwards, Mark. (undated). "The Changing Face of Environmental Performance Within the Canadian Oil Sector." Unpublished graduate student paper, in possession of author.

Eggerston, Laura. (1999). "Controversial environment bill passed by House." *Toronto Star.* June 2.

Emery, Claude. (1991). *Share Groups in British Columbia.* Library of Parliament Research Branch.

Environment Canada. (2000). *Evaluation of the Accelerated Reduction and Elimination of Toxics Initiative (ARET).* Draft report. March.

Environmental Commissioner of Ontario. (1996). *The Ontario Regulation and Policy-Making Process in a Comparative Context: Exploring the Possibilities for Reform.*

Environmental Mining Council of British Columbia. (2005). "Follow the Mining Money: An Activist Toolkit for Direct Corporate Campaigning." Website viewed August 17 <http://www.miningwatch.org/emcbc/publications/toolkit/5.htm>.

Environmental Policy Unit, Queen's University. (1996). *Lessons Learned from ARET: A Qualitative Survey of Perceptions of Stakeholders.* Working Paper Series 96-94.

Epstein, Edwin M. (1969). *The Corporation in American Politics.* Englewood Cliffs, NJ: Prentice-Hall.

Fafard, Patrick C. (2000). "Groups, Governments and the Environment: Some Evidence from the Harmonization Initiative." In Patrick C. Fafard and Kathryn Harrison, eds., *Managing the Environmental Union: Intergovernmental Relations and Environmental Policy in Canada.* Kingston: Queen's University School of Policy Studies.

Fagin, Dan, and Marianne Lavelle. (1999). *Toxic Deception: How the Chemical Industry Manipulates Science, Bends the Law and Endangers Your Health*. Monroe, ME: Common Courage Press.

Finlay, J. Richard. (1994 [1978]). "The Tasks and Responsibilities of Public Affairs." *Business Quarterly* 58: 105-10.

Fombrun, Charles J., and Violina P. Rondova. (2000). "The Road to Transparency: Reputation Management at Royal Dutch/Shell." In Majken Schultz, Mary Jo Hatch, and Mogens Holten Larsen, eds., *The Expressive Organization: Linking Identity, Reputation, and the Corporate Brand*. Oxford: Oxford University Press.

Fones-Wolf, Elizabeth. (1994). *Selling Free Enterprise: The Business Assault on Labor and Liberalism, 1945-60*. Chicago: University of Illinois Press.

FPAC [Forest Products Association of Canada]. (2003). "Expect More." *2003 Annual Review*.

Frankel, Carl. (1998). *In Earth's Company: Business, Environment and the Challenge of Sustainability*. Gabriolo Island, BC: 1998.

Galbraith, John Kenneth. (1983). *The Anatomy of Power*. Boston: Houghton Mifflin.

Gibson, Robert B. (1999). *Voluntary Initiatives: the new politics of corporate greening*. Peterborough, ON: Broadview Press.

Gitlin, Todd. (1987). *The Sixties: Years of Hope, Days of Rage*. New York: Bantam Books.

Glasbeek, Harry. (2002). *Wealth by Stealth: Corporate Crime, Corporate Law, and the Perversion of Democracy*. Toronto: Between the Lines.

Grant, Wyn. (1995). *Autos, Smog and Pollution Control: The Politics of Air Quality Management in California*. Aldershot, UK: Edward Elgar.

Graves, Robert. (1995 [1929]). *Goodbye To All That*. Oxford: Berghahn Books.

Greenpeace. (1992). *The Greenpeace Book of Greenwash*. Vancouver: Greenpeace.

Greer, Linda, and Christopher Van Löben Sels (1997). "When Pollution Prevention Meets the Bottom Line." *Environmental Science and Technology* 31(9): 418-22A.

Greve, Michael S., and Fred L. Smith, Jr., eds. (1992). *Environmental Politics: Public Costs, Private Rewards*. New York: Praeger.

Gunningham, Neil. (1998). "The Chemical Industry." In Neil Gunningham, Peter Grabosky, and Darren Sinclair. *Smart Regulation: Designing Environmental Policy*, Oxford: Clarendon Press.

Gunningham, Neil, Robert A. Kagan, and Dorothy Thornton. (2003). *Shades of Green: Business, Regulation, and Environment*. Stanford, CA: Stanford University Press.

Hajer, Maarten A. (1995). *The Politics of Environmental Discourse: Ecological Modernization and the Policy Process.* Oxford: Clarendon Press.

Hanigan, John A. (1995). *Environmental Sociology: A Social Constructionist Perspective.* London: Routledge.

Harrison, Kathryn. (1996a). *Passing the Buck: Federalism and Canadian Environmental Policy.* Vancouver: UBC Press.

———. (1996b). "The Regulator's Dilemma: Regulation of Pulp Mill Effluents in the Canadian Federal State." *Canadian Journal of Political Science* XXIX(3): 469-96.

———. (1999). "Retreat from Regulation: The Evolution of the Canadian Environmental Regulatory Regime." in G. Bruce Doern, Margaret M. Hill, Michael J. Prince, and Richard J. Schultz, eds., *Changing the Rules: Canadian Regulatory Regimes and Institutions.* Toronto: University of Toronto Press.

———. (2001). "Paper Trails: Environmental Regulation in a Global Economy." Paper presented at the Annual Meeting of the Canadian Political Science Association, Quebec City, May 27-29.

———. (2002). "Ideas and Environmental Standard-Setting: A Comparative Study of Regulation of the Pulp and Paper Industry." *Governance: An International Journal of Policy, Administration and Institutions* 15(1): 65-96.

———. (2004). "Promoting Environmental Protection Through Eco-Labelling: An Evaluation of Canada's Environmental Choice Program." In Kernaghan Webb, ed., *Voluntary Codes: Private Governance, the Public Interest and Innovation.* Ottawa: Carleton Research Unit for Innovation, Science and Environment.

Harrison, Kathryn, and George Hoberg. (1994). *Risk, Science and Politics: Regulating Toxic Substances in Canada and the United States.* Montreal and Kingston: McGill-Queen's University Press.

Haveman, Mark, and Mark Dorfman. (1999). "Breaking Down the 'Green Wall' (Part One): Early Efforts at Integrating Business and Environment at SC Johnson." *Corporate Environmental Strategy* 6(1): 5-13.

Hawken, Paul. (1993). *The Ecology of Commerce.* New York: Harper Business.

Heclo, Hugh. (1994). "Ideas, Interests and Institutions." In Lawrence C. Dodd and Calvin Jillson, eds., *The Dynamics of American Politics: Approaches and Interpretations.* Boulder, CO: West View Press.

Hessing, Melody, Michael Howlett, and Tracy Summerville. (2005). *Canadian Natural Resource and Environmental Policy.* Vancouver: UBC Press. 2nd ed.

Hirschorn, J., T. Jackson, and L. Bass. (1993). "Towards Prevention: the emerging environmental management paradigm." In Tim Jackson, ed., *Cleaner Production Strategies*. Boca Raton, FL: Lewis Publishers.

Hoberg, George. (1991). "Sleeping with an Elephant: The American Influence on Canadian Environmental Regulation." *Journal of Public Policy* 2(1): 307-42.

———. (2000). "Trade, Harmonization and Domestic Autonomy in Environmental Policy" <http://faculty.arts.ubc.ca/hoberg/george.htm>.

Hoffman, Andrew J. (1997). *From Heresy to Dogma: An Institutional History of Corporate Environmentalism*. Stanford: Stanford University Press, 2001.

———. (2000). *Competitive Environmental Strategy: A Guide to the Changing Business Landscape*. Washington, DC: Island Press.

Howlett, Michael. (1994). "The Judicialization of Canadian Environmental Policy, 1980-1989: A Test of the U.S.-Canada Convergence Hypothesis." *Canadian Journal of Political Science* 27(1): 99-125.

———. (2002). "Policy Instruments and Implementation Styles." In Debora VanNijnatten and Robert Boardman, eds., *Canadian Environmental Policy: Context and Cases*, 2nd ed. Toronto: Oxford University Press.

Howlett, Michael, and Rebecca Raglon. (1992). "Constructing the Environmental Spectacle: Green Advertisements and the Greening of the Corporate Image, 1910-1990." *Environmental History Review* 16(4): 52-68.

Howlett, Michael, and M. Ramesh. (1995). *Studying Public Policy*. Toronto: Oxford University Press.

HRSDC [Human Resources and Skills Development Canada] (last modified 2005, 07-08). *Soft Drink Industry* <http://www.hrsdc.gc.ca/asp/gateway.asp?hr=en/hip/hrp/sp/industry_profiles/soft_drinks.shtml&hs=hzp>.

Ibbotson, Brett, and John-David Phyper. (1996). *Environmental Management in Canada*. Toronto: McGraw-Hill Ryerson.

Imperial Oil. (1991). *A Discussion Paper on Global Warming Response Options*.

Inco (reviewed 1997). *Inco Environmental, Health and Safety Policy*.

IJC [International Joint Commission]. (1982). First Biennial Report on Great Lakes Water Quality. Biennial Report under the Great Lakes Water Quality Agreement of 1978 to the Governments of the United States and Canada and the State and Provincial Governments of the Great Lakes Basin. Washington, DC and Ottawa: IJC.

———. (1986). Third Biennial Report on Great Lakes Water Quality.

———. (1992). Sixth Biennial Report on Great Lakes Water Quality.

Jagers, Sverker C., Matthew Paterson, and Johannes Stripple. (2005).

"Privatizing Governance, Practicing Triage: Securitization of Insurance Risks and the Politics of Global Warming." In David L. Levy and Peter J. Newell, eds., *The Business of Global Environmental Governance.* Cambridge, MA: MIT Press.

Jang, Brent. (1997). "Oil firms split on global warming." *The Globe and Mail.* December 5.

Johns, Gary. (1996). *Organizational Behavior: Understanding and Managing Life at Work.* New York: HarperCollins.

Johnson, William. (1999). "Overview of Corporate Law: Past, Present and Future." In Kevin McGuinness, *The Law and Practice of Canadian Business Corporations.* Toronto: Butterworths.

Jones, Douglas. (1966). "The Canadian Pulp and Paper Industry." Background paper B 18-1. *Proceedings of the Canadian Council of Resource Ministers' Conference on Pollution and Our Environment.* Montreal: CCRM.

Kelley, Patricia C. (1991). "Factors that Influence the Development of Trade Associations' Political Behaviour." In J.E. Post, ed., *Research in Corporate Social Performance and Policy*, vol. 12. Greenwich, CT: JAI Press.

King, Andrew A., and Michael J. Lenox. (2000). "Industry self-regulation without sanctions: The chemical industry's responsible care program." *Academy of Management Journal* 43(4): 698-716.

Klein, Naomi. (2000). *No Logo.* Toronto: Vintage Canada.

Kollman, Ken. (1998). *Outside Lobbying: Public Opinion and Interest Group Strategies.* Princeton, NJ: Princeton University Press.

Kono, Toyohiro, and Stewart R. Clegg. (1998). *Transformations of Corporate Culture.* Berlin: Walter de Gruyter.

Korten, David. (1995). *When Corporations Rule the World.* West Hartford and San Francisco: Kumarian and Berrett-Koehler.

Labatt, Sonia. (1997). "Corporate Response to Environmental Issues: Packaging." *Growth and Change* 28(1): 67-92.

Lachance, Claude-André. (1999). Letter to "a member of the government." April 12. In possession of author.

Lafferty, William M., and James Meadowcroft. (2000). "Introduction." In William M. Lafferty and James Meadowcroft, eds., *Implementing Sustainable Development: Strategies and Initiatives in High Consumption Societies.* Oxford: Oxford University Press.

Langille, David. (1987). "The Business Council on National Issues and the Canadian State." *Studies in Political Economy* 24: 41-85.

Legett, Jeremy. (1999). *The Carbon War: Dispatches from the End of the Oil Century.* London: Allen Lane, Penguin.

Levy, David L., and Peter J. Newell. (2005). "A Neo-Gramscian Approach to Business in International Environmental Politics: An Interdisciplinary, Multi-level Framework." In David L. Levy and Peter J. Newell, eds., *The Business of Global Environmental Governance.* Cambridge, MA: MIT Press.

Levy, David L., and Peter J. Newell, eds. (2005). *The Business of Global Environmental Governance.* Cambridge, MA: MIT Press.

Lindblom, Charles. (1977). *Politics and Markets.* New York: Basic Books.

Litvak, Isaiah A. (1994 [1981]). "Government Intervention and Corporate Government Relations." *Business Quarterly.* 58: 130-37.

Lohmann, Larry. (1996). "Freedom to Plant: Indonesia and Thailand in a Globalizing Pulp and Paper Industy." In Michael H.G. Parnwell and Raymond Bryant, eds., *Environmental Change in South-East Asia: People, Politics and Sustainable Development.* London: Routledge.

Luger, Stan. (2000). *Corporate Power, American Democracy and the Automobile Industry.* Cambridge: Cambridge University Press.

Lukes, Steven. (1974). *Power: A Radical View.* London: Macmillan.

Macdonald, Doug. (1991). *The Politics of Pollution: Why Canadians Are Failing Their Environment.* Toronto: McClelland and Stewart.

———. (1996). "Beer Cans, Gas Guzzlers and Green Taxes: How Using Tax Instead of Law May Affect Environmental Policy." *Alternatives Journal* 22(3): 12-19.

———. (1997). *Policy Communities and Allocation of Internalized Cost: Negotiation of the Ontario Acid Rain Program, 1982-1985.* PhD dissertation, Faculty of Environmental Studies, York University.

———. (1998). "Business Lobbying on Environment." Paper delivered at the annual meeting of the Environmental Studies Association of Canada/L'Association canadienne d'études environnementales, Ottawa. June 3.

———. (1999). "Business as an Environmental Policy Actor: Background Paper." Round Table Discussion, Trent University. October 29-30.

———. (2001). "Coerciveness and the selection of environmental policy instruments." *Canadian Public Administration/Administration Publique du Canada* 44(2): 161-87.

———. (2002). "The Business Response to Environmentalism." In Debora L. VanNijnatten and Robert Boardman, eds., *Canadian Environmental Policy: Context and Cases Second Edition.* Toronto: Oxford University Press.

———. (2003). "The business campaign to prevent Kyoto ratification." Paper delivered at the annual meeting of the Canadian Political Science Association, Dalhousie University. May 31.

Macdonald, Douglas, and Heather Smith. (1999). "Promises made, promises broken: questioning Canada's commitments to climate change." *International Journal* 55(1): 107-24.

Macdonald, Douglas, and Debora VanNijnatten. (2005). "Sustainable Development and Kyoto Implementation in Canada: The Road Not Taken." *Policy Options*, July-August. 26(6): 13-19.

MacKinnon, Janice. (2003). *Minding the Public Purse: The Fiscal Crisis, Political Trade-Offs, and Canada's Future*. Montreal and Kingston: McGill-Queen's University Press.

Mahon, John F., and Richard A. McGowan. (1996). *Industry as a Player in the Political and Social Arena*. Westport, CT: Quorum Books.

Malmqvist, Tove. (2003). "Climate Change: Can Oil Companies Move Beyond Petroleum?" Unpublished MA thesis, Department of Political Science, University of Toronto.

Marchand, Roland. (1998). *Creating the Corporate Soul: The Rise of Public Relations and Corporate Imagery in American Big Business*. Berkeley: University of California Press.

Marcus, Alfred A., Allen M. Kaufman, and David R. Beam. (1987). *Business Strategy and Public Policy: Perspectives from Industry and Academia*. New York: Quorum Books.

Markowitz, Gerald, and David Rosner. (2002). *Deceit and Denial: The Deadly Politics of Industrial Pollution*. Berkeley: University of California Press.

Matas, Robert. (1995). "MP's environmental proposals panned." *The Globe and Mail*. October 16.

McGuinness, Kevin Patrick. (1999). *The Law and Practice of Canadian Business Corporations*. Toronto: Butterworths.

McKenzie, Judith. (2002). *Environmental Politics in Canada: Managing the Commons into the Twenty-First Century*. Toronto: Oxford University Press.

McRobert, David. (1994). Ontario's Blue Box System: A Case Study of Government's Role in the Technological Change Process, 1970-1991. Chapter 5 in "Labour Relations, Technological Change and Sustainability: Resolving the Structural Issues." Draft LLM Thesis, Osgoode Hall Law School, York University.

McRobert, David, D. Macdonald, P. Pickfield, and A. Imada. (1990). *Five Years of Failure: A Documentation of the Failure of the Ontario Government to Reduce Solid and Hazardous Waste Quantities*. Toronto: Pollution Probe.

Mellon, Margaret, Leslie Ritts, Stephen Garrod, and Marcia Valiante. (1986). *The Regulation of Toxic and Oxidant Air Pollution in North America*. Toronto: CCH Canadian Limited.

Mercier, Jean. (1997). *Downstream and Upstream Ecologists: The People, Organizations, and Ideas Behind the Movement*. London: Praeger.

Miles, Robert H., in collaboration with Kim S. Cameron. (1982). *Coffin Nails and Corporate Strategies*. Englewood Cliffs, NJ: Prentice-Hall.

Miller, Jon, and David Muir. (2004). *The Business of Brands*. Chichester: John Wiley and Sons.

Miller, Karen S. (1999). *The Voice of Business: Hill and Knowlton and Postwar Public Relations*. Chapel Hill: University of North Carolina Press.

Mills, C. Wright. (1956). *The Power Elite*. New York: Oxford University Press.

MOE [Ministry of the Environment, Ontario]. (2005). *An Introduction to the Ministry of the Environment*. Ministry website. Viewed September 14 <http://www.ene.gov.on.ca/>.

Mitchell, Neil J. (1989). *The Generous Corporation: A Political Analysis of Economic Power*. New Haven, CT: Yale University Press.

———. (1997). *The Conspicuous Corporation: Business, Public Policy, and Representative Democracy*. Ann Arbor: The University of Michigan Press.

Mittelstaedt, Martin. (1999) "Criminal polluters finding Canada the promised land." *The Globe and Mail*. March 23.

———. (2000). "Rules on hazardous waste feared too lax." *The Globe and Mail*. February 28.

Moffet, John, and François Bregha. (1999). "Responsible Care." In Robert B. Gibson, ed., *Voluntary Initiatives: The New Politics of Corporate Greening*. Peterborough, ON: Broadview Press.

Moffet, John, François Bregha, and Mary Jane Middelkoop. (2004). "Responsible Care: A Case Study of a Voluntary Environmental Initiative." In Kernaghan Webb, ed., *Voluntary Codes: Private Governance, the Public Interest and Innovation*. Ottawa: Carleton Research Unit for Innovation, Science and Environment.

Montpetit, Eric. (2003). *Misplaced Distrust: Policy Networks and the Environment in France, the United States and Canada*. Vancouver: UBC Press.

Moran, T.H. (1974). *Multinational Corporations and the Politics of Dependence: Copper In Chile*. Princeton, NJ: Princeton University Press.

Muldoon, Paul. (1994). "Incorporating Pollution Prevention into Part II of CEPA: An Agenda for Reform." In Toxics Caucus of the Canadian Environmental Network, *Reforming the Canadian Environmental Protection Act, A Submission to the Standing Committee on Environment and Sustainable Development*.

Najam, Adil. (1999). "World Business Council for Sustainable Development: The Greening of Business or a Greenwash?" *Yearbook of International Co-operation on Environment and Development, 1999/2000*. London: Earthscan.

Natural Resources Canada. (2002). News release: "Government of Canada Responds to Industry Concerns about Climate Change," accompanying release of letter from the Honourable Herb Dhaliwal, Minister, to Mr. John Dielwart, Chairman, Canadian Association of Petroleum Producers. December 18.

New Directions Group. (1991). *Reducing and Eliminating Toxic Substances: An Action Plan for Canada*. September.

———. (1997). *Criteria and Principles for the Use of Voluntary or Non-regulatory Initiatives to Achieve Environmental Policy Objectives*. October.

———. (2005). *History of the NDG*. Website, viewed July 8 <http://www.newdirectionsgroup.org/about/initiatives.php?PHPSES-SID=b8a307f5e09bc4b1c5b69a3dfa77b942>.

Newell, Peter (2000). *Climate for Change: Non-state Actors and the Global Politics of the Greenhouse*. Cambridge: Cambridge University Press.

Nguyen, Lily. (2003). "Kyoto oil sands 'scare' eases." *The Globe and Mail*. January 10.

Nocera, Joe. (2006). "If It's Good for Philip Morris, Can it Also Be Good for Public Health?" *The New York Times Magazine*. June 18.

OCETA, Ontario Centre for Environmental Technology Advancement. (1997). *Ontario Environment Industry 1997 Survey*.

OECD. (2003). *Voluntary Approaches for Environmental Policy: Effectiveness, Efficiency and Usage in Policy Mixes*. Paris: OECD.

Olewiler, Nancy. (1990). "The Case for Pollution Taxes." In G. Bruce Doern, ed., *Getting it Green: Case Studies in Canadian Environmental Regulation*. Ottawa: C.D. Howe Institute.

———. (1994). "The Impact of Environmental Regulation on Investment Decisions." In Jamie Benedickson, G. Bruce Doern, and Nancy Olewiler, eds., *Getting the Green Light: Environmental Regulation and Investment in Canada*. Ottawa: C.D. Howe Institute.

———. (2006). "Environmental Policy in Canada: Harmonized at the Bottom?" In Kathryn Harrison, ed., *Racing to the Bottom? Provincial Interdependence in the Canadian Federation*. Vancouver: UBC Press.

Paehlke, Robert. (1989). *Environmentalism and the Future of Progressive Politics*. New Haven, CT: Yale University Press.

———. (1997). "Green Politics and the Rise of the Environmental Movement." In Thomas Fleming, ed., *The Environment and Canadian Society*. Toronto: ITP Nelson.

Paehlke, Robert, and Douglas Torgerson, eds. (2005). *Managing Leviathan: Environmental Politics and the Administrative State*. Peterborough, ON: Broadview Press.

Palter, Jay. (1994). "Chlorine-Free Update." Toronto: Greenpeace.

Panitch, Leo, ed. (1977). *The Canadian State: Political Economy and Political Power*. Toronto: University of Toronto Press.

Parlour, James W. (1981). "The Politics of Water Pollution Control: A Case Study of the Canadian Fisheries Act Amendments and the Pulp and Paper Effluent Regulations, 1970." *Journal of Environmental Management* 13: 127-49.

Phyper, John-David, and Brett Ibbotson. (2003). *The Handbook of Environmental Compliance in Ontario*. Toronto: McGraw-Hill Ryerson.

Piasecki, Bruce W. (1995). *Corporate Environmental Strategy: The Avalanche of Change Since Bhopal*. New York: John Wiley and Sons.

Porter, Gareth, Janet Welsh Brown, and Pamela S. Chasek. (2000). *Global Environmental Politics*. 3rd ed. Boulder, CO: Westview Press.

Post, James E., William C. Frederick, Anne T. Lawrence, and James Weber. (1996). *Business and Society: Corporate Strategy, Public Policy, Ethics*. New York: McGraw-Hill. 8th ed.

Post, James E., Robert B. Dickie, Edwin A. Murray, Jr., and John Mahon. (1983). "Managing Public Affairs: The Public Affairs Function." *California Management Review* XXVI(1): 135-50.

Prakash, Aseem. (2000). *Greening the Firm: The Politics of Corporate Environmentalism*. Cambridge: Cambridge University Press.

Price Waterhouse. (1994). *The Canadian Pulp and Paper Industry: A Focus on Human Resources*. Ottawa: Supply and Services Canada.

Pring, George W., and Penelope Canan. (1996). *SLAPPs: Getting Sued for Speaking Out*. Philadelphia: Temple University Press.

Proctor, Robert. (1995). *Cancer Wars: How Politics Shapes What We Know and Don't Know about Cancer*. New York: BasicBooks.

Project for Environmental Priorities. (1999). "Harris Fails Environmental Test." News release. May 26 <http://www.web.net/pep>.

Pross, A. Paul. (1992). *Group Politics and Public Policy*. Toronto: Oxford University Press. 2nd ed.

Redhead, Robert. (1998). Personal communication. February 24.

Reguly, Eric. (1999). "The 'sustainable development' sham." *The Globe and Mail*. April 24. B2.

Reinhardt, Forest L. (2000). *Down to Earth: Applying Business Principles to Environmental Management*. Boston: Harvard Business School Press.

Richards, John, and Larry Pratt. (1979). *Prairie Capitalism: Power and Influence in the New West*. Toronto: McClelland and Stewart.

Roberts, Paul. (2004). *The End of Oil*. Boston: Houghton Mifflin.

Rowlands, Ian. (2000). "Beauty and the beast?: BP's and Exxon's positions on global climate change." *Environment and Planning C: Government and Policy* 18: 339-54.

Russett, Bruce, and Harvey Starr. (1992). *World Politics: The Menu for Choice*. New York: W.H. Freeman. 4th ed.

St-Pierre, Antoine. (1993). *Industrial Competitiveness, Trade and the Environment: A Look at Three Sectors of the Economy*. Ottawa: Conference Board of Canada.

Sawatsky, John. (1987). *The Insiders: Government, Business and the Lobbyists*. Toronto: McClelland and Stewart.

Schmidheiny, Stephen. (1992). *Changing Course: A Global Business Perspective on Development and the Environment*. Cambridge, MA: The MIT Press.

Schoenberge, Erica. (1997). *The Cultural Crisis of the Firm*. Oxford: Blackwell.

Schrecker, T.F. (1984). *Political Economy of Environmental Hazards*. Ottawa: Law Reform Commission of Canada.

————. (1985). "Resisting Regulation: Environmental Policy and Corporate Power." *Alternatives* 13(1): 9-21.

————. (2005). "Class, Place and Citizenship: The Changing Dynamics of Environmental Protection." In Robert Paehlke and Douglas Torgerson, eds., *Managing Leviathan: Environmental Politics and the Administrative State*. Peterborough, ON: Broadview Press.

Shaw, Daniel J. (1989). *The Canadian Pulp, Paper and Paperboard Industry*. Ottawa: Energy, Mines and Resources.

Shellenberger, Michael, and Ted Norhaus. (2004). "The Death of Environmentalism" <http://www.grist.org/news/maindish/2005/01/13/doe-reprint/>.

Simmons, Greg. (2002). *Canadian regulation of air pollution from motor vehicles*. Greenpeace and Sierra Legal Defence Fund.

Sinclair, William F. (1990). *Controlling Pollution from Canadian Pulp and Paper Manufacturers: A Federal Perspective*. Ottawa: Supply and Services Canada.

Skjaerseth, Jon Birger, and Tora Skodvin. (2003). *Climate change and the oil industry: Common problem, varying strategies*. Manchester: Manchester University Press.

Smith, Mark A. (2000). *American Business and Political Power: Public Opinion, Elections and Democracy*. Chicago: The University of Chicago Press.

Smith, Toby M. (1998). *The Myth of Green Marketing: Tending our Goats at the Edge of Apocalypse.* Toronto: University of Toronto Press.

Solway, Alison Beder. (1997). "Environmental Risk Management Systems and ISO 14000." Talk delivered at the University of Toronto. November 13.

Standing Committee on Environment and Sustainable Development. (1995). News Release, "Parliamentary Committee calls for Pollution Prevention." June 20.

Stefanick, Lorna. (1997). "Organization, administration and the environment: will a facelift suffice, or does the patient need radical surgery?" *Canadian Public Administration* 41(1): 99-119.

Stewart, Keith. (1999). "Post-Fordism and 'Green' Industry: The NDP in Ontario." Paper presented at the annual meeting of the Association for Socialist Studies, Sherbrooke, Quebec. June 8.

Stigler, G. (1971). "The Theory of Economic Regulation." *Bell Journal of Economics and Management* 2(1): 3-21.

Strick, John C. (1990). *The Economics of Government Regulation: Theory and Canadian Practice.* Toronto: Thompson Educational Publishing.

Suchman, Mark C. (1995). "Managing legitimacy: Strategic and institutional approaches." *The Academy of Management Review* 20(3): 571-602.

ten Brink, Patrick. (2002). "Prologue." In Patrick ten Brink, ed., *Voluntary Environmental Agreements: Process, Practice and Future Use.* Sheffield: Greenleaf Publishing.

Thompson, Andrew. (1980). *Environmental Regulation in Canada: An Assessment of the Regulatory Process.* Vancouver: Westwater Research.

Thompson, Geoffrey, Moira L. McConnell, and Lynne B. Heustis, eds. (1993). *Environmental Law and Business in Canada.* Aurora, ON: Canada Law Book.

Tollefson, Chris. (1994). "Strategic Lawsuits Against Public Participation: Developing a Canadian Response." *The Canadian Bar Review* 73: 200-33.

Toner, Glen. (2000). "Canada: From Early Frontrunner to Plodding Anchorman." In William M. Lafferty and James Meadowcroft, eds., *Implementing Sustainable Development: Strategies and Initiatives in High Consumption Societies.* Oxford: Oxford University Press.

Trent Environmental Policy Institute. (1999). "Proceedings and associated documents, Business as an Environmental Policy Actor, Round Table Discussion, October 29 and 30, 1999, Trent University." Paper Number 1. Peterborough, ON: Trent University.

Truman, David B. (1971 [1951]). *The Governmental Process: Political Interests and Public Opinion.* New York: Alfred A. Knopf Press. 2nd ed.

VanNijnatten, Debora. (1996). "Environmental Governance and Multistakeholder Consultation in Canada." Queen's University, School of Policy Studies, Environmental Policy Unit, Working Paper Series 96-2. May.

———. (1999). "The ARET Challenge." In Robert B. Gibson, ed., *Voluntary Initiatives: The New Politics of Corporate Greening*. Peterborough, ON: Broadview Press.

VanNijnatten, Debora, and Robert Boardman. (2002). "Introduction." In Debora L. VanNijnatten and Robert Boardman, eds. *Canadian Environmental Policy: Context and Cases Second Edition*. Toronto: Oxford University Press.

VanNijnatten, Debora, and Douglas Macdonald. (2003). "Reconciling Energy and Climate Change Policies: How Ottawa Blends." In G. Bruce Doern, ed., *How Ottawa Spends 2003-2004: Regime Change and Policy Shift*. Toronto: Oxford University Press.

VanNijnatten, Debora L., and W. Henry Lambright. (2002). "Canadian Smog Policy in a Continental Context: Looking South for Stringency." In Debora L. VanNijnatten and Robert Boardman, eds., *Canadian Environmental Policy: Context and Cases*. Toronto: Oxford University Press.

VanNijnatten, Debora L., and William Leiss, with Peter V. Hodson. (1997). "Environment's X-File: Pulp Mill Effluent Regulation in Canada." Environmental Policy Unit, School of Policy Studies, Queen's University.

Vestal, Allan W. (1993). "Public Choice, Public Interest, and the Soft Drink Interbrand Competition Act: Time to Derail the 'Root Beer Express'?" *William and Mary Law Review* 34(337): 337-91.

Vogel, David. (1989). *Fluctuating Fortunes: The Political Power of Business in America*. New York: Basic Books.

———. (1995). *Trading Up: Consumer and Environmental Regulation in a Global Economy*. Cambridge, MA: Harvard University Press.

Walley, Noah, and Bradley Whitehead. (1994). "It's Not Easy Being Green." *Harvard Business Review* 72(3): 46-52.

Watson, Tag. (1999). Personal communication. December 7.

Webb, Kernaghan. (2004). "Understanding the Voluntary Codes Phenomenon." In Kernaghan Webb, ed., *Voluntary Codes: Private Governance, the Public Interest and Innovation*. Ottawa: Carleton Research Unit for Innovation, Science and Environment.

Webb, Kernaghan, and David Clarke. (2004). "Chapter 13 Voluntary Codes in the United States, the European Union and Developing Countries: A Preliminary Survey." In Kernaghan Webb, ed., *Voluntary Codes: Private Governance, the Public Interest and Innovation*. Ottawa: Carleton Research Unit for Innovation, Science and Environment.

Welford, Richard. (1997). *Highjacking Environmentalism: Corporate Responses to Sustainable Development*. London: Earthscan.

Welford, Richard, and Richard Starkey, eds. (1996). *Business and the Environment*. London: Earthscan.

Wilson, Graham K. (1990). "Corporate Political Strategies." *British Journal of Political Science* 20(2): 281-88.

Wilson, James Q. (1996). "The Corporation as a Political Actor." In Carl Kaysen, ed.,*The American Corporation Today*. New York: Oxford University Press.

Wilson, Jeremy. (1992). "Green Lobbies: Pressure Groups and Environmental Policy." In Robert Boardman, ed., *Canadian Environmental Policy: Ecosystems, Politics and Process*. Toronto: Oxford University Press.

———. (1998). *Talk and Log: Wilderness Politics in British Columbia.* Vancouver: UBC Press.

———. (2002). "Continuity and Change in the Canadian Environmental Movement: Assessing the Effects of Institutionalization." In Debora L. VanNijnatten and Robert Boardman, eds., *Canadian Environmental Policy: Context and Cases*, 2nd ed. Toronto: Oxford University Press.

Winfield, Mark. (1993). *Who Pays for Blue?: Financing Residential Waste Diversion in Ontario.* Canadian Institute for Environmental Law and Policy.

———. (1994). "The Ultimate Horizontal Issue: The Environmental Policy Experiences of Alberta and Ontario, 1971-1993." *Canadian Journal of Political Science* XXVII(1): 129-52.

———. (2002). "Environmental Policy and Federalism." In Herman Bakvis and Grace Skogstad, eds., *Canadian Federalism: Performance, Effectiveness and Legitimacy*. Toronto: Oxford University Press.

Winfield, Mark, M. Anieksli, H. Benevides, and A. Kranjc. (2002). *Governance Tools for Sustainable Development Within the Government of Canada.* Ottawa: Pembina Institute for Appropriate Development.

Winsor, Hugh. (1999). "Ex-Liberal spearheads industry's bid against bill." *The Globe and Mail*. April 26.

Wood, Stepan. (2003). "Green Revolution or Greenwash? Voluntary Environmental Standards, Public Law and Private Authority in Canada." In Law Commission of Canada, ed. *New Perspectives on the Public-Private Divide*. Vancouver: UBC Press.

———. (2006). "Voluntary Environmental Codes and Sustainability." In Benjamin J. Richardson and Stepan Wood, eds., *Environmental Law for Sustainability*. Oxford: Hart Publishing.

Zelditch, Morris Jr. (2001). "Theories of Legitimacy." in John T. Jost and Brenda Major, eds., *The Psychology of Legitimacy: Emerging Perspectives on Ideology, Justice and Intergroup Relations*. Cambridge: Cambridge University Press.

Additional Readings

Beyond the works listed in the references, readers may wish to consult some of those listed here.

Atkinson, M.M., and W.D. Coleman. (1989). *The State, Business and Industrial Development in Canada*. Toronto: University of Toronto Press.

Bliss, Michael. (1987). *Northern Enterprise: Five Centuries of Canadian Business*. Toronto: McClelland and Stewart.

Clarke, Toby. (1997). *Silent Coup: Confronting the Big Business Takeover of Canada*. Ottawa: Canadian Centre for Policy Alternatives.

Clark-Jones, Melissa. (1987). *A Staple State: Canadian Industrial Resources in Cold War*. Toronto: University of Toronto Press.

Coleman, William D., and Henry J. Jacek. (1983). "The Roles and Activities of Business Interest Associations in Canada." *Canadian Journal of Political Science* XVI: 2.

DeSimone, Livio D., and Frank Popoff. (1997). *Eco-efficiency: The Business Link to Sustainable Development*. Cambridge, MA: MIT Press.

Dobin, Murray. (1998). *The Myth of the Good Corporate Citizen: Democracy Under the Rule of Big Business*. Toronto: Stoddart.

Doyle, Jack. (1992). "Hold the Applause: A Case Study of Corporate Environmentalism." *The Ecologist* 22(3): 84-90.

Eells, Richard. (1962). *The Government of Corporations*. New York: The Free Press of Glencoe.

Fearn-Banks, Kathleen. (1996). *Crisis Communications: A Casebook Approach*. Mahwah, NJ: Lawrence Erlbaum Associates.

Fisher, Kurt and Johan Schot. (1993). *Environmental Strategies for Industry: International Perspectives on Research Needs and Policy*. Washington, DC: Island Press.

Ghobadian, A., H. Viney, J. Liu, and P. James. (1998). "Extending Linear Approaches to Mapping Corporate Environmental Behaviour." *Business Strategy and the Environment* 17: 13-23.

Gillies, James. (1981). *Where Business Fails: Business-Government Relations at the Federal Level in Canada.* Montreal: Institute for Research on Public Policy.

Grant, Wyn. (1993). *Business and Politics in Britain.* London: MacMillan. 2nd ed.

Groenewegen, Peter, et al., eds. (1996). *The Greening of Industry Resource Guide and Bibliography.* Washington, DC: Island Press.

Harris, Richard A. (1985). *Coal Firms Under the New Social Regulation.* Durham, NC: Duke University Press.

Hatch, Mary Jo. (1997). *Organization Theory: Modern, Symbolic and Postmodern Perspectives.* Oxford: Oxford University Press.

Heath, Robert L., ed. (1988). *Strategic Issues Management: How Organizations Influence and Respond to Public Interests and Policies.* San Francisco: Jossey-Bass.

Jones, L.R., and John H. Baldwin. (1994). *Corporate Environmental Policy and Government Regulation.* Greenwich, CT: JAI Press.

Kirkland, Lisa-Henri, and Dixon Thompson. (1999). "Challenges in Designing, Implementing and Operating an Environmental Management System." *Business Strategy and the Environment* 8: 128-43.

Loudon, A.A. (1987). "The Chemical Industry and the Environment." Paper presented at the European Conference on Industry and Environmental Management, Interlaken, Austria. October 12.

Lusterman, Seymour. (1987). *The Organization and Staffing of Corporate Public Affairs.* New York: The Conference Board.

Lynn, Leonard H., and Timothy J. McKeown. (1988). *Organizing Business: Trade Associations in America and Japan.* Washington, DC: American Enterprise Institute for Public Policy Research.

Macdonald, Doug. (1997). "Business as an actor in the Canadian environmental policy community: a proposed research agenda." Paper delivered at the annual meeting of the Environmental Studies Association of Canada/L'Association canadienne d'études environnementales, Ottawa. June 7.

———. (2002). "The Environmental Policy Interest of the Regulated Firm." Paper delivered at the annual meeting of the Canadian Political Science Association, University of Toronto. May 31.

Marcus, Alfred A. (1996). *Business and Society: Strategy, Ethics and the Global Economy.* Chicago: Irwin.

McCahery, Joseph, Sol Picciotto, and Colin Scott, eds. (1993). *Corporate Control and Accountability: Changing Structures and the Dynamics of Regulation.* Oxford: Clarendon Press.

Mitnick, Barry, ed. (1993). *Corporate Political Agency.* London: Sage.

Moss, Scott J. (1981). *An Economic Theory of Business Strategy: An Essay in Dynamics Without Equilibrium.* Oxford: Martin Robertson.

Murray, V.V., ed. (1985). *Theories of Business-Government Relations.* Toronto: Trans-Canada Press.

Murray, V.V., and C.J. McMillan. (1983). "Business-Government Relations in Canada: A Conceptual Map." *Canadian Public Administration* 26(4): 591-609.

Nagelschmidt, Joseph S., ed. (1982). *The Public Affairs Handbook.* Washington, DC: Amocom.

Nattras, Brian, and Mary Altomare. (1999). *The Natural Step for Business: Wealth, Ecology and the Evolutionary Corporation.* Gabriola Island, BC: New Society Publishers.

Newell, Peter, and Matthew Paterson. (1998). "A climate for business: global warming, the state and capital." *Review of International Political Economy* 5(4): 679-703.

Perrow, Charles. (1986). *Complex Organizations: A Critical Essay.* New York: Random House. 3rd ed.

Pfeffer, Jeffrey, and Gerald R. Salancik. (1978). *The External Control of Organizations.* New York: Harper and Row.

Post, James E. (1993). "The State of Corporate Public Affairs in the United States: Results of a National Survey." *Research in Corporate Social Performance and Policy* 14: 79-89.

Reinhardt, Forest L. (1999). "Market Failure and the Environmental Policies of Firms: Economic Rationales for 'Beyond Compliance' Behavior." *Journal of Industrial Ecology* 3(1): 9-21.

Ryan, Mike H., Carl L. Swanson, and Rogene A. Buchholz. (1987). *Corporate Strategy, Public Policy and the Fortune 500.* Oxford: Basil Blackwell.

Schmidheiny, Stephen, and Federico J.L. Zorraquín. (1996). *Financing Change: The Financial Community, Eco-Efficiency and Sustainable Development.* Cambridge, MA: MIT Press.

Scott, Richard W. (2003). *Organizations: Rational, Natural and Open Systems.* Upper Saddle River, NJ: Prentice Hall. 5th ed.

Simon, Herbert A. (1964). "On the Concept of Organizational Goal." *Administrative Science Quarterly* 9(1): 1-22.

Stanbury, W.T. (1986). *Business-Government Relations in Canada.* Toronto: Methuen.

Stead, W. Edward, and Jean Gardner Stead. (1992). *Management for a Small Planet: Strategic Decision Making and the Environment.* Newbury Park, CA: Sage.

Toner, Glen, and G. Bruce Doern. (1986). "The Two Energy Crises and

Canadian Oil and Gas Interest Groups: A Re-examination of Berry's Propositions." *Canadian Journal of Political Science* XIX(3): 467-93.

Vogel, David. (1987). "Political Science and the Study of Corporate Power: A Dissent from the New Conventional Wisdom." *British Journal of Political Science* 17(4): 385-408.

Williamson, Oliver E. (1990). "The Firm as a Nexus of Treaties: an Introduction." In Masahiko Aoki, Bo Gustafafson, and Oliver E. Williams, eds., *The Firm as a Nexus of Treaties*. London: Sage.

Index

sulphur dioxide, 27, 99,
103, 135
Suncor, 167
Sunset Chemical Protocol,
159
sunsetting, 127, 156–62, 176
Superfund legislation, 88
sustainable development,
13, 33, 123–26, 186
in advertising, 148
belief in, 191–92
defining, 13, 151–53
as false consciousness, 53
as strategy, 183–84
Sustainable Development
Technology Fund, 125
symbols, 38

taxaphrene, 158
taxes
corporate, 137
cutting, 56–57, 137–38
on pollution, 139–40,
145–46
on raw materials, 109
tax incentives, 26
Thatcher, Margaret, 16, 185
theoretical perspectives,
20–29
threats, 3, 19
as explanatory factor, 176
to products, 178
3M, 62
throw-away society, 106–7
tobacco industry, 29, 36,
45, 75, 188
Toronto Conference, 96
tourism, 13
Toxics Caucus, 159
toxic substances, 3–4, 13,
91, 134, 140, 186
chemical industry and,
114
in mill waste, 116–17
regulation of, 70, 72, 97
sunsetting of, 156–62
trade associations, 87–89,
118

Trudeau government, 71,
76, 97, 146, 163
Truman government, 47
trusts, 31, 43

Union Carbide, 62, 113, 115
United Nations Conference
on Environment and
Sustainable Develop-
ment, 95, 126. See also
Rio Conference
United Nations Environ-
ment Program, 12, 96
United Nations Framework
Convention on Climate
Change (UNFCCC), 1,
28, 135, 167. See also
Kyoto Protocol
United States
advertising in, 148–49
automobile industry in,
82–83, 103–4, 135
influence of, 2
regulation in, 66, 71, 74,
135

Vail, Theodore, 43
Vander Zalm, Bill, 117
virtual elimination, 157
Vogel, David, 50
volatile organic compounds,
135
voluntarism, 138–46, 160,
166–67
Voluntary Challenge and
Registry (VCR), 135,
141, 144, 166–67, 171
voluntary environmental
agreements (VEAs), 143
voluntary programs, 9, 26,
82, 101, 105, 135,
166–67

Walkerton incident, 13, 32,
133
waste disposal, 6, 27, 97,
106–7
Waste Diversion Act, 111

waste reduction, 64
Waterfront Remedial
Action Programs
(WRAPS), 121
water pollution, 13, 79–81,
82, 133
drinking water and, 13,
25, 32, 70, 97, 133,
135
weather, 154–55
Weyerhauser, 148, 149
Wilson, Graham, 41
Wilson, James Q., 50–51
Wilson, Jeremy, 135
win-win arguments, 63
wise use groups, 181
Wiwa, Ken Saro, 150
wood-waste pollution,
79–81
World Business Council on
Sustainable
Development (WBCSD),
4, 62–63, 126, 157
World Meteorological
Organization, 96

zero discharge, 127, 157